Unorthodox
Lawmaking

Unorthodox Lawmaking

New Legislative Processes in the U.S. Congress

Second Edition

Barbara Sinclair
University of California, Los Angeles

A Division of Congressional Quarterly Inc.
Washington, D.C.

To
Dick Fenno,
teacher, mentor, friend

CQ Press
A Division of Congressional Quarterly Inc.
1414 22nd St. N.W.
Washington, DC 20037
(202) 822-1475; (800) 638-1710

www.cqpress.com

Printed in the United States of America

Library of Congress Cataloging-in-Publication Data

Sinclair, Barbara, date.
    Unorthodox lawmaking : new legislative processes in the U.S. Congress / Barbara Sinclair. — 2nd ed.
      p.   cm.
    Includes bibliographical references and index.
    ISBN 1-56802-572-6   ISBN 1-56802-510-6 (pbk.)
    1. Legislation—United States. 2. United States—Politics and government—1993– I. Title.
KF4945.S58.2000
328.73'077—dc21   00-044480

Contents

---

c h a p t e r   t h r e e

c h a p t e r   f o u r

c h a p t e r   f i v e

c h a p t e r   s i x

c h a p t e r   t w e l v e

The Consequences of Unorthodox Lawmaking

Tables

Preface

DURING THE TWENTY-PLUS YEARS that I have been doing research on Congress and teaching courses about the institution, the gap between the legislative process that I observe on Capitol Hill and the legislative process described in U.S. government textbooks has become a chasm. Like most teachers, I tried to give my students a sense of the contemporary legislative process in all its variety while still presenting the "textbook" model as the standard. That approach, I came to believe, is no longer adequate or accurate.

The reception the first edition of this book received from my colleagues persuaded me that most share my perception; thus this second edition.

This book describes how the legislative process in the U.S. Congress really works today. In it I show how the process has changed in recent years, explore the reasons for the change, and examine its consequences. Although based on original research, the book is written with the nonspecialist in mind. No extensive knowledge of Congress is presupposed. I believe that it will help prepare readers to pursue further studies of Congress if they so choose, but my primary aim is to enable them to make sense of congressional politics and to judge claims about congressional performance.

I refer to the contemporary legislative process as "unorthodox lawmaking" to distinguish frequently employed contemporary procedures and practices from what is still often presented in textbooks as the standard process. The term emphasizes the extent of recent changes and gives me a handy way of referring to a set of procedures and practices that are either new or much more frequently employed than they used to be. In fact, the legislative process for major legislation is now less likely to conform to the textbook model than to unorthodox lawmaking.

This new edition is similar to the first in intent, organization, and argument. I have updated all the data series through the end of the 105th Congress (1997–1998), have replaced some old examples with more current ones, and have replaced two of the case studies with new ones. I have also brought the examination of changes and trends up to date, especially by discussing heightened partisanship and its consequences in the Senate. I retained some of the case studies and examples from the first edition because I believe they help to illuminate how unorthodox lawmaking works in a variety of political contexts.

The book begins with two short case studies that provide a vivid example of how much the legislative process has changed. Chapter 1 describes the passage of clean air legislation in 1970 and in 1990 and then, through a comparison of the process on the two bills, introduces unorthodox lawmaking and the questions it raises. Chapters 2–5 explain the procedures and practices that make up the new legislative process. Chapter 2 begins with the introduction of a bill and proceeds step by step through the process in the House, at each stage examining and illustrating frequently used procedures. Chapter 3 traces the path a bill takes through the Senate. Before 1970 one could speak of a standard legislative process that most major legislation traversed, but as these chapters show there are now many routes from introduction to enactment. Once the House and Senate have passed legislation, the two different versions must be reconciled, as I explain in Chapter 4. Chapter 5 addresses omnibus legislation, the budget process, and legislative-executive summits. Chapter 6 explores the historical origins of the procedures and practices that characterize contemporary lawmaking and documents the change over time in their frequency. Chapters 7–11 analyze unorthodox lawmaking through a series of case studies. Accounts of the process on the 1993 national service bill, on the "patients' bill of rights" (managed care reform) legislation in 1999, and an omnibus drug bill passed in 1988 illustrate the range and variability of the contemporary legislative process. Case studies of the enactment of President Clinton's economic program in 1993, of the Republicans' attempt in 1995 to pass a balanced budget that included restructuring Medicare, Medicaid, welfare, and other major programs, and of the 1997 balanced budget deal between Clinton and Congress show how the budget process works and demonstrate its contemporary use as an instrument of comprehensive policy change. Chapter 12 examines the influence that the changes in procedures and practices have had on legislative outcomes and on how Congress functions.

I chose to describe the contemporary legislative process early in the book, in Chapters 2–5, followed by a chapter that analyzes the trajectory of change and the reasons for it. For those who prefer their history first, the order of those chapters can be reversed, with Chapter 6 read before Chapters 2–5. Chapters 7–9, the case studies of nonbudget legislation, could easily be read after Chapters 2–4 and before Chapter 5, which deals with the budget process.

In addition to the quantitative analysis of the process on major legislation described in Chapter 1, this book is based on my observations and experiences as an American Political Science Association congressional fellow in the office of the House majority leader in 1978–1979; in the office of the Speaker in 1987–1988 on an informal basis; and on interviews with members of Congress, their staffs, and informed observers over the course of more years than I am now willing to admit. I owe Jim Wright, Speaker of the House from 1987 to 1989, and his staff an enormous debt for giving me the opportunity to observe the legislative process from the inside. I am also grateful to all of those very busy people who made time to talk to me over the years and from whom I learned so much. All unattributed quotations are from interviews I conducted.

I would especially like to thank Peter Robinson, formerly of the House Parliamentarian's Office and of Speaker Wright's staff, and Stanley Bach, Richard Beth, and Walter Oleszek of the Congressional Research Service. All are incredibly knowledgeable and extremely generous in sharing their expertise. Stan Bach, Michael Kraft, and Sandy Maisel read the first-edition manuscript and gave me invaluable comments and advice. I want them to know how much I appreciate their detailed and thoughtful reviews; they significantly improved the manuscript. Robin Kolodny, Bruce Oppenheimer, and Steve Smith, who read the proposal and much of an early draft, provided perceptive and helpful advice. Cary R. Covington, Rebekah Herrick, and David Menefee-Libey reviewed the first edition and provided me with many useful suggestions for improving the second. Stan Bach read the new case studies with his discerning eye and commented on them with his combination of great knowledge and common sense. I am truly grateful. Much of the quantitative material has been presented in papers at professional meetings; I thank the many colleagues who commented on those papers. I continue to learn from my colleagues in the congressional scholarly community; there are too many to list here, but I thank them all. Of course, none of these people is responsible for any remaining errors. Finally, I would like to thank Brenda Carter and Gwenda Larsen, of CQ Press, and Nola Healy Lynch, who copyedited the text. They have been great to work with.

Unorthodox Lawmaking

chapter one

Clean Air: An Introduction to How the Legislative Process Has Changed

I N 1970 CONGRESS PASSED A PATH-BREAKING Clean Air Act, legislation Congressional Quarterly called "the most comprehensive air pollution control bill in U.S. history" (*Congressional Quarterly Almanac* 1970, 472).

Reported by the House Interstate and Foreign Commerce Committee, the bill was considered on the House floor under an open rule allowing all germane amendments. Of the nine amendments offered, eight were defeated, most on voice votes; only one technical amendment was accepted. The bill passed the House 375–1.

In the Senate the Public Works Committee reported a bill stronger than the House legislation or the administration's draft. After two days of floor debate, during which ten amendments were accepted by voice vote and two rejected by roll calls, the Senate voted 73–0 to pass the strong bill. The conference committee, consisting of five members of the House committee and nine senators, came to an agreement on a bill much closer to the Senate's stringent version than to the House's milder bill, and both chambers approved the conferees' version by voice vote.

Although the bill was far stronger than the legislation he had initially proposed, President Richard Nixon signed the Clean Air Act, "one of the most far-reaching laws ever passed by Congress to regulate the domestic economy," in the words of a prominent journalist. The act set auto emission standards so stringent that it forced the development of new technology, and it directed the Environmental Protection Agency to establish national air quality standards (Cohen 1992, 13).

* * *

1

In 1989, when the 101st Congress began work on a major revision of the Clean Air Act, the political and institutional environment had changed, and the path the legislation traversed to enactment was very different from that of its 1970 predecessor. In the Senate the slightly renamed Public Works and Environment Committee again reported a strong bill. The bill was considered on the Senate floor for six days, but the majority leader, George Mitchell, D-Maine, could not muster the sixty votes needed to overcome a threatened filibuster. To construct a bill that could pass the chamber, the majority leader began negotiations with the administration and with a large and shifting group of senators. Members of the Environment Committee participated on a continuous basis, but many other senators with an interest in specific issues also took part. After a month of talks, an agreement was reached. To guard against any unraveling of the compromise, Mitchell and President George Bush pledged to oppose floor amendments, even those that reflected their policy preferences.

Mitchell offered the compromise worked out in the talks as a substitute amendment to the bill the Environment Committee had reported. He negotiated a complex unanimous consent agreement (UCA) for considering the bill on the floor. That UCA did not limit either debate or amendments; it simply required senators to put the amendments they wished to offer on a list. This provided a modicum of order to floor consideration of the bill. After ten days' debate over a month's time, the Senate passed the bill 89–11. Of about 250 amendments on the list, 25 were offered and pushed to a roll call vote; nine of these passed. None was a "deal breaker."

In the House the legislation was referred to three committees, rather than just one, as the 1970 bill had been. The Energy and Commerce Committee, successor to Interstate and Foreign Commerce, was the lead committee, and after protracted internal negotiations it reported legislation that represented a compromise among its factions. One key issue, however, had been decided by extremely close votes in both the subcommittee and the full committee, and Speaker Tom Foley, D-Wash., was concerned that the issue might well lead to a bitter party-splitting battle on the floor. He thus instructed the lead representatives of the two Democratic factions, Henry Waxman of California, chair of the subcommittee, and John Dingell of Michigan, chair of the full committee, to work out a compromise. In order to pressure them to act expeditiously, Foley set a deadline for floor action on the legislation. The Speaker and his aides then worked with Waxman and Dingell to help them come to an agreement. The other committees, also under Speaker-imposed deadlines, reported their legislative language.

Unlike its 1970 predecessor, the 1990 clean air legislation went to the floor under a rule that restricted amendments to the nineteen listed in the Rules Committee report and that carefully structured how they would be considered. The crucial Waxman-Dingell deal was offered as an amendment on the floor and approved 405–15. In all, six amendments were pushed to a roll call vote and five passed; none of these threatened the key compromises. The House then approved the bill 401–21.

Speaker Foley chose 130 conferees to represent the seven committees with some jurisdiction over the bill's subject matter; nine members from two committees represented the Senate. Protracted negotiations produced a bill that passed both chambers easily. A dramatic expansion of the Clean Air Act, the 1990 bill for the first time set up a program for controlling acid rain, established a stringent new program to control emissions of toxic air pollutants, and set new standards and timetables for improving urban air quality (*Congress and the Nation* 1993, 469, 473–474). Although it was considerably stronger than the draft he had proposed, President Bush signed the legislation.

* * *

These examples illustrate how greatly the legislative process has changed over the past two decades.[1] The legislative process on the 1970 Clean Air Act perfectly fits the bill-becomes-a-law diagram that is still a staple of American politics and legislative process textbooks (see Table 1.1). The 1970 bill was considered by a single committee in each chamber. It came to the House floor as drafted and approved by the committee, and it was considered there under an open rule allowing all germane amendments. The Senate also considered the bill as drafted by its committee; no senator mounted a filibuster; no amending marathon occurred. After both chambers had passed the bill, a small group of senior members of the two committees got together in conference and worked out a compromise between the House and Senate versions.

The process on the 1990 bill, by contrast, was much more complex and not amenable to a nice, neat diagram. The legislation was considered by several committees in the House, and in both chambers compromises arrived at through informal processes altered the bills after the committees reported their legislation. Floor procedures were complex and tailored to the specific bill at issue. In the Senate the real possibility of a filibuster shaped the process, making it necessary for Majority Leader Mitchell to build through negotiations an oversized coalition. The final conference agreement was worked out by a much larger and more diverse group of members than in 1970.

---

1. These accounts are based largely on primary documents, interviews (in the case of the 1990 act), and the following secondary sources: Congressional Quarterly's accounts, Cohen (1992), and Smith (1995, chap. 12).

TABLE 1.1   The 1970 Clean Air Act as an Example of the Textbook Legislative Process

Action	House	Senate
Committee	HR17255 referred to the Committee on Interstate and Foreign Commerce. Hearings held March 16–21 and April 14, 1970. Bill marked up. Bill reported June 3, 1970. Rules Committee grants open rule.	S4358 referred to the Senate Public Works Committee. Hearings held March 16–20, March 23–26, and April 17, 1970. Bill marked up. Bill reported September 17, 1970.
Floor	Considered in Committee of the Whole and passed by the House June 10, 1970.	Debated on the floor September 21–22 and passed September 22, 1970.
Conference	Conferees appointed. Conference meets. Conference agreement reached. Conferees file report December 17, 1970.	
Floor	House approves conference report December 18, 1970.	Senate approves conference report December 18, 1970.
Presidential	Sent to the president. President signs December 31, 1970.	

In the contemporary Congress the textbook diagram describes the legislative process for fewer and fewer of the major bills. The seemingly unorthodox legislative process on the 1990 Clean Air Act is actually more characteristic of contemporary major legislation than the supposedly standard textbook process that the 1970 Clean Air Act went through. To be sure, even during the textbook era not all legislation followed the relatively simple, straightforward process depicted by Table 1.1; there have always been alternative paths. Their use, however, was extraordinary, not ordinary; most major legislation followed the textbook process.[2]

---

2. Shortcut processes to handle noncontroversial legislation did and have continued to exist.

Today the bill that, like the 1970 Clean Air Act, is reported by a single committee and considered on the floor under a simple open rule still exists but is not likely to be major legislation. Rather than being sent to one committee in each chamber, many measures are considered by several committees, especially in the House, while some measures bypass committee altogether. Not infrequently, after a bill has been reported but before it reaches the floor, major substantive changes are worked out via informal processes. Omnibus measures of great scope are a regular part of the legislative scene, and formal executive-congressional summits to work out deals on legislation are no longer considered extraordinary. On the House floor most major measures are considered under complex and usually restrictive rules, often tailored to deal with problems specific to the bill at issue. In the Senate bills are regularly subject to large numbers of not-necessarily-germane floor amendments; filibuster threats are an everyday fact of life, affecting all aspects of the legislative process and making cloture votes a routine part of the process. This book explores how and why the legislative process in the U.S. Congress has changed since the 1970s and examines the consequences of those changes.

Although the recent changes in the legislative process were preceded by a long period of stability, they are by no means unique. The Constitution does not specify how Congress is to carry out its core task of lawmaking; beyond a few basic requirements, it allows each house to determine its own rules and procedures. During its history of more than 200 years, the Congress has altered its legislative process a number of times.

In the very early years the legislative process in both the House and Senate emphasized the full membership's responsibility for lawmaking. The full membership debated a subject on the floor, decided whether legislation was warranted, and, if it was, laid out substantive guidelines. Then a special or select committee was appointed to draft legislation according to those guidelines (Cooper and Young 1989; Risjord 1994).

Even in the early decades not all business could be given so much time and attention; minor business was sent first to small committees. The House then began to create standing—that is, permanent—committees to handle recurrent complex issues, and the Senate began to send to a particular select committee all matters relating to the subject for which the committee had been initially created. During the second decade of the 1800s in the House and not much later in the Senate, standing committees became predominant. The committees did the initial work on legislation; only after they were finished did the rest of the membership have their say.

Floor procedure, too, has changed over time. In the early years both chambers' floor proceedings were relatively fluid and unstructured; even the House placed few limits on members' debate time (Binder 1996). Considering bills in the order they were introduced, the House was able to dispose of all of its business. Soon, however, House floor procedures became problematic. In 1811 the House adopted its first significant restrictions on floor debate, and throughout the nineteenth century the chamber struggled to develop a fair and efficient way of setting and ordering its floor agenda. Not until the 1880s and 1890s did the House develop its premier device for scheduling major floor legislation: special rules from the Rules Committee (Oppenheimer 1994). Special rules, which required a simple majority of the House membership for approval, allowed legislation to be taken up out of order; this innovation made it possible for the majority party and its leaders, if they controlled the Rules Committee in fact as well as in form, to control the House schedule.

Senate floor procedure changed in much less basic ways over the course of its history (Bach 1994). The chamber's lack of limits on debate, initially the result of no considered decision, became over time a revered defining characteristic (Binder 1997). In the early years the Senate's small size made it unnecessary to limit the time members could debate an issue. Eventually, however, senators' extended debate prerogative became a problem. By then, the prerogative was well entrenched; the formidable barrier the rules themselves erected against change was fortified by the widely accepted myth that extended debate reflected the framers' intent (Binder and Smith 1997). Under extraordinary pressure from the president and the public, the Senate in 1917 for the first time changed its rules in such a way as to make cutting off debate possible. The resulting cloture procedure, however, was cumbersome and required a two-thirds vote for success.

Why has the legislative process changed over time? The long evolution of the legislative process is far too complex to review here, and scholars do not agree about just why things happened as they did (Cooper 1981; Gamm and Shepsle 1989). Certainly increases in workload, alterations in the political and social environment, and the strategic behavior of parties and of members as individuals were important determinants. For example, increases in the congressional workload and in the size of its own membership put pressure on the House to modify procedures that had adequately served a smaller, less busy legislature. Majorities, especially partisan majorities, found their legislative goals stymied by chamber rules that facilitated minority obstructionism. These majorities were able to change such rules in the House but were largely blocked in the Senate. On a more abstract, theoretical level, changes in the legislative process can be seen as the responses of members to the problems and opportunities the institutional structure and the political environment present to them as they pursue, as individuals or collectively, their goals of reelection, influence in the chamber, and good public policy (Fenno 1973; Sinclair 1995).

The alterations in the legislative process since the 1970s are the latest installment in an ongoing story. They shed light not only on the contemporary legislative process (what is happening on Capitol Hill today) but also on the broader political process. The study of rules changes also provides insight into how democratic institutions like the Congress evolve and adapt.

Chapters 2 through 5 describe the procedures and practices that make up the new legislative process and document their frequency. Before 1970 one could speak of a standard legislative process that most major legislation followed. It is now more accurate to speak of legislative processes in the plural. Bills today follow many routes from introduction to enactment; the legislative process is characterized by variability, not uniformity. Multiple examples give the reader a sense of when the new procedures and practices are employed.

In Chapter 6 the historical origins of contemporary lawmaking are explored and the change in frequency of particular practices over time is documented. Chapters 7 through 11 use case studies to analyze unorthodox lawmaking. The 1993 national service bill, managed care legislation (the "patients' bill of rights") in 1999, and an omnibus drug bill in 1988 illustrate the range and variability of the contemporary legislative process. The process on these three bills ranges from similar in many respects to the old standard process, though with some unorthodox elements, on national service to a radically unorthodox "designer" process on the drug bill. The enactment of Clinton's economic program in 1993 and budget politics under divided control—including the Republicans' attempt in 1995 to pass a balanced budget that included a restructuring of Medicare, Medicaid, welfare, and a number of other major programs and the 1997 balanced budget deal between Clinton and Congress—show how the budget process works and illustrate its contemporary use as an instrument of comprehensive policy change.

Chapter 12 examines the impact that the new procedures and practices have on legislative outcomes and on how Congress functions. Congress is the least-liked branch of the national government; only a fraction of the American people express confidence in the Congress. Americans are not happy with either the congressional process or the policy produced (Hibbing and Theiss-Morse 1995). Is unorthodox lawmaking, in part, responsible, either directly or indirectly? Does it enhance or inhibit the likelihood of a bill becoming law? What other effects does the change in process have on how the Congress functions? Does it foster or discourage deliberation, the development and bringing to bear of expertise, the inclusion of a broad range of interests, and informed and timely decision making?

Americans expect a lot from Congress. Congress should represent the people and pass laws that both reflect the will of the people and work. That is, citizens expect members of Congress to bring into the legislative process the views, needs, and interests of the people they are elected to represent, and they expect Congress to pass laws that are responsive to popular majorities and deal promptly and effectively with pressing national problems. Has unorthodox lawmaking made Congress more or less capable of carrying out the formidable tasks with which it is charged?

A Note on Data

I argue here that the legislative process on major legislation has changed. To show that is so, I need to define major legislation and then document change over time. Major measures are defined by the list of major legislation in the *CQ Weekly* (before 1998 *Congressional Quarterly Weekly Report*), augmented by those measures on which key votes occurred (again according to the *CQ Weekly*). This provides a list of about forty-five to fifty-five bills (and some other measures such as budget resolutions and constitutional amendments) for each Congress that close contemporary observers considered major. I then examine the course these major measures traversed in selected Congresses. I supplement my data by drawing where possible on the work of other scholars.

The Congresses selected are the 91st (1969–1970), a prereform Congress; the 94th (1975–1976), the first reformed Congress; the 97th (1981–1982), the first Congress of the Reagan presidency and one in which the Republicans controlled the Senate; the 100th (1987–1988) and the 101st (1989–1990), the last Reagan and first Bush Congresses; the 103rd (1993–1994), the first Clinton Congress and the only Congress in the series in which one party controlled the presidency and both houses of the Congress; the 104th (1995–1996), the first Congress in forty years with Republican control of both houses; and the 105th (1997–1998).

Multiple Paths:
The Legislative Process
in the House of Representatives

THE LEGISLATIVE PROCESS IN THE CONTEMPORARY Congress is varied and complex. The old textbook process depicted in Table 1.1 was predictable and linear, with one stage following another in an inevitable sequence. At many stages now there is no single, normal route but rather a number of different paths that legislation may follow. The best way to understand the contemporary legislative process is to begin with the introduction of a bill and proceed step by step through the process in each chamber, examining frequently used options at each stage. That is what this and the following three chapters do.

This is not a book on parliamentary procedure; procedures that are obscure and seldom employed are of no interest here. Rather, my aim is to make understandable the procedures and practices that occur on the major legislation considered during any contemporary Congress.[1]

For convenience, we begin the journey in the House of Representatives. Most legislation and other measures—budget resolutions and constitutional amendments—may begin in either chamber. The Constitution requires that tax legislation originate in the House, the people's chamber, and by custom the House also acts first on appropriations—that is, spending—bills. The Senate, however, is fully co-equal as a policy initiator. Even

---

1. I have relied heavily on Tiefer (1989) and Gold et al. (1992) for the fine points of procedure. The interested reader should also consult Oleszek (1996). The people at the Congressional Research Service, especially Stanley Bach, Richard Beth, and Walter Oleszek, were invaluable sources of information. Peter Robinson was also extremely helpful.

in the tax area, the Senate can initiate policy change by amending a minor House-passed tax bill. Yet because the House tends to act before the Senate (Strom and Rundquist 1977), we start with action in that chamber. Although action on the same issue may take place simultaneously in the two chambers, formal action on legislation is a sequential process: the House and the Senate cannot act on the same bill at the same time.

Bill Introduction

To introduce a bill, a member of the House simply drops it into the "hopper," a wooden box at the front of the chamber, when the House is in session.[2] Bill introduction has not changed in recent years. Only members of the House may introduce bills or resolutions in the House, and a member may introduce as many measures as he or she wishes. Thus even the president needs to find a member of the House to introduce his legislation, though doing so is seldom a problem.

In fact, the legislation members introduce has many different origins. Some bills are introduced at the behest of interest groups or even individual constituents; some come from federal government agencies and departments; some represent a member's own personal policy priorities. The legislative process in Congress is open and permeable. Although only members of Congress can perform official acts like introducing bills and voting, members' behavior is influenced by the president, interest groups, constituents, the media, and public opinion. That makes all of them significant actors in the legislative process.

Bill Referral

Once introduced, the bill is referred to the committee or committees of jurisdiction. Because committees are the primary shapers of legislation

---

2. The term *bill* is here used for bills, which are designated by the prefixes HR (for House of Representatives) and S (for Senate), and for joint resolutions, designated H.J.Res. and S.J.Res. There is no practical difference between the two in process and in effect; both become law. I try to use the term *measure* to indicate a broader class of legislative entities, including bills but also concurrent resolutions (H.Con.Res. or S.Con.Res.), which do not become law, and constitutional amendments. In process terms the difference between bills and joint resolutions, on the one hand, and concurrent resolutions and constitutional amendments, on the other, is that the last two do not require the president's signature. Resolutions, designated H.Res. or S.Res., deal with matters entirely within the purview of one body and do not require action by the other.

and because they differ in membership and perspective, which committee receives the bill can make a difference to the legislative outcome. The parliamentarian, a professional, nonpartisan employee of the House, handles referrals under the supervision of the Speaker, whose prerogative it is to make this decision. Referrals are governed by the rules of the House, specifically Rule X, which specifies what subject matters fall within the purview of each committee, and by precedents. Thus, referral decisions are usually fairly routine, but especially when new issues arise, there is some discretion (King 1994).

Multiple Referral

In 1975 the House changed its rules and permitted the referral of legislation to more than one committee. The prominent issues had changed: many had become more complex, and they no longer fit neatly into the jurisdiction of a single committee. Since that rules change, multiple referral has become increasingly common, especially on major legislation. By the Congresses of the late 1980s (1987–1990), about 18 percent of all measures were referred to more than one committee (Young and Cooper 1993, 214). When only major legislation is considered, the likelihood of multiple referral is even higher. In most Congresses since the late 1980s about three out of ten major measures were multiply referred; in the 104th Congress, half were.[3]

Most routine multiply referred measures (about 80 percent) are sent to two committees (Davidson and Oleszek 1992, 132). Again, major legislation is different; in the Congresses of the late 1980s and early 1990s (100th, 101st, 103rd), more than half of multiply referred legislation went to three or more committees and, in some cases, to many more. President Bill Clinton's reinventing government legislation (the Government Reform and Savings Act of 1993), for example, went to seventeen House committees; his health care bill was referred to ten. The big trade bill passed by the 100th Congress (1987–1988) was referred to six committees, and five other committees wrote trade-related legislation that was incorporated into the omnibus trade bill. In 1989 a bill to provide aid to Poland and Hungary was sent to seven committees. In the 104th and 105th Congresses (1995–1996, 1997–1998) fewer major bills were sent to multiple committees; 29 and 17 percent, respectively, of multiply referred major bills went to three or more committees. However, in the 104th, the bill to abolish the Department of Commerce was referred to eleven committees and immigration reform to seven.

---

3. Tables with the complete data series for this and most of the other "unorthodox processes" discussed in this chapter can be found in Chapter 6.

It is easy to understand why many committees had jurisdiction over the bill to reinvent government; the bill concerned many federal agencies, each one under the purview of a different committee. But why was the trade bill referred to many committees? Even more curious, why was legislation to aid two countries in eastern Europe multiply referred? The trade bill not only concerned unfair trade practices and authority to negotiate trade agreements. It also contained provisions on the retraining of workers displaced by plant closings and on grants to schools and colleges to improve the teaching of math, science, and foreign languages. The trade bill mandated negotiations with foreign governments to establish a competitive exchange rate for the dollar and to create an independent agency to buy loans owed by developing countries at a discount, required the identification of foreign owners of U.S. businesses and real estate, and prohibited government agencies from buying from companies in foreign countries whose governments restrict purchases from U.S. businesses (Cranford 1987, 813). On the Poland-Hungary bill, the Foreign Affairs Committee, which has jurisdiction over foreign aid, played the lead role, but Ways and Means was involved because of its jurisdiction over granting special trade benefits to foreign countries; programs for scholarships for Polish students, for technical training for Polish farmers and businesspeople, and for the promotion of U.S. exports to Poland and Hungary involved still other committees.

The original 1975 multiple referral rule instructed the Speaker to refer a bill to all committees with jurisdiction. Before 1995 the Speaker had three types of multiple referral to use (Davidson and Oleszek 1992). The most frequent type was a joint referral: a bill was sent to two or more committees simultaneously. Or a bill could be divided up and various sections and titles sent to different committees. Such split referrals have been relatively rare; dividing up complex legislation can be difficult. More common were sequential referrals: a measure is assigned to two or more committees in sequence. Typically, the first committee has the most jurisdiction and consequently the largest legislative role. The Speaker could combine types of referrals. Thus, legislation might be sent initially to the two or more committees with the most jurisdiction under a joint referral and then sequentially to other committees with lesser jurisdictional interests.

As amended in 1977, the multiple referral rule allowed the Speaker to set a reporting deadline for committees under any sort of referral. By custom, time limits were set on sequential but not on joint or split referrals. Since the Speaker could decide the type of referral to use, he exercised discretion as to time limits.

The 1995 rule, the aim of which was to streamline the process, abolished the old form of joint referral and instructed the Speaker to designate a primary committee (Evans and Oleszek 1995). As interpreted, the rule actually allows for several primary committees under a split referral. During the first 100 days of the 104th Congress, split referrals were frequently used. The welfare reform bill, for example, was split among the Ways and Means Committee, the Economic and Educational Opportunities Committee, and the Agriculture Committee. Joint referrals and, to an extent, sequential referrals have been replaced by the referral of legislation to a primary committee (based on "the weight of the bill") and *additional initial referral* to one or more other committees.

Committees that receive legislation on additional initial referral may consider it immediately; they need not wait for the primary committee to report before beginning their work. In that sense the new process is similar to the old joint referral procedure. However, when the primary committee reports, the other committees are, at the Speaker's discretion, subject to time limits; if time limits are imposed, the committee must report within the specified time or be automatically discharged, that is, have the legislation taken away from it. The usual form of such a referral reads, "referred to the [primary] committee, and in addition to the [secondary] committees, for a period to be subsequently determined by the Speaker, in each case for consideration of such provisions as fall within the jurisdiction of the committee concerned." Once the primary committee has reported, Republican Speakers have imposed time limits on the other committees if they have not yet reported. Especially in the 104th Congress, those time limits were often short, in some cases one day. There seem to have been fewer turf fights during the period of Republican control than in previous years, but whether the new rule was responsible is unclear. Certainly, during the 104th Congress, with a new majority in control, committee chairs were under intense pressure from the party leadership and the membership to not allow turf fights to interfere with passing bills on the Republican agenda. In any case, prominent turf fights under Republican control have featured substantive committees—especially the Transportation and Infrastructure Committee—pitted against the Appropriations or Budget Committees and so did not involve multiple referral.

What does multiple referral mean for how committees work and for how legislation is processed? Clearly, on much of the most important legislation of a Congress, committees must work together if they are to legislate successfully. Some committees—ones that frequently share jurisdiction—have developed standard operating procedures for working together. However, if the committees involved have substantially different and noncongruent perspectives, the relationship can be difficult and may make getting any legislation to the floor harder. In 1990, for example, the Ways and Means Committee and the Education and Labor Committee preferred distinctly different approaches to child care legislation; during months of negotiation, neither side was willing to budge. An agreement was finally reached only after the Speaker intervened and forced closure.

Some participants and knowledgeable observers contend that the multiple referral rule encourages committees to be even more turf conscious and to make even more, often tenuous, claims for jurisdiction than they otherwise would. Certainly in the House, members maintain their influence in the legislative process by aggressively asserting their committees' jurisdictional claims to legislation. Whether multiple referral has markedly exacerbated this tendency we cannot know; but without it there would still be turf fights and no method of handling them.

On the plus side, when legislation is referred to a number of committees, multiple perspectives are brought to bear on complex problems. More interests have a voice and a more diverse group of members a say at the committee stage, where it counts most. Given the complexity of today's problems, this is certainly a benefit even if some delay is the cost.

For the Speaker, who is responsible for referral decisions, the high frequency with which major legislation is multiply referred presents both problems and opportunities. Until the 1995 rules change, a committee received a referral almost automatically; neither rules nor custom gave the Speaker discretion to withhold referrals. Yet when legislation is referred to several committees, the number of people who must come to agreement is multiplied, complicating and often slowing down the legislative process. Multiply referred legislation can present a variety of procedural problems on the floor. Frequently, multiple referral forces the role of jurisdictional and substantive mediator on the Speaker. That role, however, brings with it influence as well as headaches. And, of course, multiple referral also gives the Speaker the opportunity to set time limits for the reporting out of legislation. That power helped the Republican leadership speed things along during the first 100 days of the 104th Congress. Under the new rule the Speaker has more discretion, particularly in terms of which additional committees receive referrals. Of course, he is still subject to pressure from members protecting their committee's clout (Evans and Oleszek 1995).

Bypassing Committee

Although legislation is now frequently considered by more than one committee, sometimes bills bypass committee consideration altogether. In the late 1980s almost one of five major measures was not considered by a committee in the House. Among the Congresses of the 1990s, the frequency drops to about one in twenty in the 103rd Congress and to about one in ten in the 104th and 105th. However, as we will see, that low rate is somewhat deceiving.

The circumstances under which the committee of jurisdiction is bypassed in the House are varied. A majority of the House membership can bypass an unresponsive committee by the discharge procedure: any member may file a discharge petition calling for a measure to be brought out of committee and to the floor; when half the House members—218—have signed the petition, the measure is taken away from the committee and considered on the floor. In the 97th Congress (1981–1982), in the 102nd (1991–1992), and again in the 103rd (1993–1994), a constitutional amendment to require a balanced federal budget was brought to the floor through the discharge procedure. In all three cases the committee of jurisdiction—the House Judiciary Committee—opposed the measure and had refused to consider or report it.

A House rules change in 1993 may have increased the chances that the discharge procedure would succeed—at least on high-visibility issues. Previously, names on a discharge petition—and thus the names of those who had not signed—were kept confidential until 218 was reached. The rules change specified that the list of who had signed would be public from the first signature, making it easier to pressure members to sign on hot-button issues. Still, the discharge procedure is seldom successful (Beth 1994).

The threat of a discharge petition can pressure a committee and the majority party leadership to bring to the floor measures they would rather not consider. During the 106th Congress (1999–2000), supporters of campaign finance reform and of managed heath care regulation used discharge petitions to convince the Republican leadership to bring their issues to the floor. Although neither petition received the required number of signatures, when the number got close the majority leadership capitulated. If a discharge petition does get 218 signatures, its proponents—and not the majority leadership—control the floor.

When a committee is successfully bypassed, the decision to do so is usually made by the majority party leadership.[4] The rationale for doing so varies widely. In early 1987, at the beginning of the 100th Congress, the Democratic Party leadership brought a clean water bill and a highway–mass transit bill directly to the floor, hoping to score some quick

---

4. The most frequent means the leadership uses is extraction by the Rules Committee—that is, by the Rules Committee making the bill in order even though it has not been reported by committee (Tiefer 1989, 268–269).

victories. Both bills had gone through the full committee process and had passed by large margins in the preceding Congress. Thus, the committees could hardly claim they had been cut out of the process. In 1988 the Democratic Party leadership took the Senate's version of the Civil Rights Restoration Act directly to the floor because time for action was getting short, and the leaders wanted to pass the bill without change to avoid a conference. The leadership feared delay in the Senate were further Senate action required. Most supporters were convinced that a bill more to their liking than the Senate version could never overcome a Senate filibuster nor a presidential veto.

In 1982 the House Democratic leadership and the chairman of the tax-writing Ways and Means Committee were unwilling to take the lead— and the blame—for a major tax increase made necessary by President Ronald Reagan's huge tax cut of the year before. Thus, despite the constitutional requirement that the House initiate tax legislation, the Senate actually did so by attaching tax-increase provisions as amendments to a minor House-passed revenue bill. The result was that the House Ways and Means Committee was effectively bypassed on the initial drafting of the legislation; members of that committee did have an impact on the legislation in the House-Senate conference committee that worked out the final version.

Once in a while the majority party leadership believes an issue to be too politically delicate for the committee or committees of jurisdiction to handle. In 1988 the Speaker entrusted the drafting of the House Democrats' alternative to Reagan's plan for aiding the Nicaraguan contras to a task force headed by the deputy whip; no committee was involved. The political risks inherent in strongly opposing the president on a highly charged and highly visible foreign policy issue, as House Democrats were doing, were too great to leave the decision making to a committee.

Although most items in the Contract with America, the House Republicans' legislative agenda in the 104th Congress, went through the formal committee process, committee deliberation was largely pro forma. The unfunded mandates bill, for example, was referred to four committees on January 4, 1995, the first day of the session; the Government Reform and Oversight Committee ordered it reported on January 10, having spent only one meeting marking up the bill; Rules followed suit two days later; on January 19 floor consideration began. In fact, the bills in the Contract were actually drafted before the Congress began (the Contract was put together in the summer of 1994), and the Republican leadership was unwilling to brook changes of any magnitude (Owens 1996). During the 1994 campaign, the leaders had promised action on all the items in the first 100 days, an extremely ambitious schedule that allowed for little real deliberation in committee, and they feared being accused of not keeping their promises if significant changes were made.

The Republican leadership often used task forces to work out legislation in the 104th but in most cases did not formally bypass committee deliberation. For example, a "design team" led by Speaker Newt Gingrich, R-Ga., worked out the contours of the Medicare reform bill. Immigration policy also was crafted by a task force; according to a participant, about 80 percent of the task force's recommendations were incorporated in the bill reported by the Immigration Subcommittee of the Judiciary Committee. The membership of the task forces and of the key committees of jurisdiction often overlap. The task force device allows the leadership to involve other interested members in the process and puts pressure on committees to act expeditiously and with sensitivity to the sentiments of the party majority.

Because the issue is substantively, procedurally, and politically complex, Speaker Gingrich set up a task force headed by Chief Deputy Whip Dennis Hastert, R-Ill., to draft managed care reform legislation in the 105th Congress and brought that legislation directly to the floor, bypassing the committees of jurisdiction. When Hastert became Speaker in the next Congress, he promised to follow regular order and not bypass committees. Yet the same constellation of problems eventually forced Hastert to turn to unorthodox processes in drafting managed care legislation, and he too effectively bypassed the committees. (See Chapter 8 for the full story.) In response to the Columbine High School shootings in the spring of 1999 and to the Democrats' effort to pass and gain credit for strong gun control legislation, Hastert brought a weak gun control bill directly to the floor, bypassing the Judiciary Committee—with the full acquiescence of Chairman Henry J. Hyde, R-Ill.

Postcommittee Adjustments

After a bill has been reported from committee, supporters often make substantive adjustments. The practice has become almost routine, with more than a third of major legislation subject to such postcommittee adjustments in most recent Congresses and almost half in the 104th Congress. Occasionally, legislation will be taken back to committee for formal revision. Much more frequently, changes will be negotiated and then incorporated into a substitute bill or an amendment. The substitute may supersede the committee bill and become the version (called the base bill) taken to the House floor, or it may be incorporated into the committee bill by the rule; alternatively, the substitute or the amendment may be offered by supporters on the floor.

Such postcommittee adjustments are made to enhance the legislation's chances of passage. Almost always both committee and party leaders are involved, with the majority party leadership often taking the lead. Major legislation that involves difficult political, substantive, or procedural problems is most likely to require such alterations. The committee leaders have, in most cases, done in committee what they were willing and able to do to ensure passage; and the majority party leaders are ultimately held responsible for passing the legislation their party members and the House as an institution need and want.

Multiple referral has drawn the majority party leaders into the substantive side of the legislative process; when the committees to which major legislation has been jointly referred cannot come to an agreement among themselves, the party leadership may have to take over the job of negotiating enough of an agreement to avoid a bloody battle on the House floor. A 1987 bill to restructure the farm credit system provides a good example. The House Agriculture Committee reported legislation that included a provision setting up a secondary market in farm mortgages. Securities issues are in the jurisdiction of the Banking and Commerce committees, and the legislation was sequentially referred to both. The leaders of these two committees and of the Agriculture Committee were, however, far apart substantively; it took strong leadership intervention to get an agreement. The majority whip brokered the deal that was taken to the floor as an amendment. The amendment and the bill passed easily. Similarly, on the child care legislation mentioned earlier, the two committees with major jurisdiction took very different approaches to the problem and could not come to an agreement; the party leadership had to intervene to break the stalemate, and that intervention involved making substantive adjustments to the legislation. In 1995 the House Republican leadership produced the party's welfare reform bill by combining bills passed by three committees and, in the process, altered some controversial provisions (Katz 1995, 815).

Controversy and saliency often prompt the need for postcommittee adjustments. Supporters may find that their bill as it emerged from committee does not command enough votes to pass. In 1988, for example, a welfare reform bill as reported from committee was viewed as too expensive by many in the House. Supporters believed it would be severely amended or fail if it went to the floor without change. The legislation could not be allowed to die. Democrats were committed to welfare reform. The committees had put a great deal of effort and time into drafting the bill, and the party leadership believed it would enhance the party's image. After extensive negotiations the leadership came up with a strategy: offer an amendment to cut the program enough to satisfy those Democrats who believed they needed to vote for cuts but not so much that the legislation's erstwhile supporters could no longer vote for it. The amendment was offered on the floor; once it passed, the bill did also.

Relatively minor postcommittee adjustments were sufficient to amass the necessary support in the House for Clinton's national service program and Goals 2000 education legislation at the beginning of his presidency. In his second year, however, even major adjustments were not enough to save his top legislative priority. Different versions of comprehensive health care legislation were reported by three committees (one committee reported two different bills); the party leadership attempted to put together a single bill that could pass but was unsuccessful. The issue and the Clinton approach had become too controversial.

In the 104th Congress the Republican leadership often found it necessary to make postcommittee adjustments in legislation. To pass a big rescission bill (a bill cutting already appropriated spending) in 1995, the leadership had to agree to drop restrictive anti-abortion language and to accept a "lockbox" provision dictating that the savings go to deficit reduction and not to fund tax cuts. The first was necessary to get the votes of GOP moderates, the second to pick up some votes from conservative Democrats (Hager 1995a, 796–797). When the constitutional amendment imposing term limits on members of Congress emerged from the Judiciary Committee in a form that the majority of the Republican Party found unacceptable, the Rules Committee, at the direction of the leadership, dropped the committee draft and substituted another version (Salant 1995, 787). In early 1996 committee-approved provisions were deleted from the antiterrorism bill and from the immigration bill before they were taken to the floor. In the former case the leadership was eager to pick up the votes of the most conservative Republicans, who opposed giving the federal government any new powers. The weakening of the antiterrorism bill proved to be insufficient, and an amendment largely gutting the bill was adopted on the House floor. In the case of immigration legislation, business groups opposed a committee-approved provision requiring the verification of the legal immigration status of workers in five states. When the head of the Immigration Task Force complained about the change that would make the plan voluntary, the chair of the Immigration Subcommittee said, "The idea was to get the bill to the House floor with solid support" (Eilperin 1996, 1).

With his razor-thin partisan majority in the 106th Congress, Speaker Dennis Hastert often found postcommittee adjustments necessary to pass important bills. Moderate Republicans threatened to vote against the Ways and Means Committee's 1999 tax bill because, they claimed, it concerned itself too little with deficit reduction. They were brought back on board with language that made the tax rate cut dependent on a declining national debt (Taylor 1999c, 1783–1785). Passing appropriations bills in 1999 required a series of adjustments in committee-drafted bills. (For more, see Chapter 6.)

Legislation that involves many issues is likely to be both highly consequential and controversial and, as such, not infrequently requires postcommittee fine-tuning. The broad scope of such omnibus measures, which are discussed more in Chapter 5, means that most members have a keen interest in at least some provisions. Putting together a version that is satisfactory to most members of the majority party and to a majority of the House may be difficult for the reporting committee or committees. Budget resolutions that lay out a blueprint for federal spending in the following year—how much will be spent, for what, whether there will be a tax increase, and what the deficit will be—and reconciliation bills that bring law into accord with the budget blueprint (and thus may include changes in a multitude of programs as well as tax increases) are the sort of omnibus measures that frequently require postcommittee adjustments orchestrated by the majority party leadership. The case studies in Chapters 10 and 11 of the 1993 reconciliation bill, which in essence contained President Clinton's economic program; of the even more ambitious 1995 reconciliation bill incorporating congressional Republicans' balanced budget plan; and of the 1997 balanced budget deal provide a number of examples.

Special Rules

In the House the majority party leadership schedules legislation for floor debate. When a committee reports a bill, it is placed at the bottom of one of the House calendars, the Union Calendar if major legislation. Considering legislation in the order it is listed on the calendar would make little sense, since optimal floor scheduling dictates attention to a host of policy and political factors. The House has developed ways of getting legislation to the floor that provide the needed flexibility. The primary ways of bringing legislation to the floor are through suspension of the rules and through special rules from the Rules Committee, both procedures that the majority party leadership controls.

Noncontroversial legislation is usually considered under suspension of the rules. In 1991–1993, for example, 52 percent of all bills that passed the House did so by way of the suspension procedure. Much of the legislation considered under suspension is narrow in impact or minor in importance. Examples include H.Con.Res. 146, a concurrent resolution authorizing the 1996 Special Olympics Torch Relay to be run through the Capitol grounds, or S1341, a bill to provide for the transfer of certain lands to the Salt River Pima-Maricopa Indian community and the city of Scottsdale, Arizona. Legislation of more far-reaching significance also may be considered under suspension of the rules. This happens if the bill is so broadly supported that using much floor time is unwarranted. One example is HR2778, a 1995 bill affecting members of the armed forces performing services for the peacekeeping effort in the Republic of Bosnia and Herzegovina. The bill entitled them to certain tax benefits normally granted to those who serve in a combat zone.

The motion to suspend the rules is in order on Mondays and Tuesdays. Legislation brought up under this procedure is debated for a maximum of forty minutes. No amendments are allowed, and a two-thirds vote is required for passage.

The Speaker has complete discretion over what legislation is considered under suspension. When a committee chair has a bill he or she considers appropriate for suspension, the chair makes a request to the leadership. The Speaker is guided by party rules restricting the use of the procedure. The Democratic Caucus and the Republican Conference both have rules specifying that, to be considered under suspension of the rules, bills should be bipartisan, have strong committee support, and cost less than $100 million. These rules can be waived, but the requirement of a two-thirds vote for passage limits what can be successfully passed under suspension of the rules.

Most major legislation is brought to the House floor by a special rule that allows the measure to be taken up out of order. The Rules Committee reports such rules, which take the form of House resolutions. A majority of the full membership must approve each one.

The rule sets the terms for a measure's floor consideration. A rule always specifies how much time is to be allowed for general debate and who is to control that time. One or two hours of general debate are typical, though major measures are sometimes granted considerably more time. The time is always equally split between the chair and the ranking minority member of the committee that reported the legislation; if several committees worked on the bill, each will control some of the general debate time.

A rule may restrict amendments, waive points of order (against what would otherwise be violations of House rules in the legislation or in how it is brought up), and include other special provisions to govern floor consideration. The extent to which a rule restricts amendments and the manner in which it does so also may vary. An open rule allows all germane amendments, while a closed rule prohibits all amendments other than those offered by the reporting committee. Between the two extremes are rules that allow some but not all germane amendments to be offered; the Rules Committee labels each a modified open rule or a modified closed rule, depending on just how restrictive the rule is. Some rules of this kind allow only specific amendments enumerated in the Rules Committee report to be offered. Others allow only amendments that have been submitted to the Rules Committee or printed in the *Congressional Record* by a specific time. Still other rules set a time limit on the amending process and allow all germane amendments that can be offered during that time period.

In the contemporary House most rules are somewhat restrictive; in the Congresses of the early 1990s, two-thirds or more of all rules were modified open or modified closed or, occasionally, closed. Republicans had chafed under restrictive rules and promised to be more open if they took control of the House. The proportion of all rules that were restrictive did go down a bit in the 104th and 105th Congresses as Republicans had promised. Restrictive rules were even more likely to be used on major legislation than on all legislation, and that did not change when the Republicans took control. In the 1990s three-fourths or more of all major bills were considered under a restrictive rule.

When major legislation is ready for floor consideration, a decision on what type of rule to use must be made. Given the variety in contemporary rules, the choices are many. The Rules Committee is officially charged with making the decision, and the leaders of the reporting committee make their preferences known. But since the majority party members of Rules are selected by the Speaker, the party leadership strongly influences what is decided. On major legislation the decision on the character of the rule is considered crucial to the bill's success; not surprisingly, the leadership decides.

Because there are many options in the design of a rule, special rules can increasingly be tailored to the problem at hand. Thus, when a bill is referred to several committees, setting the ground rules for floor consideration can present a host of complicated and delicate problems (Bach and Smith 1988, 18–23). Debate time must be divided. When two or more committees have reported different provisions on a given matter, a decision also must be made about which committee's language will constitute the base text and how the other committees' versions will be considered. The first rule for the consideration of the 1992 energy bill, which had been referred to nine committees, split five hours of general debate among the committees. The Energy and Commerce Committee received one hour; the other eight were allotted a half hour each. The committees worked out as many of the conflicts among themselves as they could. In the remaining cases, the Rules Committee decided which committee's version would go into the base bill that would serve as the original bill for the purpose of amendment on the floor. Other committees could offer their language as amendments on the floor. The rule limited the amendments to those listed in the Rules Committee's report, set debate time for each amendment—ranging from five to twenty minutes per side—and specified that those amendments "shall not be subject to amendment except as specified in the report" (*Congressional Record,* May 20, 1992, H3462).

The rule for the juvenile justice/gun control legislation considered in June of 1999 demonstrates that complex rules are not limited to multiply referred legislation. Speaker Hastert decided the House needed to respond legislatively to the Columbine High School shootings. The Senate had passed gun control legislation, and Democrats and moderate Republicans were clamoring for the House to follow suit. Yet a host of procedural and political problems confronted him. The only legislation a committee had so far reported was HR1501, a noncontroversial bill providing grants to combat juvenile crime. A big majority of House Republicans opposed gun control, but moderate Republicans believed their electoral survival depended on a response to the public's demand to do something after the shootings; even conservatives felt the need to respond, though not by passing gun control legislation (Carney 1999, 1426–1432).

Hastert decided to bring gun control provisions and other measures aimed at combating juvenile crime to the floor, even though they had not been reported by committee. The rule specified that HR1501, the noncontroversial bill, be considered first; forty-four specific amendments were made in order to HR1501. One of these was the McCollum amendment, which incorporated the Republicans' new juvenile crime measures, such as increased minimum sentences for juveniles and allowing prosecutors to try juveniles as adults in federal courts; thirty-eight of the other amendments allowed were made in order as amendments to the McCollum amendment, meaning that the McCollum amendment was in effect the base bill. The rule further stated:

> Each amendment may be offered only by a Member designated in the report, shall be considered as read, shall be debatable for the time specified in the report equally divided and controlled by the proponent and an opponent, shall not be subject to amendment except as specified in the report. . . . All points of order against the amendments printed in the report are waived. (*Congressional Record,* June 15, 1999, H4339)

Many of the amendments were intended to give their sponsors and others who voted for them something to tell their constituents when asked about their response to Columbine. For example, an amendment allowed states and municipalities to display the Ten Commandments on public property. (It was approved 248–180.)

After HR1501 was disposed of, the rule specified that HR2122, the Speaker's gun control bill, be considered. Eleven amendments were made in order, and consideration was governed by a provision like that above, which specified who had the right to offer each amendment and set time limits. The most important amendments were the NRA-backed Dingell amendment, which would weaken the bill's gun control provisions, and the Democrats' McCarthy amendment, which would strengthen them. The Republican leadership wanted to make sure that its members had a menu of proposals to choose from. The Republican leaders believed that if the Dingell weakening amendment were adopted, it would sink the bill. Republicans chose to allow John Dingell, a senior Democrat, to offer his amendment rather than have a Republican offer the weakening amendment, to obscure partisan responsibility for weakening or killing gun control.

Finally, the rule stipulated that if both bills passed, they would be combined and sent to the Senate as one bill. The bills had been split so that the gun control provisions would not endanger the juvenile justice measures. As it turned out, the gun control bill failed. When the Dingell amendment was adopted and the McCarthy amendment failed, the resulting legislation was too weak for pro–gun control Democrats but still too strong for adamantly anti–gun control Republicans.

The Uses of Special Rules

Special rules can be used to focus attention and debate on the critical choices, to save time and prevent obstruction and delay, and sometimes to structure the choices members confront on the floor in a way that promotes a particular outcome. When the rule gives members a choice among comprehensive substitutes but bars votes on narrow amendments, it is focusing the debate on alternative approaches, on the big choices rather than the picky details. In recent years rules allowing a choice among comprehensive substitutes have been used to bring to the floor tax bills, budget resolutions, civil rights bills, and social welfare legislation on issues such as parental leave, the minimum wage, and child care.

Rules that restrict amendments and waive points of order save time and prevent obstructionism. Before Republicans gained a House majority in the 1994 elections, they had promised, if they took control of the chamber, to use less restrictive rules than had the Democrats when in power. Yet House Republicans also promised to pass the Contract with America during the first 100 days of the 104th Congress. When they brought one of the early Contract items to the floor under an open rule, Democrats naturally enough offered multitudes of amendments. Thereafter, the Republican-controlled Rules Committee usually included in its otherwise unrestrictive rules a time limit on total amending activity.

Any restrictions on amendments, even simply the requirement that amendments be submitted to the Rules Committee several days before being offered on the floor, help the bill's proponents by reducing uncertainty. Proponents can focus their efforts and plan strategy more efficiently; opponents lose the element of surprise.

In addition to reducing uncertainty, carefully crafted rules can structure choices to advantage a particular outcome. The 1988 case of welfare reform legislation discussed earlier illustrates how. Most Democrats— enough to constitute a clear majority of the House—favored passing a welfare reform bill; they believed it constituted good public policy. Many, however, believed that, for reelection reasons, they had to go on record as favoring a reduction in the costs of the program. By allowing a vote on an amendment to cut the program moderately but barring one on an amendment that made draconian cuts, the rule gave those members who needed it the opportunity to demonstrate fiscal responsibility and also ensured that legislation most Democrats favored would be enacted.

In 1995 Republicans, now in the majority, used a cleverly constructed restrictive rule to protect their rescission bill. The rule specified that anyone wishing to restore spending that had been cut in the bill had to offset the cost by cutting something else in the same section of the bill. Thus, no money could be transferred to social programs from defense spending or from disaster relief for California, for example, since these programs were in different sections of the bill.

The rule for the Republicans' omnibus tax-cut bill in 1995 disallowed an amendment on one of its most controversial provisions. The bill gave families earning up to $200,000 a year a $500 per child tax credit; moderate Republicans wanted to reduce the eligibility to families making less than $100,000; conservative Republicans were adamantly opposed to any cap. Since Democrats agreed with moderate Republicans, had the amendment been made in order it would have passed, and then conservative Republicans might have opposed the bill. The Republican leadership gambled that moderate Republicans would not desert their party and simply refused them a vote on their amendment. In 1997, the bill outlawing so-called partial-birth abortions was brought to the floor under a closed rule; the Republican leadership wanted to bar a vote on a

Democratic amendment, attractive to some moderate Republicans, that would have made an exception for cases in which the mother's health was at risk.

Occasionally a closed rule can be used to defeat a bill. In 1997, to get the necessary support for the rule bringing the budget reconciliation bills to the floor, the Republican leadership had to promise a group of deficit hawks a floor vote on their draconian budget enforcement bill. That bill, which even its supporters conceded needed refinement, was brought to the floor under a closed rule, which made it impossible for supporters to improve it through amendments; it went down in flames on an 81–347 vote (*Congressional Quarterly Almanac* 1997, 2–49).

In 1998, the Republican leadership used the opposite strategy to attempt to defeat the Shays-Meehan campaign finance reform bill. Threat of a discharge petition forced the leadership to bring it to the floor, but because the leadership acted before the petition got 218 votes, the leadership, not the bill's supporters, controlled the floor. The rule allowed 11 substitute amendments, each of which could be amended; a second rule made at least 248 amendments in order. Campaign finance supporters cried foul, arguing that the Republican leadership's plan was for the debate to drag on forever and the bill to fall victim to some of the "poison pill" amendments intended to split the support coalition. Yet, even though debate did drag on and on—the House debated the bill sporadically from May 21 to August 8—and dozens of killer amendments were offered, the coalition held together and passed the Shays-Meehan bill (*Congressional Quarterly Almanac* 1998, 18-6–18-16).

New Parliamentary Devices

New parliamentary devices developed in recent years have made special rules even more flexible and potent tools for structuring choices. A "king-of-the-hill" provision in a rule specifies that a series of amendments or entire substitutes are to be voted on ad seriatim and the last one that receives a majority prevails. This device makes possible a direct vote on each of several alternatives; in ordinary parliamentary procedure, if an amendment or substitute receives a majority, no further alternative amendments to that part of the bill already amended can be offered. Clearly, when the king-of-the-hill procedure is employed, the amendment or substitute voted on last is advantaged. The procedure also makes it possible for members to vote for more than one version, which is sometimes politically advantageous. When Democrats were in the majority, budget resolutions were often considered under king-of-the-hill rules. Members were thus guaranteed a vote on each of the substitute versions of the resolution made in order by the rule. The House Budget Committee version was always placed in the advantageous last position.[5]

The rule for the 1991 civil rights bill illustrates how the procedure can be used strategically. The rule stipulated that the three substitutes made in order were to be offered in a specific order under the king-of-the-hill procedure. The rule gave liberals a vote on their much stronger version but put that substitute first in line. Having cast a vote in favor of the tough bill favored by civil rights activists, these members then could support the leadership's more moderate compromise. The rule next gave House Republicans and the Bush administration a vote on their preferred version. It put the Democratic compromise last—that is, in the advantaged position.

In the 104th Congress Republicans began using a "queen-of-the-hill" variant, which allows a vote on all the versions but specifies that whichever version gets the most votes, so long as it receives a majority, wins. The rules for the welfare reform bill and the term-limits constitutional amendment took this form; in the former case, a liberal Democratic substitute, a more conservative Democratic substitute, and the Republican version were considered under the queen-of-the-hill procedure. On term limits, votes on four versions were made in order. In both cases the option the Republican leadership supported was placed last, which is still the preferred position. Supporters of the last option, unlike those of earlier ones, know how many votes they need to win.

In the 105th Congress, a queen-of-the-hill rule was used on the term-limits constitutional amendment. Rules Committee chair Gerald Solomon, R-N.Y., explained the political rationale:

> The Committee on Rules was faced with a situation where there are nine States which have passed ballot initiatives requiring Members from those States to support a particular version of the term limits constitutional amendment specified in the ballot initiative, or else they would have to have a special designation next to their names on the ballot the next time they run at the next election which would read "disregarded voter instructions on term limits." (*Congressional Record*, Feb. 12, 1997, H459)

The queen-of-the-hill procedure allowed members from these states to vote for their state's specific version. The various versions were even labeled by state; the first to be voted on was the Arkansas version.

---

5. When the leadership was confident that it could defeat all the alternatives and no postcommittee adjustments in the budget resolution were needed, the Budget Committee version was not offered as an amendment at all but constituted the base bill.

Another new device—a self-executing rule—provides that when a rule is adopted by the House, the accompanying bill is automatically amended to incorporate the text of an amendment either set forth or referenced in the rule. The procedure provides a simple way of inserting last-minute corrections or compromises into a bill and prevents a direct and separate vote on the language in question. Thus, in 1999 after the Republicans' tax bill was reported from committee, the leadership, in order to amass the votes needed to pass the bill, worked out a compromise with moderate Republicans. The language was incorporated into the legislation by a self-executing provision in the rule. The Republican leadership has used the device frequently, as the case study in Chapter 11 shows. During the 105th Congress, 20 of 149 rules for initial consideration of legislation included self-executing provisions; a number of these were rules for appropriations bills.

On the Floor

Floor consideration of a bill begins with debate on the rule. One hour is allotted, half controlled by a majority member of Rules and half by a minority member. The majority member explains and justifies the rule, the minority member gives his or her party's position, and then both yield time to other members who wish to speak. If neither the rule nor the legislation is controversial, much less than the full hour may be used. If the legislation is controversial but the rule is not, members frequently will use the time to discuss the legislation substantively. Since so many of today's rules are restrictive and complex, they are often highly controversial, and debate may well revolve around the character of the rule itself and consume the entire hour. During this period, no amendments to the rule are in order.

The House must approve the rule before consideration of the legislation can begin. The Rules Committee member managing the debate on the rule for the majority party will move the previous question. If successful, the motion cuts off debate, and the House then proceeds to vote on the rule itself. The only way to amend the rule is to defeat the previous question motion. If opponents defeat the previous question motion, they control the floor and may propose the special rule they would like to see. Losing on the motion to order the previous question is devastating for the majority party and seldom happens; a member who votes against his or her party on this crucial procedural motion is not quickly forgiven.

One memorable vote on the previous question occurred in 1981 on the reconciliation bill that implemented President Reagan's economic program. The key battle on that legislation was over the rule. Reagan and

House Republicans wanted a single vote on Reagan's package of spending cuts; they could then make the vote a test of whether members supported or opposed the popular president's program to rescue the economy. Democrats, who controlled the House, proposed a rule that forced a series of votes on cutting specific popular programs. Knowing they were likely to lose at least some of those votes and thereby major chunks of Reagan's economic plan, Republicans decided to try to defeat the previous question on the rule. With the help of some conservative Democrats, they were successful and so were able to substitute their own rule that called for a single vote on the package as a whole.

Votes on the previous question are usually far less visible, and disgruntled majority party members can be persuaded by their leadership to vote yes on that motion and show their displeasure, if they must, by voting against the rule. Fearing they lacked the votes to pass their rule for the consideration of the Department of Interior appropriations bill in the summer of 1995, Republicans nevertheless made an attempt to do so — but only after forcefully explaining to their freshmen members that they had better not join the minority in voting against the previous question (Burger 1995, 22). The rule was, in fact, defeated. The leadership then worked out a compromise among House Republicans, got the Rules Committee to incorporate it in a new rule, brought that to the floor, and passed it. When the majority party lost the rule, it did not lose control of the floor as it would have had it lost the previous question vote.

Once the previous question has been approved, the House votes on the rule itself. When the rule is not controversial, the vote may be by voice; on controversial rules the votes will be recorded. These recorded votes are still often called roll call votes, although the House seldom calls the roll as it did in the days before electronic voting. Because rules are frequently contentious, recorded votes are likely. In the 100th, 101st, 103rd, and 104th Congresses (1987–1990, 1993–1996), 168 major measures were brought to the floor under special rules, and 128 (76 percent) of the rule votes were decided by recorded votes.

The majority party sometimes loses votes on rules but not often. The vote on the Interior appropriations rule was the only one that Republicans lost during the 104th; from 1981 to 1992, Democrats lost on average just over one rule per year. During the highly charged 103rd Congress (1993–1994) Democrats lost five rules, and during the 105th with its narrow partisan majority Republicans lost five.

Increasingly, majority party members are expected to support their party on such procedural votes. Over the period 1987 to 1996 (but excluding the 102nd Congress), the mean vote by majority party members in favor on rule passage votes was 97 percent. Votes on rules tend to fall along party lines, especially when the rule is restrictive. Of rules for major legislation in the 100th and 101st Congresses, 48 percent saw a majority of Democrats supporting the rule and a majority of Republicans opposing it; in the 103rd and the 104th Congresses, 60 percent of rule votes saw a majority of the majority party voting in favor and a majority of the minority party voting against. Over those four Congresses, 74 percent of modified closed rules were decided by such party votes.

If the House approves the rule, it thereby resolves itself into the Committee of the Whole, where the debate and amending of the legislation takes place. A sort of parliamentary fiction, the Committee of the Whole has the same membership as the House but somewhat more streamlined rules. The quorum for doing business in the Committee of the Whole is 100 members rather than the House quorum of 218 members (half the full membership). In the Committee of the Whole when a member is recognized to offer or speak on an amendment, it is for only five minutes. The Speaker does not preside over the Committee of the Whole, but since he chooses the presiding officer and always picks a majority party member, the majority party remains in control of the chair.

General debate begins the consideration of the bill in the Committee of the Whole. The rule has specified who controls the time. The chair of the committee or subcommittee that reported the bill serves as floor manager for the majority and actually controls the time allotted to the committee majority; his or her minority counterpart controls the minority's time. The majority floor manager begins with a prepared statement explaining what the legislation does and why it deserves to pass.

The minority floor manager then makes a statement, which may range from wholehearted agreement with his or her opposite number to an all-out attack on the bill. When the committee has come to a broad bipartisan agreement, general debate may be a veritable lovefest, with committee members congratulating each other on the wonderful job they did and on the admirably cooperative way in which they did it. When the committee reporting the legislation is split, especially if it is split along party lines, the tone of floor debate will be contentious and sometimes bitter. If the legislation is the product of several committees, each will have floor managers, each of whom will make an opening statement.

After opening statements the floor managers yield time—usually in small amounts—to other members who wish to speak. By and large, the majority floor manager yields time to supporters of the legislation and to majority party members, while the minority floor manager yields time to minority party members and, assuming the bill is controversial, to opponents of the bill. Often not all majority party members support the bill and not all minority party members oppose it. Therefore, both managers may yield time to opponents of their position. An opponent today, especially if a fellow party member, may be a supporter tomorrow and should not be alienated.

When general debate time has expired, the amending process begins. What happens next depends on the rule. If all germane amendments are allowed, members are recognized to offer amendments. House rules give the chair of the Committee of the Whole discretion to determine the order of recognition, but by custom members of the reporting committee are given preference in gaining recognition, and they are recognized in order of seniority (Tiefer 1989, 231). Once a member is recognized to offer his or her amendment, the member has five minutes to explain it. The floor manager has five minutes to reply, then other members may speak. They gain time by offering pro forma amendments "to strike the last word" or "to strike the requisite number of words." The member who offers a pro forma amendment does not actually want it to pass, but by offering it he or she gets five minutes to speak on the amendment that is really at issue.

A House member may offer an amendment to the amendment being considered. Such a second-degree amendment may be intended sincerely to improve the amendment to which it is offered. Alternatively, the purpose behind a second-degree amendment may be to lessen the impact or even negate altogether the effect of the original amendment. If a bill's supporters believe they cannot defeat a popular but, in their view, harmful amendment, they may try to come up with a second-degree amendment to at least weaken its effect.

Debate on an amendment under the five-minute rule may go on for a considerable period of time, but eventually when everyone who wants to has spoken, a vote on the amendment occurs.

Sometimes a floor manager has no objections to an amendment or actually supports it and will simply "accept" the amendment without asking for a recorded vote. In that case the amendment is usually approved by voice vote. If the floor manager—or another member—opposes the amendment, a vote will be demanded. The first vote may be by voice, but if the amendment is at all controversial, the losing side in a voice vote will demand a recorded vote. Only twenty-five members are needed to force a recorded vote.

The House uses an electronic voting system. Members have individualized cards that look rather like a credit card; they insert their card into one of the ten voting stations attached to the backs of seats on the House floor and punch the "yea," "nay," or "present" button. The vote is recorded by a computer, and it also shows up as a green, red, or amber light next to the member's name on a huge lighted display behind the Speaker's dais.

After the amendment has been disposed of, another member is recognized to offer another amendment. Under an open rule the amending process continues as long as there are members who want to offer amendments and who are on the floor prepared to do so. The House can by majority vote cut off debate, though amendments that have been "preprinted" in the *Congressional Record* at least one day before floor consideration are guaranteed ten minutes of debate (Tiefer 1989, 401–403). Unlike senators, House members have limited patience for protracted floor debate. In January 1995 Republicans brought the unfunded mandates bill to the floor under an open rule; after six days of debate and with 170 amendments still pending, they voted to cut off debate.

A more frequently used way of controlling the length of the amending process is through the rule. Under many rules the amending process proceeds pretty much as described above except that the amendments allowed are limited, perhaps to those preprinted in the *Congressional Record*. In other cases the rule specifies which amendments are in order and which member may offer each. In these cases the rule frequently specifies a time limit on debate on a specific amendment—perhaps twenty minutes, or an hour for a major amendment. The rule also is likely to prohibit amendments to the amendments made in order.

What happens in the Committee of the Whole thus varies depending on the number of committees involved and the character of the rule. Clearly, a structured rule makes floor proceedings more orderly and predictable.

After general debate and whatever amending is allowed have been completed, the Committee of the Whole rises and reports back to the House. The Speaker again presides and the rules of the House again are in effect. Amendments adopted in the Committee of the Whole must be approved by the House, which gives opponents of an amendment a second chance to defeat it. Usually, however, the House votes on all the amendments adopted as a package and approval is certain. Occasionally, if a vote was very close and the amendment makes major and unacceptable changes in the legislation, an effort to change the outcome will be made. In 1995 Democrats, with some help from moderate Republicans, successfully passed in the Committee of the Whole an amendment to an appropriations bill deleting controversial language barring the Environmental Protection Agency from enforcing various environmental laws. The amendment won on a close 211–206 vote and the provision was important to many staunchly antiregulatory Republicans, so the leadership called for a second vote in the House and defeated the amendment on an even closer 210–210 vote. (Motions die on a tie vote.) In that case the leadership used a bit of strategic scheduling and got lucky; although no Republicans switched their votes, several Democrats who had supported the amendment the first time were absent for the second vote. Usually, however, amendments that win in the Committee of the Whole win again in the House. After all, the membership of the two bodies is identical.

The minority may then offer a motion to recommit the legislation to committee with or without instructions. A motion to recommit without instructions is essentially a motion to kill the bill and seldom prevails. By this point too many members have a stake in the legislation's enactment; if it lacked majority support, it would probably not have gotten so far. A motion to recommit with instructions—that is, instructions to report the bill back with specified changes—is, in effect, a motion to amend the bill. It is the minority's last chance to change the legislation. The motion may propose substituting the minority's version of the bill for the majority's, or it may propose much more modest changes. Again, because it is the minority's motion, it seldom wins—though more frequently than the motion to recommit without instructions. Assuming the legislation survives, a vote on final passage is taken, usually by recorded vote. Legislation that gets this far will almost certainly pass.

Constitutional amendments requiring a two-thirds vote often are defeated on a floor vote in the House, but bills that require only a majority seldom are; in the 100th, 101st, 103rd, and 104th Congresses, the only major bills to be defeated at this stage were two competing proposals to aid the Nicaraguan contras, one President Reagan's and the other sponsored by the Democratic leadership in 1988; the first 1990 budget summit agreement (though that technically was the defeat of a conference report); and the campaign finance bill in the 104th, legislation the leadership opposed. The narrow partisan majority in the 105th resulted in a higher number of defeats; four bills lost at this stage, including two that were leadership priorities (school vouchers and the waiving of environmental regulations on emergency flood control projects).

If the legislation does pass, a motion to reconsider is made and laid upon the table. This ensures that the issue cannot be reopened. The legislation is then sent to the Senate.

Unorthodox Lawmaking in the House

If the textbook legislative process can be likened to climbing a ladder, the contemporary process is more like climbing a big old tree with many branches. The route to enactment used to be linear and predictable; now it is flexible and varied. To be sure, the textbook model was never a complete description of how bills became laws. There have always been alternative routes. In the past, however, the alternatives were infrequently used on major legislation. Now variation is the norm. As the case studies in Chapters 7 through 11 show, no two major bills are likely to follow exactly the same process.

Although the new practices and procedures arose in response to different problems and opportunities (see Chapter 6), their consequences are similar. The new practices and procedures in the House facilitate lawmaking. Most make it easier for the majority party's leadership to advance its members' legislative goals. The leadership now has more flexibility to shape the legislative process to suit the particular legislation at issue. When climbing a ladder there isn't much one can do if a rung is broken; when climbing a tree with many branches, if one route is blocked there is always another to try.

chapter three

Routes and Obstacles: The Legislative Process in the Senate

IN THE SENATE LEGISLATION MUST TRAVERSE the same basic path as in the House, and the alternatives at the various stages are, in many cases, similar—at least on the surface. Yet the Senate is a quite different body from the House (Matthews 1960; Sinclair 1989; Smith 1989). Smaller in membership, the Senate is less hierarchical and less formal. Senate rules give senators as individuals great power: a senator may hold the floor indefinitely unless the Senate invokes cloture, which requires an extraordinary majority; further, any senator may offer an unlimited number of amendments to almost any piece of legislation, and those amendments need not even be germane. Current norms allow senators to use extended debate and floor amendments expansively (Sinclair 1989).

The differences in the two bodies are reflected in their legislative processes. The Senate does much of its business by unanimous consent—both an acknowledgment and an augmentation of the power of senators as individuals. Any one senator can block a unanimous consent request. The Senate is not a majority-rule chamber like the House. In the House the majority can always prevail; in the Senate minorities can often block majorities.

Bill Introduction

In the Senate, as in the House, only members—that is, senators—may introduce legislation, and each may introduce as many measures as he or she pleases. Senators may introduce their bills from the floor or just submit them to the clerks while the chamber is in session. The sources of legislation—the executive branch, interest groups, constituents, the legislator's pet projects—are similar in the two chambers. Because senators represent whole states and serve on more committees than the typical House member, they tend to offer legislation concerning a broader range of issues.

Bill Referral

When a bill is introduced or arrives from the House of Representatives, it is normally referred by the presiding officer, on the advice of the parliamentarian, to the committee of predominant jurisdiction. Senate rules do not encourage multiple referral as House rules do.

Multiple Referral

Sometimes bills are sent to more than one committee in the Senate. A 1977 rule provides that the joint party leadership (that is, the majority and the minority leaders acting together) can by motion propose that legislation be multiply referred, but this route is never used (Davidson 1989, 379–380). When legislation is multiply referred, it is done by unanimous consent; the consent request may specify time limits for each committee's consideration of the legislation as the 1977 rule had allowed. Agreements are usually negotiated by the affected committee leaders; in the Senate party leaders seldom take an active role (Davidson 1989, 388). "One just can't imagine the Senate giving its leaders the kind of power the Speaker has with respect to referral—determining what committees can do what to legislation, sometimes even to specifying what language they can work on, specifying committee reporting deadlines, and the like," a knowledgeable observer explained in an interview with the author.

In the Senate several different committees sometimes consider bills that, while not identical, deal with the same topic. For example, in 1995 three committees—Judiciary, Governmental Affairs, and Energy and Natural Resources—reported out regulatory reform legislation. Even when not technically multiply referred, such legislation entails many of the same complications.

Multiple referral is less frequent in the Senate than in the House; only a little more than one in ten major measures were sent to more than one committee in recent Congresses. Much of the legislation sent to multiple committees in the House is referred to only one committee in the Senate; the reverse is seldom the case.

Legislation that is multiply referred in the Senate is also less likely than in the House to be sent to a large number of committees. The big trade bill in the 100th Congress was referred to nine committees in the Senate, and the bills implementing the North American Free Trade Agreement (NAFTA) and the General Agreement on Tariffs and Trade (GATT) were each sent to six. More typical, however, is referral to two committees.

Part of the difference in the frequency of multiple referral in the Senate and the House is a result of differences in how jurisdictional boundaries are drawn in the two chambers; the Senate made significant changes in 1977, and its committee jurisdictions are somewhat more consonant with contemporary issues. But the difference also reflects more basic differences between the chambers; in the Senate when legislation impinges on the jurisdiction of more than one committee, the committee chairs often informally work out any problems among themselves.

Bypassing Committee

In the Senate, as in the House, committees are sometimes bypassed altogether. In recent Congresses about one in seven major measures went to the Senate floor without going through committee; in the 104th Congress (1995–1996), however, more than one in four did so. In the Senate bypassing a committee is technically simple; if any senator objects to committee referral (more precisely, objects on the floor to further proceedings on the measure after the second reading, which occurs right before the bill would be referred to committee), the bill goes directly to the calendar (Tiefer 1989, 594). When legislation reported by a Senate committee awaits floor action and a companion House-passed bill arrives in the Senate, this procedure is frequently used to put the bill directly on the calendar rather than sending it to a committee that has already dealt with the issue. In a similar vein, when a Senate committee is still working on a bill and the House sends over its version, the House-passed bill is commonly held at the desk by unanimous consent. The use of these procedures does not, of course, constitute bypassing the committee in any real sense.

Any senator's power to put legislation directly on the calendar simply by objecting to the bill's being referred to committee would seem to make bypassing committee easy. However, the majority leader, through his scheduling powers, effectively has a veto over senators bringing bills to the floor directly by this route. Although procedurally simple, the direct route really requires the majority leader's assent to work.

Senate committee chairs, with the majority leader's agreement, sometimes use this rule to speed up the legislative process, particularly on relatively uncontroversial legislation. In early 1987, for example, a clean water bill that had overwhelmingly passed late in the previous Congress but had been vetoed by Reagan was brought directly to the floor. In 1988 legislation protecting whistleblowers had passed, but again late in the year, and Reagan killed it by pocket veto. When the next year the sponsors and the Bush administration worked out a compromise, the bill was no longer at all controversial, so supporters took it directly to the floor. On fair housing legislation in 1988, extensive negotiations among Senate committee leaders, administration officials, and interest group representatives produced a broadly supported compromise, which was taken directly to the floor. Doing so enabled the bill to pass before the August recess and avoid the end-of-the-session rush. Republicans, newly in the majority in 1995, were determined to pass quickly legislation requiring that Congress abide by various regulatory laws; the House had passed its bill on the first day of the session. A similar bill had passed before and had bipartisan support, so the Senate by unanimous consent placed the legislation directly on the calendar. Despite this maneuver, the Senate still took a week to pass the bill.

Political considerations may dictate bypassing committee. In the wake of the Oklahoma City bombing, President Clinton proposed antiterrorism legislation. To demonstrate his and the Republican Party's concern about the issue as well as his ability to get things done, then–majority leader Bob Dole of Kansas wanted swift action. He and Judiciary chairman Orrin G. Hatch, R-Utah, drafted legislation and took it to the floor, bypassing committee consideration. In 1999 Majority Leader Trent Lott of Mississippi took a "partial-birth" abortion bill and a bill to establish a "Social Security lockbox" directly to the floor, bypassing committee. In both cases, the desire to score political points dictated the timing; in the latter case, Lott also bypassed the committee because Finance Committee Chairman William Roth of Delaware opposed the bill.

Occasionally, the Senate bypasses committees to, in effect, avoid multiple referral. An omnibus drug bill in 1988 involved the jurisdiction of more than half the committees; rather than referring the legislation to all the various committees with jurisdiction, Senate leaders bypassed committee consideration. Instead, the bill was based on the recommendations of party task forces and drafted through months-long, bipartisan negotiations among key senators. Although the senators who were involved were largely the ones who would have taken the lead had the legislation gone to the committees, the informal process allowed for more flexibility (see Chapter 9).

Senators have available another—and, in some ways, even easier—way to bypass committee; they can offer their legislation as an amendment to another bill on the floor. In most cases the "amendment" need not even be germane. The original Gramm-Rudman budget-balancing legislation was never considered by committee; Texas Republican Phil Gramm, its lead sponsor, simply offered it on the floor as an amendment to legislation raising the debt ceiling. In 1984 Democrats, then in the minority in the Senate, brought civil rights legislation that Republicans opposed to the floor as an amendment to a continuing appropriations resolution, a must-pass bill. In 1999, Sen. Edward M. (Ted) Kennedy, D-Mass., attempted to attach an increase in the minimum wage to several unrelated bills.

Senate handling of the ethics–pay raise issue in 1989 represented a combination of these procedures. When the bill came over from the House (without any Senate provisions, since each chamber handles its own internal matters), the Senate leaders placed it directly on the calendar, thus bypassing committee. Time was short, and the issue was too delicate for a committee to handle. Then the majority and minority leaders jointly offered a leadership amendment to apply House provisions banning pay-raises and honoraria to the Senate (*Congressional Quarterly Almanac* 1989, 57). Insufficient votes to pass their amendment later forced them to scale back the pay raise, again through a floor amendment.

As these examples suggest, the legislative process is often less formal in the Senate than in the House. Individual members are more important and committees less important than in the House. Given the power that senators as individuals wield and each senator's enormous workload, informal negotiations and agreements sometimes supplant more formal procedures.

Postcommittee Adjustments

To enhance its chances of passage, legislation in the Senate, as in the House, may be altered after it has been reported from committee. In recent Congresses about a third of major measures were subject to such postcommittee adjustment; in the 104th Congress (1995–1996) the proportion shot up to 60 percent but, in the 105th, it fell again.

The effort to craft a postcommittee compromise may be led by the party leadership. On the clean air bill in 1990, Majority Leader Mitchell orchestrated the complex negotiations that finally produced a bill that could pass the Senate (Cohen 1992, 81–98). He was similarly active on child care legislation in 1989, putting together a substitute based on elements of the Finance and Labor Committees' versions when it became clear the liberal Labor Committee's bill could not pass on its own. In 1995, when Republican supporters of two line-item-veto bills could not work out their differences, Majority Leader Dole helped craft a draft quite different from either one (Taylor 1995, 855).

More frequently than in the House, in the Senate committee leaders or even individual senators take the lead. In 1993, for example, Senate

Banking Committee leaders faced the daunting task of passing highly unpopular legislation to provide funds to finish the savings and loan bailout. In a time of big deficits and not enough money for popular programs, no senator relished voting for what appeared to be a bailout of the greedy savings and loan industry, even though, in effect, the bailout was an obligation resulting from the federal government's guarantee of the safety of deposits. After the Senate Banking Committee had reported the legislation, it became clear it would not pass, so the chair and the ranking minority member, after negotiations with the Clinton administration, offered a less generous substitute on the floor and thereby engineered passage. Similarly, when Clinton's national service program ran into some trouble on the Senate floor, Senator Kennedy, chair of the Senate Labor Committee, made changes via an amendment that picked up the needed votes. In 1999, Sen. John McCain, R-Ariz., chair of the Commerce Committee, had to make a number of postcommittee compromises to pass legislation setting liability limits for potential Y2K problems, thus protecting high-tech companies. As he explained on the Senate floor:

> Mr. President,[1] we are about to culminate the work of many months: investigation, drafting, negotiation, and compromise. . . .
>
> I want to remind my colleagues that many compromises have been made in this bill since it passed out of the Commerce Committee. It is certainly not as strong a bill as that passed by the House. These compromises have been made in order to get a bill that can have bipartisan approval and can be signed into law. (*Congressional Record,* June 15, 1999, S6976)

Of course, the strategy of altering the bill substantively to increase support is not always successful; it may not be possible to make sufficient changes to pick up needed new votes without altering the measure in a way that alienates its supporters. In 1995 Senate supporters of a balanced budget constitutional amendment engaged in a succession of very public negotiations as they scurried to get the necessary votes. Majority Leader Dole and the chair of the Judiciary Committee, as well as other core supporters, crafted an amendment restricting the judiciary's power over the constitutional amendment's enforcement and thereby won the support of Sen. Sam Nunn, D-Ga. Despite lengthy attempts, they were never able to satisfy senators concerned about the impact of the balanced budget amendment on the Social Security system, and the amendment failed.

Passage of a constitutional amendment requires a two-thirds vote, an intentionally high barrier to success. Ordinary legislation, if it is controversial, may well need an extraordinary majority as well. Senators now use

---

1. Because the Constitution designates the vice president of the United States as the president of the Senate, the presiding officer of the Senate is always addressed as "Mr. President," even though the vice president seldom presides.

their right of extended debate—their right to talk and thus block action indefinitely—much more frequently than in the past. Since cutting off debate requires sixty votes, supporters of legislation must build a coalition that is bigger than a simple majority. Doing so will likely require extensive compromise and may require the sort of postcommittee adjustments discussed here. On the national service legislation sponsors never had a problem getting a majority; they had to make more concessions in order to amass the sixty votes it takes to overcome a threatened filibuster (see Chapter 7). Republicans could have passed strong Y2K legislation if only a majority had been required; of course, they still would have had to worry about a presidential veto.

Scheduling Legislation for the Floor

The Senate does not use special rules to bring legislation to the floor. The majority leader, by motion or unanimous consent, just takes the bill to be considered off the calendar. Senate precedent provides the majority leader with the right of first recognition; when several senators seek recognition, the majority leader is recognized first and the minority leader second. Otherwise, Senate rules require the presiding officer to recognize the first senator to seek recognition, giving the presiding officer much less discretion than his House counterpart has. (When the Senate is debating legislation, the bill's managers have the right to be recognized after the leaders but before other senators.)

Although the procedure seems simpler than that used by the House, the Senate majority party leadership actually has much less control over the scheduling of legislation and over the terms for its consideration. On any debatable motion any senator can hold the floor indefinitely unless or until sixty senators vote to shut off debate. The motion to proceed to consideration of a bill is debatable, so senators can filibuster against bringing legislation they oppose to the floor.

This fact shapes the process by which legislation is actually scheduled for floor debate in the Senate. The majority leader usually moves bills off the calendar for floor consideration by unanimous consent; a study of 247 matters considered by the Senate in the 98th Congress (1983–1984) found that 98 percent came up by unanimous consent (Tiefer 1989, 563).

The Consultation Process

Since any senator can block a unanimous consent request, the majority leader, if he wishes floor business to proceed smoothly, must check with all interested senators before bringing legislation to the floor. He always consults with leaders of the reporting committee and with the minority leader; in the Senate effective scheduling requires bipartisan cooperation, and that requires intensive consultation between the majority and minority leaders.

Unlike the House, where floor scheduling is a task of the majority party leadership alone, the Senate cannot function if the two leaders do not work together. The more contentious and the more partisan the issue, the more consultation is required. During the impeachment trial of President Clinton, Majority Leader Lott and Minority Leader Tom Daschle of South Dakota checked with each other multiple times a day.

Since any senator can object to considering the legislation and since time constraints make it impossible for the leaders to check with every senator on every piece of legislation, senators without an obvious interest in the bill are expected to inform their party leadership if they do have an interest. For every bill the party secretaries, who are employees of the majority and minority leaders, keep a record of senators who have asked to be informed before the bill is brought to the floor, and these senators must be consulted. For good measure, once the majority and minority leaders have agreed on a unanimous consent agreement, that information is put on the "hot line," an automated telephone line to all senators' offices; the recorded message specifies the terms of the agreement and asks senators who have objections to let their leader know in a given period of time.

Senate party leaders contend that their only responsibility to senators who have asked to be informed is to tell them when the leaders are ready to bring a bill to the floor, and that may well be all a particular senator expects. The senator may simply want to be sure the legislation comes up when he or she is in town.

In other cases, however, a senator may object to the legislation's floor consideration at any time or until the bill's supporters have altered it to his or her liking. The notification by a senator to his or her party leader is called a hold; a typical hold letter, addressed to Majority Leader Trent Lott and copied to the majority secretary, reads:

Dear Trent:

I will object to any time agreement or unanimous consent request with respect to consideration of any legislation or amendment that involves [the matter in question], as I wish to be accorded my full rights as a Member of the Senate to offer amendments, debate and consider such legislation or amendment.

Many thanks and kindest personal regards.

[signature]

The party secretaries confer every morning and inform each other about new holds on legislation or nominations. They do not, however, reveal the names of their members that have placed the holds, so a hold may remain anonymous.

Holds are not specified in Senate rules; they are an informal custom. What gives holds their bite is the implicit or explicit threat to filibuster the motion to proceed. The majority leader sometimes will go ahead with the legislation despite a hold, but he then may face a filibuster on the motion to proceed and, if that is overcome, a filibuster on the bill itself. Even if both filibusters can be overcome, the time consumed is substantial. Especially when floor time is short—before a recess or near the end of the session—only the most essential legislation is likely to be considered as worthy of so much time. After all, if scarce time is used trying to end a filibuster, other legislation will be sacrificed. Supporters of legislation are under increasing pressure to make concessions that will remove the threat of a filibuster. As time becomes scarcer, a hold increasingly becomes a veto.

Senators' willingness to hold up one matter in order to extract concessions on another, sometimes known as hostage taking, has further complicated Senate floor scheduling. For example, in 1995 Jesse Helms, R-N.C., chairman of the Senate Foreign Relations Committee, sponsored a State Department reorganization bill that the Clinton administration and many Democrats opposed. Helms brought the legislation to the floor, but after two attempts at imposing cloture failed, Majority Leader Dole stopped floor consideration. Frustrated, Helms began bottling up ambassador nominations, the START II treaty, and the Chemical Weapons Convention. Democrats responded by blocking action on a flag desecration constitutional amendment and a Cuba sanctions bill, both priorities for Helms. Negotiations and concessions eventually unstuck the impasse, though only the Cuba sanctions bill actually became law. In the summer of 1996, Majority Leader Dole allegedly sought to stack the Senate conference delegation on the Kennedy-Kassebaum health insurance reform bill with supporters of medical savings accounts (MSAs), which Republicans favored but a Senate majority had rejected on a floor vote. Senator Kennedy, a strong opponent of MSAs, threatened to filibuster the naming of conferees until an acceptable compromise on MSAs was reached. In response, Sen. Don Nickles, R-Okla., objected to the naming of conferees on the minimum wage bill until conferees on the Kennedy-Kassebaum bill had been appointed. Again negotiations eventually led to a resolution.

The majority leader thus schedules legislation under severe constraints. When he rises to make a unanimous consent request that the Senate proceed to consider a particular bill, he has almost always cleared it with his party colleagues and received agreement from his minority counterpart, who has cleared it with his party members.

Nominations

The Constitution gives the Senate the power to advise and consent on high-level presidential appointments. This has come to mean that the Senate by majority vote must approve presidential nominations of cabinet secretaries and other high-level executives, ambassadors, and judges, including Supreme Court justices.

Divided government and party polarization have made the confirmation process an increasingly confrontational one. Senators use holds to block nominations they oppose, even if a Senate majority clearly supports the nomination. Thus cloture votes showed a sizable majority for the confirmation of Henry Foster as surgeon general, but lacking the sixty votes necessary to cut off debate, the nomination died. James Hormel, an openly homosexual man nominated by President Clinton as ambassador to Luxembourg, almost certainly commanded majority support, but opposition from extreme conservatives led Majority Leader Lott to refuse to bring the nomination to the floor for a vote. (Using his power to make recess appointments, Clinton appointed Hormel to the post "temporarily" while Congress was out of session.) During the Reagan and Bush administrations, Democrats blocked judicial nominees that they considered too conservative; in the second half of the 1990s, Republicans blocked many of Clinton's nominees because they believed them too liberal. In a number of these cases, the nomination never made it to a floor vote.

Increasingly often in recent years senators have taken to holding nominations hostage in order to extract concessions on other matters from the administration. That is, senators block nominees they do not oppose in order to gain a bargaining chip vis-à-vis the administration. The nomination of William Holbrook as ambassador to the UN in 1999 was held up over matters having nothing to do with him. Sen. Charles Grassley, R-Iowa, wanted the administration to respond to his concerns about the treatment of a State Department whistleblower; Senators Mitch McConnell, R-Ky., and Lott hoped to extract from the president a promise to appoint their candidate to the Federal Election Commission. Senator Hatch, chairman of the Judiciary Committee, held up most judicial nominees during the first half of 1999 in order to force the president to appoint his choice, a person strongly opposed by environmentalists, to the bench. Even members of the president's own party occasionally use the strategy. In fall of 1997, for example, Sen. Ron Wyden of Oregon wanted the Pentagon to reopen an investigation into a military transport plane crash that had killed a constituent. Finding the Pentagon's responsiveness to his request unsatisfactory, Wyden put a hold on the nomination of Gen. Henry Shelton to become chairman of the Joint Chiefs of Staff. That got the Pentagon's attention; Wyden's problem was quickly resolved and Shelton's nomination was released (*Roll Call*, Sept. 29, 1997).

Unanimous Consent Agreements

The Senate often considers legislation under a formal unanimous consent agreement (UCA). The majority leader, his staff, or committee leaders under his general supervision negotiate an agreement setting terms for the consideration of the legislation. A UCA may specify time for general debate and time limits for the debate of specific amendments; it may bar nongermane amendments or nongermane amendments that are not explicitly listed; and it may specify the time for votes on specific amendments and on final passage (Tiefer 1989, 573–584; Smith and Flathman 1989). Here is an example of a fairly typical unanimous consent agreement. It was offered and agreed to on June 10, 1999:

> Mr. President, I ask unanimous consent that the Senate proceed to the consideration of Calendar No. 91, S. 886, the State Department reauthorization bill, at a time determined by the two leaders, and that the bill be considered under the following limitations: that the only first-degree amendments in order be the following, and that they be subject to relevant second-degree amendments,[2] with any debate time on amendments controlled in the usual form, provided that time for debate on any second-degree amendment would be limited to that accorded the amendment to which it is offered; that upon disposition of all amendments, the bill be read the third time, and the Senate proceed to vote on passage of the bill, as amended, if amended, with no intervening action.
>
> I submit the list of amendments.
>
> The list is as follows:
>> Abraham-Grams: U.S. entry/exit controls.
>> Ashcroft: 4 relevant.
>> Baucus: 3 relevant.
>> Biden: 5 relevant.
>> Bingaman: Science counselors—embassies.
>> Daschle: 2 relevant.
>> Dodd: 3 relevant.
>> Durbin: Baltics and Northeast Europe.
>> Feingold: 4 relevant.
>> Feinstein: relevant.

---

2. Relevance is, in most cases, a less strict standard than is germaneness.

Helms: 2 relevant.
Kerry: 3 relevant.
Leahy: 5 relevant.
Lott: 2 relevant.
Managers' amendment.
Kennedy: relevant.
Moynihan: relevant.
Reed: 2 relevant.
Reid: relevant.
Sarbanes: 3 relevant.
Thomas: veterans
Wellstone: 3 relevant.
Wellstone: trafficking.
Wellstone: child soldiers. (*Congressional Record*, S6821)

As this list of amendments suggests, unanimous consent agreements in recent years have become increasingly individualized as Senate leaders seek to accommodate individual senators' demands (Smith and Flathman 1989, 361). Each interested senator may bargain for particular amounts of debate time on his or her amendments and even expect to have the date and time when those amendments will come up specified.

Some unanimous consent agreements are a great deal more complicated than the State Department bill UCA. The UCA for the patients' bill of rights in 1999 set a specific time for debate to begin and limited general debate to three hours. The agreement also specified that all first-degree amendments be offered in an alternating fashion, with Senator Daschle to offer the initial first-degree amendment; all first- and second-degree amendments were limited to 100 minutes each, and second-degree amendments were limited to one second-degree amendment per side, per party. Last, the UCA set a time for the final vote and even provided for votes on several nominations (see Chapter 8).

Comprehensive unanimous consent agreements that are worked out before the bill comes to the floor and that govern the entire process of consideration are relatively rare (Smith and Flathman 1989, 366; Evans and Oleszek 1999). More often, the leader will be able to work out only a partial agreement before debate begins. As consideration progresses, senators are likely to become clearer about what amendments they want to offer and how much time they will need, and further agreements may become possible. Thus, several partial UCAs may govern a bill's consideration. As an expert participant explained:

Usually you have a UCA only to bring something to the floor, and then maybe you have another one that will deal with a couple of important amendments, and then perhaps a little later, one that will start limiting amendments to some extent, and then perhaps one that specifies when a vote will take place. So it's done through a series of steps, each of which sort of leaves less and less leeway.

A unanimous consent agreement provides some of the predictability that a special rule provides in the House. The difference between the measures is that a simple majority can approve a special rule while a UCA requires unanimous consent—one senator can veto it. This difference, of course, has an enormous impact on the legislative process in the two chambers.

Clearly, unanimous consent agreements make the majority leader's job easier; once a UCA is in effect, he has a much better idea of how long the legislation will take on the floor. The bill's supporters value the reduction in uncertainty that a UCA accomplishes. But why do other senators agree to unanimous consent agreements? For other senators, with their extremely busy schedules and their own legislative priorities, the more predictable schedule and the more efficient use of time that UCAs make possible are important benefits and may dictate acquiescing in a UCA even for a bill the senator does not support. But, if the senator strongly opposes the legislation, he or she can always object.

The Senate Floor

Assume the Senate has agreed to consider the legislation. Floor debate begins in the same way it does in the House: with opening statements by the majority and minority floor managers. As in the House, the chair and the ranking minority member of the committee or subcommittee usually manage the legislation on the floor, but in the Senate a bill sponsor who holds no such official position may act as floor manager. The floor managers yield time to other senators who wish to speak.

Debate is unlimited unless constrained by a unanimous consent agreement, and even then it will not be as restricted as in the House. Senators' statements are likely to be considerably longer than those of representatives. When the Senate is engaged in a great debate, such as on the resolution in 1991 to authorize the Persian Gulf War, the lack of tight time limits makes for better and certainly more dramatic debate. On less momentous occasions Senate debate can drag on interminably, and the lack of time limits provides no incentive for senators to prepare their remarks carefully.

Especially if the Senate is operating without a complex UCA, debate on amendments is quite unstructured. The floor manager will usually know when a senator intends to offer an amendment, and if that senator is not on the floor at the appropriate time, the floor manager is likely to wait! The House, in contrast, waits for no member and certainly not for a rank-and-file member who wants to offer an amendment.

Quorum calls are used to kill time. A senator can make a point of order that a quorum is not present, and the presiding officer will ask the clerk to call the roll.[3] The Senate does not use electronic voting. The clerk will very slowly call the names of the senators while everyone waits for the senator who is supposed to be offering the amendment to show up. When the senator comes in, the quorum call is vacated (that is, called off), usually without a quorum ever having shown up. Similarly, when senators need some time in the midst of floor consideration to negotiate in private, quorum calls make possible a kind of time-out. For example, the floor manager and a senator offering an amendment may want to see if they can work out a compromise version of the amendment that both find acceptable.

Amendment Rules and Their Consequences

Senate rules, under most circumstances, allow any senator to offer as many amendments as he or she wishes to legislation on the floor. For most bills the amendments need not even be germane to the legislation; that is, if a senator wants to offer a civil rights provision to an agriculture bill, Senate rules do not prohibit it. Amendments to general appropriations bills (that is, spending bills) must be germane according to Senate rules, but senators often prefer not to enforce the rule. Many unanimous consent agreements do bar nongermane amendments unless they are explicitly listed, and after cloture is invoked amendments must be germane. The Congressional Budget and Impoundment Control Act of 1974 (hereafter the Budget Act) requires that amendments to budget resolutions and reconciliation bills be germane.

In fact, senators frequently offer nongermane amendments. Throughout his long Senate career Jesse Helms has used nongermane amendments on hot-button topics such as busing, homosexuality, pornography, and abortion to get his issues to the floor and force senators to vote on them. In the late 1980s he successfully attached to an education bill an amendment outlawing dial-a-porn services (900-number telephone services that provide explicit sexual messages for a fee). But Helms is by no

---

3. In fact, a quorum is seldom present since senators are in their offices or in committee working. Even if a quorum is present, the presiding officer must have the roll called; only under cloture may the presiding officer determine the presence of a quorum by counting.

means alone; most senators use the tactic at least occasionally. In early 1993 then–minority leader Dole attempted unsuccessfully to attach an amendment on homosexuals in the military to family and medical leave legislation. His purpose was to embarrass President Clinton and, if possible, to impede passage of the bill. In this case Majority Leader Mitchell successfully countered Dole's strategy by offering an amendment to Dole's amendment that, in effect, removed its sting. In 1994 senators offered to the bill reauthorizing the Elementary and Secondary Education Act amendments limiting the application of the Davis-Bacon labor law, inserting provisions of the omnibus crime bill that had been dropped by crime bill conferees, and prohibiting the secretary of education from issuing new regulations to carry out the Vocational Education Act.

Senators' ability and willingness to offer nongermane amendments have major implications for the majority leadership's control of the schedule and of the agenda more broadly. The leadership cannot keep issues off the floor by refusing to schedule legislation. A senator can simply offer the legislation as a nongermane amendment. In the 104th Congress Majority Leader Dole and most Republicans would have dearly loved to keep off the floor the issue of open hearings on the ethics case involving Sen. Bob Packwood, R-Ore. But Sen. Barbara Boxer, D-Calif., offered it as a floor amendment to the defense authorization bill and forced a recorded vote. Sen. Carl Levin, D-Mich., and other supporters of lobbying reform and gift ban legislation forced Dole to schedule that legislation although he would have preferred not to. They threatened to add the provisions as an amendment to the telecommunications bill, one of Dole's highest priorities. The agreement that Dole announced on June 9, 1995, committed the Senate to considering lobbying reform and the gift ban no later than July 28 and explicitly barred consideration of such measures before then (*Congressional Record,* June 9, 1995, S8086).

As the Senate became more partisan in the 1990s, the Senate minority party became increasingly adept at using the Senate's loose amending rules to force its issues onto the floor. In 1996 Senate Majority Leader Dole and most Senate Republicans did not want to vote on a minimum wage increase that most opposed but that was popular with the public. Senate Democrats were prepared to offer the minimum wage increase as an amendment to every important piece of legislation brought to the floor and, to avoid a vote, Dole was forced to put off votes, bringing the legislative process in the Senate to a standstill. Eventually, Dole's successor as majority leader, Senator Lott, capitulated, the bill came to a vote, and it passed handily. Using similar tactics, the minority Democrats, sometimes with the help of dissident Republicans, have forced debates on campaign finance reform, gun control, tobacco taxes, and their patients' bill of rights, all issues the majority party would rather have avoided. (See Chapter 8 for a case study of this strategy.) Amending rules make it much more difficult for the majority party and the leadership to control the agenda in the Senate than in the House.

Senators today fully exercise their right to offer as many amendments as they wish on the floor, though the majority are relevant to the legislation at issue. On major legislation the number of amendments offered and pushed to a recorded vote is often high, and amending marathons (when ten or more amendments are offered and pushed to a recorded vote) are far from rare. In the 103rd through the 105th Congresses (1993–1998), on average 35 percent of the major measures considered on the Senate floor were subject to ten or more amendments decided by recorded vote.

What sort of legislation is likely to provoke a high rate of amending activity, and does such activity usually represent an attempt to legislate or to stop legislation? Legislation that must pass, as well as legislation that seems highly likely to pass, more often than other legislation evokes high amending activity, suggesting that senators are using such bills as vehicles for legislating. Appropriations bills, which must be enacted to keep the government functioning, make up a regular part of legislation on which amending marathons take place.

Legislation that is very broad in scope often provokes extensive amending activity; the big trade bill in the 100th Congress, budget resolutions, and major tax bills are examples. More than forty amendments were offered and pushed to a recorded vote on the trade bill and on the budget resolutions of 1993, 1995, and 1997; almost fifty were offered on the enormous tax bill of 1981 and forty-four on the 1995 reconciliation bill. And, of course, controversial legislation stimulates amending activity as opponents attempt to alter or even kill it, or at least to place supporters on the record on controversial provisions. In the 103rd Congress amending marathons accompanied much of Clinton's controversial agenda; campaign finance legislation, family leave, the stimulus program, national service, the Goals 2000 education program, and the omnibus crime bill, among others, had ten or more amendments offered to them on the floor. In 1999, juvenile justice legislation considered in the aftermath of the Columbine High School shootings was subject to thirty-one amendments that were pushed to a roll call, including a number of gun control amendments.

The 1993 reconciliation bill that implemented Clinton's economic program had all three characteristics: it was must-pass legislation in the view of the majority party, it was extremely broad in scope, and it was very controversial. Twenty-five amendments were offered and pushed to a recorded vote. Some were sincere attempts to alter the legislation. Amendments in this category included one that knocked out a provision requiring small businesses to report all transactions over $600 to the Internal Revenue Service and another amendment, offered by the majority leader, that was crafted to pick up the votes to pass the bill. Other amendments were intended to gut the legislation or, if they did not pass, at least force supporters to go on the record on some very unpopular provisions. For example, Republicans offered amendments to eliminate the gas tax, to strike the provision raising the proportion of Social Security benefits that are taxable for high-income retirees, and to exempt small businesses from the increased taxes in certain circumstances. All were defeated, but Democrats were forced to take some tough votes.

In the 104th and succeeding Republican-controlled Congresses, Democrats reciprocated. Republicans had hoped quickly to pass legislation that barred the federal government from placing requirements or mandates on the states unless the federal government paid the cost. Democrats forced fifty-nine hours of debate and roll call votes on more than forty amendments. Republicans were put in the uncomfortable position of voting against amendments that exempted from the bill federal mandates regulating radioactive substances; federal regulations designed to mitigate child pornography, child abuse, and illegal child labor; and mandates that regulated known human carcinogens (Hosansky 1995, 276, 307–309).

Senate party leaders cannot protect their members from tough votes in the way that House leaders sometimes can. To be sure, bill proponents often move to table an amendment. This is a nondebatable motion, and if an amendment is successfully tabled—which requires a majority vote— debate on it is cut off and it is killed without a vote ever being taken on the amendment itself. However, the tactic makes an ineffective fig leaf for senators who oppose the amendment but fear the political consequences of voting against it.

The consideration of reconciliation bills is governed by Budget Act rules that are highly complex and require sixty votes to waive. Many of the amendments offered to reconciliation bills can be killed by making a point of order against them for violating the Budget Act, and this is routinely done. The amendment's sponsor can, however, demand a recorded vote on waiving the act. While the requirement of sixty votes to waive makes it relatively easy to defeat the motion, senators are forced to go on the record. The parliamentary language does not provide much of a screen to hide the opposition of senators to the substance of the amendment. (In fact, a senator who believes that waiving budget rules is a mistake, and thus votes against such motions on principle regardless of the substance of the amendment at issue, may have a hard time convincing constituents of his motive.)

Each senator's prerogative under the rules to offer as many amendments as she or he desires on almost any piece of legislation has many uses and, in fact, is employed to a variety of ends. Committee and party leaders know that the Senate's permissive amending rules give disgruntled senators a potent weapon. Therefore, before the bill reaches the floor, leaders have a considerable incentive to bargain and compromise with any senator who expresses dissatisfaction. Senators not on the committee of jurisdiction can influence the shape of legislation at the prefloor stage in a way not possible for similarly situated House members. If a senator alerts a bill's sponsor, informally or through a hold, that she has a problem with certain of a bill's provisions, the sponsor must seriously consider trying to placate her. A single dissatisfied senator, even if she is junior and a minority party member, can cause a great deal of trouble.

Extended Debate and Cloture

A bill's supporters must concern themselves not just with the barrage of amendments opponents may offer on the floor but also with the possibility that opponents will use extended debate to block action altogether. In the Senate debate ends on a matter when every senator has said all he or she wants to say or after cloture is invoked. The cloture process is the only way in which debate can be shut off in the Senate over any senator's objection.

Any senator may circulate a cloture petition. When the senator has gathered sixteen signatures the petition is filed; after a one-day layover, the Senate votes. On most matters three-fifths of the entire Senate membership (usually sixty) must vote for cloture for the motion to pass. If the measure at issue changes Senate rules, two-thirds of those present and voting are required to shut off debate.

Even after a successful cloture vote, debate does not necessarily end immediately. Senate rule 22, the cloture rule, places a cap of thirty hours on consideration after the cloture vote. The thirty hours does include time spent on quorum calls and voting as well as on debate. The rule also requires that amendments considered after cloture must be germane.

If cloture fails, the bill's supporters may try again. There is no limit on the number of cloture petitions that may be filed on one measure, and sometimes supporters file a new petition even before a vote has been taken on a previous one so as to minimize the delay caused by the requirement that there be a day in session between the filing of the petition and the vote. In 1987 and 1988 Majority Leader Robert C. Byrd, D-W.Va., made eight attempts to impose cloture on campaign finance reform legislation before he gave up. In 1999 Republicans tried and failed to impose cloture three times on Y2K legislation before McCain decided he had to compromise; on the Social Security "lockbox," Republicans tried unsuccessfully five times.

The cloture process is time-consuming and cumbersome. Furthermore, if the opponents are determined, supporters may need to impose cloture at more than one stage in the measure's progress through the chamber. Thus, extended debate can occur on the motion to proceed to consider the measure, on specific amendments, on the measure itself, on various motions related to going to conference, and on the conference report. No single measure has ever been subject to filibusters at all these stages, but it is not uncommon for cloture to be sought at several stages. On the "motor voter" bill in 1993, for example, cloture votes took place on the motion to proceed, on the measure itself, and on the conference report.

The purpose of the cloture rule is to give the Senate some way to end a filibuster—the use of extended debate to block or delay legislation. Yet filibusters are not as easy to identify as one might think, especially since modern filibusters seldom resemble the famous ones of the past (Beth 1995). The word *filibuster* conjures up images of Sen. Huey Long, D-La., in the 1930s reading from the Constitution, quoting the Bible, and offering "pot liquor" recipes; of Sen. Strom Thurmond, D-S.C., in the 1950s holding the floor for twenty-four hours at a stretch; or of round-the-clock sessions with senators sleeping on cots in the Capitol as occurred during the great civil rights battle of 1964. Modern filibusters are seldom so dramatic, and threats to filibuster now frequently take the place of actual filibusters. A hold may keep legislation off the floor altogether.

Sometimes after a bill is brought to the floor, nothing happens: no senators step forward to offer their amendments, but proponents make no move to call a vote on passage. This happened with the 1990 clean air bill reported by the Environment Committee. In such cases supporters of the legislation know they lack the votes to invoke cloture and so refrain from forcing a showdown; opponents are consequently saved the trouble of staging an overt filibuster. Eventually, supporters must take their chances, give up on the bill, or negotiate with opponents, as happened on the clean air bill.

Because filibuster threats are frequent and may also be nebulous, a bill's supporters may file for cloture before opponents have clearly indicated they intend to engage in extended debate, and undoubtedly sometimes when opponents actually had no such intention. The requirement that all amendments must be germane after cloture is invoked sometimes encourages supporters to try for cloture. Finally, when senators spend a long time debating and amending a measure, they may simply be performing their deliberative function rather than trying to kill the measure. Many filibusters have as their purpose forcing a compromise on the legislation rather than killing it outright. Therefore, distinguishing between deliberation and filibustering becomes even harder.

Filibusters, defined as those instances where an attempt to invoke cloture has been made, are now very frequent in the Senate. Recent Congresses (103rd through 105th) have averaged twenty-eight each (Beth 1995; DSG 1994; *Congressional Quarterly Almanac,* various years). The number of cloture votes averaged almost fifty per Congress, indicating that on many measures more than one cloture vote was taken.

Filibusters occur on a broad variety of matters. Not just legislation but presidential nominations may be subject to extended debate. In 1995 Republicans killed by a filibuster the nomination of Henry Foster to be surgeon general of the United States. A majority of senators was ready to confirm Foster, but since only fifty-seven voted to cut off debate, no vote on confirmation ever took place. Extended debate is not confined to the great issues of the day; senators sometimes hold up minor and parochial legislation or more major bills for parochial reasons. A bill adjusting Hoover dam rates was filibustered; senators concerned that Cuba would interfere with radio broadcasting in their states filibustered a bill setting up Radio Marti to broadcast to Cuba; and a Maryland senator filibustered the Metropolitan Washington Airports Transfer Act. As the 102nd Congress was rushing to adjourn in October 1992, Sen. Alfonse D'Amato, R-N.Y., held the floor for fifteen hours and fifteen minutes to protest the removal from an urban aid tax bill of a provision he said could have restored jobs at a New York typewriter plant (Kuntz 1992, 3128). The bill containing the agreement on appropriations bills between President Clinton and Congress in November 1999, a bill that had to pass before the Congress could adjourn for the year, was filibustered by the senators from Minnesota and Wisconsin because it included the Northeast Dairy Compact, which they claimed hurt their dairy farmers, and by Sen. Max Baucus, D-Mont., because the bill excluded provisions making satellite TV more accessible to rural areas.

Major legislation is especially likely to encounter an extended debate–related problem—a hold, a filibuster threat, or a filibuster. In the late 1980s and early 1990s just under 30 percent ran into some extended debate–related problem that was identifiable from the public record; in the first Congress of the Clinton presidency, half of major measures did. A Republican filibuster killed Clinton's economic stimulus package; Republicans used the filibuster or a threat thereof to extract concessions on voter registration legislation ("motor voter") and the national service program, for example. Republican attempts to kill or water down legislation via a filibuster were not always successful, of course. For example, the Republican filibuster of the Brady bill imposing a seven-day waiting period for buying a gun collapsed when a number of Republican senators began to fear the political price of their participation.

Time pressure makes extended debate an especially effective weapon of obstruction at the end of a Congress, and the greater the backlog of significant legislation, the more potent any threat of delay is. At the end of the 103rd Congress, Republican filibusters killed campaign finance and lobbying reform bills. Although unsuccessful in the end, Republicans filibustered and tried to prevent passage of a massive crime bill, the California Desert Protection Act, and a comprehensive education bill. In some cases filibusters were waged to prevent legislation from being sent to conference or, more frequently, to prevent approval of the conference report. Republican threats of obstructionist floor tactics contributed to the death of important bills revamping the Superfund program, revising clean drinking water regulations, overhauling outdated telecommunications law, and applying federal labor laws to Congress.

In the 103rd Congress the filibuster was used as a partisan tool to an extent unprecedented in the twentieth century. In the 104th and 105th Congresses, Democrats, then in the minority, returned the favor. About half of major legislation encountered extended debate–related problems; Democrats killed regulatory overhaul and property rights legislation and forced majority Republicans to compromise on a number of major bills. Democrats forced concessions on product liability legislation, the Freedom to Farm bill, and telecommunications legislation, among others. In 1999, Y2K legislation passed the Senate only after Republicans agreed to compromises and the Social Security lockbox bill failed because Republicans were unwilling to satisfy Democrats.

The filibuster is not a tool of the minority party alone, however. In 1994, for example, product liability reform was killed when liberals filibustered. Majority Republicans have repeatedly filibustered campaign finance legislation. In June of 1999, Phil Gramm, a senior member of the majority party, blocked passage of a broadly supported bill allowing the disabled to keep their Medicaid and Medicare benefits when they take paid jobs, until supporters agreed to drop the funding mechanism he disliked (*Washington Post*, June 17, 1999). Even more than the Senate's permissive amending rules, the right of extended debate provides the individual senator with a powerful weapon few can refrain from using. Increasingly, extended debate has become a routinely employed partisan tool as well. As a consequence, controversial measures almost always need sixty votes to pass the Senate, and amassing the necessary support often requires significant concessions.

If legislation reaches the point of a passage vote, it almost certainly will pass. In recent Congresses almost all of the major measures that lost on passage votes in the Senate were constitutional amendments, which require a two-thirds vote. The one exception, a bill barring employment discrimination against homosexuals, was opposed by most majority party senators and was brought to the floor as part of a package deal.

Unorthodox Lawmaking in the Senate

Because the Senate's legislative process has always been less formal than the House's and thus more flexible, the distinction between the orthodox and the unorthodox is less clear in the Senate than in the House. Senators have always had the right under the rules to talk as long as they wished, offer multitudes of amendments, and propose nongermane amendments. They have always used those prerogatives. Yet all the evidence we have indicates that the frequency of such behavior has increased enormously in recent decades. The contemporary legislative process in the Senate is of necessity predicated on the assumption that senators will regularly and fully exploit their prerogatives. The extensive consultation that is a standard part of legislative scheduling, the "individualized" unanimous consent agreements, and the deference to senators as individuals are all responses to senators' hyperexploitation of their prerogatives under the rules. In addition, in recent years, the parties—especially the minority party—are fully exploiting Senate rules to further their partisan objectives. When employed by an organized and sizable group of senators, the Senate's permissive rules become a formidable weapon.

Unlike unorthodox lawmaking in the House of Representatives, the changes in the legislative process in the Senate, on balance, make legislating more difficult. Given senators' willingness to exploit their prerogatives and the lack of much cost to them within the chamber of doing so repeatedly, successful lawmaking requires accommodating individual senators and the minority party, and most controversial legislation requires a supermajority for Senate passage. To be sure, other changes in the legislative process (the increased frequency of postcommittee adjustments, for example, and sometimes the bypassing of committees) seem to facilitate lawmaking. Such changes are a response to the problems created by senators' exploitation of their debate and amending prerogatives and may ameliorate but certainly do not solve those problems.

chapter four

Getting One Bill: Reconciling House-Senate Differences

SINCE THE HOUSE AND SENATE differ in membership and rules, major legislation is unlikely to emerge in identical form from the two chambers. Even if exactly the same bill were introduced in the House and the Senate, the changes necessary to pass it would be likely to result in differences by the time it worked its way through the two chambers' quite different legislative processes. Yet, before the bill can become law, both chambers must approve the identical wording; after all, a law cannot exist in several different versions. How would people know which they were expected to obey?

A number of alternative ways of reconciling House-Senate differences are used. One chamber can simply accept the other chamber's version of the legislation. A procedure based on amendments between the chambers entails a kind of public bargaining back and forth. A conference committee of members from both chambers can be appointed and charged with coming up with a compromise, which is then taken back to both chambers for approval.

Nonconference Reconciliation Procedures

On minor legislation or when the differences between the chambers are small, one chamber may be willing to accept the other's bill. Early in 1995 the House accepted the Senate's version of legislation applying labor and other regulatory laws to Congress. The two chambers' bills were very similar, and House and Senate Republicans were eager to complete an early legislative victory. Similarly, in 1997, the House accepted the Senate's "partial-birth" abortion bill; the changes the Senate had made were not major, and the bill's supporters wanted to avoid having the Senate act on the bill again. This means of settling interchamber differences is especially likely to be used late in a Congress, when time is tight and the alternative is the probable death of the bill. Such circumstances may prompt one chamber to accept the other's version even of major legislation; if the choice is to let the legislation die and start over in the next Congress or to take a less preferred version, supporters may well opt for the latter. In 1980 the House in a lame-duck (that is, after the election) session accepted the weaker Senate version of the massive bill on Alaska lands. Since Republicans had won control of the Senate in the elections, House supporters of a strongly pro-environment bill knew they would fare worse if they waited until the next year. They also knew that, if they did anything other than simply accept the Senate bill, Senate opponents of a strong bill could easily use extended debate to kill the legislation in the few remaining days of the session. The power of extended debate as an obstructionist tool, especially late in the session, can put the House at a disadvantage, confronting the chamber with the choice of accepting Senate legislation as is or taking a chance that opponents in the Senate will kill it if more action is required.

House-Senate differences on most minor and some major legislation are reconciled through a process known as amendments between the chambers. Assume the House has passed legislation and sent it to the Senate. The Senate then amends the bill, perhaps by substituting its own version for the House's, and sends it back to the House. At this point the House floor manager of the bill may ask that the House by unanimous consent (or under suspension of the rules or by a special rule) "agree to the Senate amendment with an amendment." The Senate amendment referred to is actually the Senate version of the bill, and the amendment the House is adding is the House's initial offer of a settlement of interchamber differences. Generally, the House will stick to its own position or move least on those issues its members care about most; it will move toward the Senate position on issues considered less important by House members. If the House agrees to the motion, the bill as amended goes back to the Senate, and the Senate can either accept the House offer or respond with an offer of its own.

Although the parliamentary language soon becomes mind-bogglingly complex, what is actually going on is fairly straightforward bargaining, with each chamber making offers in succession. The legislation may go back and forth between the chambers several times (Tiefer 1989, 778). Often the differences are resolved through informal, behind-the-scenes negotiations between House and Senate committee leaders and then incorporated in the amendment one house sends the other. For example, in late 1988 a marathon series of informal negotiations settled the differences between the chambers on the omnibus drug bill. The highly complex deal was then incorporated into an amendment that the House adopted and sent to the Senate in the last hours of the session, and the Senate then accepted (Lawrence 1988c, 3145, 3170).

Conference Committees

The most common way of resolving interchamber differences on major legislation is by conference committee (Longley and Oleszek 1989). In recent Congresses (103rd, 104th, and 105th), 78 percent of major measures that got to the resolution stage were sent to conference; in some of these cases, amendments between the chambers were also used. By and large, conferences are restricted to settling differences on major legislation. This pattern can be seen through an examination of all measures. When Steven Smith looked at all the bills passed in 1985–1986, he found that only about 12 percent of all measures went to conference (Smith 1995, 406).

Both chambers must approve sending legislation to conference; the first house requests a conference and the second agrees. Usually this approval is obtained by unanimous consent, but it can be done by motion and a majority vote, though in the Senate the motion can be filibustered.

The Appointment of Conferees

In both chambers the presiding officer appoints conferees; House rules give the Speaker sole power to do so; the Senate's presiding officer must receive unanimous consent. In the Senate, with its weak presiding officer, committee leaders, sometimes with the participation of the party leaders, actually make the choice. The chair of the committee of origin, after "consultation" with the ranking minority member, "recommends" a list of conferees to the presiding officer, who accepts it without change. By tradition, conference committees are bipartisan; the ratio of majority to minority members roughly reflects the ratio in the chamber, and the majority allows the minority to choose its own members. The process is similar in the House, except the Speaker has more discretion. House rules explicitly require the Speaker to appoint "no less than a majority of members who supported the House position as determined by the Speaker." The rule continues: "The Speaker shall name Members who are primarily responsible for the legislation and shall, to the fullest extent feasible, include the principal proponents of the major provisions of the bill as it passed the House" (Gold et al. 1992, 339). Since the decision about which members meet these criteria is solely the Speaker's, the rule actually gives him more leeway to choose, if he so desires, junior members or members not on the committee of origin. During the 104th Congress, Speaker Gingrich was unusually assertive in exercising the Speaker's discretion; he appointed freshmen and even, on occasion, Democratic supporters of the legislation that the minority had kept off its conference delegation. In 1999, after managed care legislation that the Republican party leadership opposed passed the House, Speaker Hastert employed his discretion to keep Republican supporters of the successful bill off the conference committee; despite protests from a number of the sixty-eight Republicans who broke ranks to support the Norwood-Dingell bill, neither Charlie Norwood, R-Ga., the chief sponsor, nor Greg Ganske, R-Iowa, another prominent backer, was appointed. Senate leaders have also, from time to time, attempted to stack conference delegations, as Majority Leader Dole did on the Kennedy-Kassebaum health care reform bill in 1996. However, the fact that so many conference-related motions are debatable and can be filibustered holds Senate leaders in check. Dole's attempt to stack the conference delegation with supporters of medical savings accounts, which he favored but a majority of the Senate had voted against, was stymied by Senator Kennedy's threat to filibuster the naming of conferees.

In both chambers most of the conferees will be members of the committee that reported the bill and, by and large, fairly senior ones. Today both chambers include leaders of the subcommittee responsible for the bill. Therefore, the conference delegation will not simply consist of the most senior members of the committee, as was often the case before the mid-1970s.

The multiple referral of legislation and the frequency of bills of very broad scope complicate the conference process. When several committees have considered the legislation, all expect representation on the conference committee. The consequence is very large conference delegations, especially from the House, where multiple referral is more prevalent. On the conference committee for the 1988 trade bill were 44 senators from nine Senate committees and 155 House members from fourteen House committees (Tiefer 1989, 798–799). Although this is an extreme example, multicommittee conference delegations are common. Of the fifty-one nonappropriations bills that completed conference in 1981–1982, twenty—almost 40 percent—had conference delegations from more than one committee (Tiefer 1989, 799). Of these twenty, ten had multicommittee representation from both chambers, nine from the House only and one from the Senate only. When Republicans took control of the House, they attempted to reduce the size of conference delegations to speed action, seemingly with some success. Yet some bills are so broad in scope and affect the jurisdiction of so many committees that large conference delegations are unavoidable. The reconciliation bill that implemented the spending provisions of the 1997 balanced budget deal was the product of eight committees in each chamber. The Senate conference delegation consisted of seven general conferees and three conferees from each of eight committees; eight general conferees and thirty-four conferees from eight committees represented the House. Thus the conference numbered seventy-three members in total.

When the Senate has added nongermane amendments to a bill, House conferees are often appointed from the appropriate House committees even if the original bill was reported from only a single House committee. A 1991 State Department authorization bill had been reported solely by the House Foreign Affairs Committee, but when the much-amended bill came back from the Senate, the Speaker appointed as conferees members from the Banking, Judiciary, Post Office and Civil Service, and Ways and Means committees as well (Gold et al. 1992, 70). The financial services reform bill that became law in 1999 was considered by the Banking and Commerce Committees in the House; the Speaker appointed conferees from those two committees but also from the Agriculture and Judiciary Committees.

The Speaker's discretion in the choice of conferees and in the charge he gives them is increased significantly when multiple committees are involved. Although he is effectively bound—by custom and expectations, not by rules—to appoint conferees from all the committees that reported the legislation, he decides the number of conferees from each and the breadth or narrowness of each conferee's authority (that is, over all of the bill or only specific parts). Conference appointments for large, complex bills often specify in great detail the precise titles or sections that particular conferees can negotiate as well as which conferees have authority to negotiate on the entire bill (see, for examples, Gold et al. 1992, 340–341; Smith 1995, 413). In addition, when many committees receive conference representation, the Speaker can more easily add conferees who are not members of any of the committees that reported the bill—perhaps a leadership representative or the sponsor of a major amendment.

Reaching Agreement

The conferees are charged with coming up with a compromise between the House and Senate positions that can win the assent of a majority in both chambers. Sunshine rules instituted in the mid-1970s require that conference committee meetings be open to the public. However, because a public forum inhibits the hard bargaining that is often necessary, much negotiation takes place informally behind the scenes. To reach a compromise, members may need to retreat from positions they have advocated, often ones they have argued for strongly and ones with ardent interest group and constituency support; that is easier done behind closed doors. Sometimes formal, open conference meetings simply ratify deals worked out elsewhere.

The difficulty of reaching agreement depends, of course, on how far apart the two chambers' bills are, as well as on how strongly the participants feel about their positions. Certain kinds of differences lend themselves to compromise more easily than others. When an appropriations bill goes to conference, it typically includes hundreds of items in disagreement, but the differences in dollar figures are usually resolved easily by splitting the difference or trading off among items. The tough fights are more likely to be over substantive provisions (for example, the Hyde amendment barring federal funding for abortions).

When the two chambers take completely different approaches to a problem, the conference faces the most difficult task; splitting the difference is meaningless in that context. In 1995 the House passed a line-item-veto bill that would allow the president to make a proposal to rescind spending for specific items previously approved by Congress. Unless both chambers of Congress voted to overturn the proposal, it would become law. The Senate's line-item-veto bill was very different. The Senate proposed that, after passage, appropriations bills be broken down and sent to the president as hundreds of separate bills, thus enabling him to veto individual items. Clearly, there was no way of splitting the difference between the two approaches; the conferees had to choose one or the other or come up with a different approach altogether.

Differences between the two chambers' bills on volatile political issues can also complicate resolution. The juvenile justice bills the two chambers passed in 1999 differed on the hot-button issue of gun control: the Senate had added tough gun control provisions on the floor; the House bill contained no gun control language, that chamber having voted down all of the gun control provisions on the floor. Similarly, on the most politically sensitive issue—whether patients should be able to sue their health maintenance organizations (HMOs), House and Senate managed care regulation bills diverged completely (see Chapter 8).

Conferences with many conferees from a number of different committees are much more unwieldy than the traditional small, one-committee conferences. Often with the really large delegations, many conferees have authority over only a limited part of the bill, and the conference splits up into subconferences. The trade bill conference in 1988, for example, operated through seventeen subgroups. Even then, someone must coordinate the work, making sure progress is made and that the parts are reassembled into a coherent whole at the end. The committee chairs have the primary responsibility, but the party leadership and the leaders' senior staff often are actively involved as well.

As the legislative process has changed, drawing party leaders more deeply into the process, members have come to expect that their leaders will take a hand at the conference stage when legislation is in trouble. Stalemate between the two chambers often requires leadership intervention. When conferences on four appropriations bills bogged down in late 1995 over the abortion issue, House Majority Leader Dick Armey of Texas and Senate Republican Whip Trent Lott stepped in to broker agreements that both adamantly anti-abortion House Republicans and more moderate Senate Republicans could accept (Koszczuk 1995b, 3376). In March 1996 Senate Majority Leader Dole almost single-handedly broke the stalemate on the line-item-veto bill. Having established himself as the almost certain presidential nominee of the Republican Party, Dole made getting a bill out of conference and to the president a top priority and so a test of his ability to get things done. Under these special political circumstances Republican senators, even those with severe substantive doubts about the bill, were unwilling to hold out against Dole's position of basically agreeing to the House version of the bill. Doing otherwise would have crippled their nominee. The line-item-veto bill was approved by the conferees and signed by the president, who in negotiations with Majority Leader Dole and Speaker Gingrich had decided what the effective date of the legislation would be.

Party leaders now regularly take a hand in resolving differences on the big budget bills that make up an increasingly important part of Congress's agenda. On really high visibility bills, members now expect leadership involvement in settling interchamber differences. When the choices facing conferees are highly salient and consequential ones that affect the political fate of members and of their party, party leaders are likely to make the final decisions. In order to get quick agreement on the 1999 tax bill, the centerpiece of the congressional Republicans' agenda, Hastert and Lott decided on a small conference, with party leaders serving as conferees. The House delegation consisted of five members of the Ways and Means Committee, three members of the Education and the Workforce Committee (because the bill included numerous education-related provisions), and Majority Leader Armey. Senators Roth and Daniel Patrick Moynihan, D-N.Y., respectively the chair and the ranking minority member of the Senate Finance Committee, and Majority Leader Lott made up the Senate delegation.

In conference, decisions require the assent of both the House and the Senate, the position of a chamber being determined by the majority of its conferees. (Because of this voting rule, the fact that the House usually has more conferees than the Senate does not give it an advantage.) The final agreement must also be approved by a majority of the conferees of each chamber. Conferees formally indicate their approval by signing the conference report, which consists of the compromise legislative language agreed upon by the conferees.

Rarely, conferees are unable to reach an agreement, and the legislation dies in conference. In the late 1980s, for example, the Senate added to an airline consumer protection bill an amendment requiring drug testing of airline employees. House conferees were adamantly unwilling to accept the provision. The conferees were unable to come to an agreement, and the bill died in conference. In 1994 legislation to overhaul the regulation of mining on federal lands died in conference; however, the problem was not the conferees' inability to agree but the threat of a Senate filibuster of any reachable agreement. In recent Congresses fewer than one major measure per Congress on average died in conference. By the time legislation gets to conference, many people, including many of the conferees, have a considerable stake in the legislation's enactment. Therefore, a compromise is usually found even when House and Senate versions are very different.

In the Republican-controlled 104th Congress resolving differences between the House and Senate proved to be especially difficult. The reasons illuminate the differences between the chambers in terms of their membership and rules and how those differences affect legislative outcomes. During the 1994 campaign, Republicans (House incumbents as well as House candidates) had committed themselves to enacting the Contract with America should they become the majority party in the chamber. Fueled by a large, ideologically fervent freshman class, a membership believing itself to be mandated to carrying out the Contract, and an ideologically dedicated and skillful leadership, the new majority pushed through the House in undiluted form all of the Contract's provisions except term limits, and many other nonincremental policy changes as well. House rules allow a cohesive majority to work its will, and the Republicans in 1995 were certainly cohesive.

The freshmen Republican senators, at eleven a big class by Senate standards, and many of their more senior colleagues also wanted to see major policy change. The rules of the Senate, however, made the sort of swift and uncompromising action the House had undertaken impossible in the Senate. The majority leader had to keep six to eight moderate Republicans on board to pass legislation. To avoid a filibuster or to get the sixty votes for cloture, he also had to appease Senate Democrats. As a result, much of the House's "revolutionary" legislation was significantly altered in the Senate.

During the 104th, conference committees repeatedly confronted the task of reaching agreement when the differences between the two chambers' legislation were vast and the positions on both sides strongly held. On the line-item-veto bill, as we saw, the two chambers took completely different approaches. On product liability and on the regulatory moratorium, the compromises necessary to enable the legislation to pass the Senate watered down broad and stringent House legislation to the point that many House Republicans no longer supported the bills.

Compared with many of the bills in the Contract, appropriations bills proved to be even more contentious in conference. Because appropriations bills, which fund the government, must pass, House Republicans decided to use them as vehicles to enact a host of desired policy changes quickly and to protect those provisions from a presidential veto. Although appropriations bills are not supposed to include "legislative" provisions (called riders), Congress frequently uses this tactic; what was different in the 104th was the large number of riders House Republicans attached to appropriations bills and the scope and magnitude of the legislative changes they tried to bring about in that way. The bills that went to conference carried riders on highly controversial issues. The most salient riders concerned restrictions on abortion, on Environmental Protection Agency (EPA) enforcement of environmental laws, and on the right to lobby of nonprofit groups that receive federal grant funds; but many others created problems between the House and Senate as well. Agreement on the Treasury–Postal Service and general government appropriations bill was held up for weeks because of an amendment by Rep. Ernest Jim Istook Jr., R-Okla. The Istook amendment would have cut off federal grants to groups that used even a small part of their budgets to lobby. Senate conferees adamantly refused to accept the amendment, aimed as it was at liberal groups, and House conferees, concerned about passing the conference agreement in the House, just as adamantly refused to drop it. In the end House leaders agreed to drop the amendment. The bill died nonetheless, and the departments and agencies it covered were funded through continuing resolutions.

The executive branch is often an important participant in conference and, during periods of divided control, another source of difficulties in reaching agreement. The president has no official role, but, if conferees want their legislation to become law, they must satisfy the president sufficiently to avoid a veto or be prepared to muster a two-thirds vote in both chambers. When control of the White House and Congress is divided between the parties, especially when partisan differences are sharp, the president often wields his greatest power over legislation at the conference stage. The term *veto bargaining* became current during George Bush's presidency to describe the Bush administration's frequent attempts to extract concessions from the Democratic Congress by threatening a veto.

After the Republicans gained control of Congress in the 1994 elections, President Clinton showed himself to be an adept veto bargainer. Most bills and all major legislation show the effects of administration involvement, usually at the conference stage. In 1998 the conferees for a bill authorizing funds for agricultural research and making up a shortfall in the federal crop insurance program added a provision restoring food stamp eligibility for 250,000 legal immigrants who had been denied such eligibility by the 1996 welfare reform bill; they did so because Clinton persuaded them that otherwise he would veto the bill, which was of great importance to their constituents. In 1999 Clinton forced a narrowing of the liability limits in the Y2K bill and a beefing up of the privacy protections and of the community reinvestment provisions of the financial services modernization legislation as the price of his signature. The Clinton administration has been especially involved in conferences on appropriations bills, often extracting more money for education and other favored programs from a hostile Republican Congress.

Conferees' Power and Its Limits

Conferees have considerable power over the substance of legislation. House and Senate rules specify that conferees are limited in the agreement they reach to the differences between the House and Senate versions of the legislation. However, in those cases—the majority—where the Senate has passed a substitute to the House bill (rather than a series of specific amendments to the House bill), Senate rules interpret this quite broadly. In the House the conferees can get around the rule by taking their conference report to the floor under a special rule from the Rules Committee that waives it. Although House members or senators can (by majority vote) instruct their conferees about the substance of the legislation, these instructions are not binding (Tiefer 1989, 780–833; Gold et al. 1992, 337–347). Since many conference committees finish their work late in a Congress when everyone works under severe time constraints, senators and representatives not on a conference committee often lack the time to study the conference report and thus to be able to challenge it.

Once a majority of the House conferees and a majority of the Senate conferees have formalized their approval by signing the conference report, it is returned to both chambers, where the full membership must decide whether to accept what their representatives have done. At this point no amendments are in order; the membership votes up or down on the compromise as a package.[1] Although the overwhelming majority of conference reports are approved, occasionally one is sent back to conference, a parliamentary move available only to the chamber that acts first, or simply voted down.

In 1993 the House voted to cut off funding for the superconducting supercollider; the conference committee, however, included funding for the supercollider in the energy and water appropriations conference report. The House refused to accept that outcome and recommitted the report to the conference, which complied with House wishes.

In 1995 the House rejected several conference reports on appropriations bills. For example, Democrats joined by environmentalist Republicans and some deficit hawks twice recommitted the conference report on the Interior Department appropriations bill. At issue was a moratorium on the purchase by private companies of federal land for mining at very low prices. During floor consideration of the bill, an amendment extending an already existing moratorium had passed, but the conferees dropped it in conference. When the conference report was brought back to the House, the coalition that had approved the amendment held together and recommitted the bill to conference. The conferees then agreed on the moratorium but with some caveats; the coalition, however, refused to accept half measures and again recommitted the bill to conference with instructions on the moratorium and on another issue as well. This time the conferees got the message; they reinstated the moratorium, and their conference report won House approval. The bill, however, was later vetoed by the president for other reasons.

In 1998 provisions concerning contraceptive coverage by federal health plans, Haitian refugees, and term limits for top staff of the Federal Election Commission were at issue when the chambers considered the conference report for the fiscal 1999 Treasury–Postal Service appropriations bill. The first time the House considered the conference report, it defeated the rule. After changes were made, the House approved the

---

1. The exceptions are appropriations bills on which the conferees have exceeded the scope of the differences between the two chambers' bills or to which the Senate has added amendments that constitute unauthorized appropriations or legislation and bills on which the Senate has added nongermane amendments. House rules allow separate votes on those matters (Tiefer 1989, 833–848).

conference report, but in the Senate, Harry Reid, D-Nev., blocked consideration. In the end, the bill was wrapped into an omnibus appropriations bill.

These cases notwithstanding, the recommittal or defeat of a conference report is rare. Yet, as infrequent as the rejection of a conference report is, its occasional occurrence serves to remind conferees that they must be sensitive to the policy preferences of their chambers' membership. Conferees have very considerable discretion but only within the limits set by the full membership's tolerance.

The Final Step

After both the House and Senate have approved legislation in identical form, it is sent to the president, who can sign it, do nothing, or veto it. If he signs it or holds it for ten weekdays while Congress is in session, the legislation becomes law. However, if Congress has adjourned sine die (that is, indefinitely, which happens at the end of the Congress), the president can kill legislation by holding it for ten weekdays without signing it. In those cases the president is said to cast a pocket veto.[2]

When the president casts a formal veto, the legislation is sent back to the Congress with the president's message of disapproval and his reasons for having cast the veto. For the legislation to become law, both houses must override the veto by a two-thirds vote.

No rules require that Congress vote to override a president's veto within a specified period of time. In the past the vote tended to come fairly soon after the veto. For years this was the expectation and the practice. Recently, however, the chamber that originated the bill (which must vote to override first) has sometimes held the bill to gain political advantage. In 1996, for example, Republican leaders did not schedule veto override votes on the "partial-birth" abortion bill until late September, only weeks before the elections. This was a bill that had passed both houses way back in March and had been vetoed in April.

Mustering a two-thirds vote in both chambers on a controversial matter is a formidable task. George Bush had only one veto overridden during his four years as president even though he was politically quite weak

---

2. Recent presidents have asserted the right to pocket veto legislation when the Congress has adjourned but not sine die (between the two sessions, for example); Congress has contested this in court (Gold et al. 1992, 248–250). The Supreme Court has not ruled on the central issue, so the constitutional status of such a pocket veto is uncertain.

during much of his presidency. In 1995, despite being enormously weakened by the devastating 1994 elections, Clinton suffered only one override; from 1996 through 1999, only one more of his vetoes was overridden. A bill's supporters know that if they want to enact legislation, they must either satisfy the president or be prepared to amass enough support in both houses to override his veto. The former will usually seem the easier task. Thus, the veto gives the president considerable influence in the legislative process.

Reconciling Differences: How Much Change?

Change in the legislative process within the two chambers has spilled over and affected the process of reconciling interchamber differences. Multiple referral and members' desire for broad participation have led to bigger conference delegations, especially on the part of the House. The unwieldiness of such large delegations and committees' jurisdictional concerns have prompted conferences to work in subconferences, which on the House side have authority to make decisions only on specifically delineated parts of the legislation. The coordinating problems such an undertaking entails draw the party leadership, the only central leadership in the chambers, into a process that used to be committee dominated. The party leaders' greater involvement in the legislative process within their chamber—in working out postcommittee compromises that facilitate passage, for example—leads to a greater role for them in conference as well. If it took leadership intervention to put together the compromise necessary to pass the bill, sustaining the compromise in conference and passing the resulting conference report will often require leadership involvement, too.

c h a p t e r   f i v e

Omnibus Legislation, the Budget Process, and Summits

UNORTHODOX LAWMAKING IS NOT CONFINED to the sorts of innovations and modifications in standard procedures and practices examined in previous chapters but encompasses new forms of legislation and new ways of making decisions as well. The contemporary Congress now often legislates through enormous omnibus bills, something it rarely did in the past. Entirely new processes—the budget process and summits—have become prominent.

When legislative decisions are made through omnibus legislation, the budget process, and summits, decision making is more centralized than it is ordinarily; central leaders—congressional party leaders and often the president—play a more important role, frequently the decisive role. These modes of legislating make it possible for Congress to enact comprehensive policy change, always a difficult task for a decentralized institution; they also may reduce the opportunities for careful scrutiny of the legislation's provisions and for broad participation by rank-and-file members.

Divided government, partisan polarization, and big deficits are the most important of the environmental factors that fostered these developments. Although the budget has been balanced, so long as divided government and intense partisanship persist, the major political conflicts of a Congress likely will continue to revolve around omnibus legislation, the budget process, and summits.

Omnibus Legislation and the Budget Process

The legislation that Congress deals with varies from the short and simple—the two-sentence bill that designates "the Federal building located at 300 East 8th Street in Austin, Texas, as the 'J. J. "Jake" Pickle Federal Building' "—to the extraordinarily long and complex.[1] The 1990 Clean Air Act was about 800 pages long, and nonexperts would need a translator to make sense of it; the bills enacting President Ronald Reagan's economic program in 1981 and President Bill Clinton's in 1993 were both considerably longer.

Legislation that addresses numerous and not necessarily related subjects, issues, and programs, and therefore is usually highly complex and long, is referred to as omnibus legislation. Although there is no consensus technical definition of what constitutes an omnibus bill, every Congress watcher would classify as omnibus the 1988 trade bill that spanned the jurisdiction of thirteen House and nine Senate committees and the antidrug bill passed the same year. The latter covered drug abuse education and prevention; treatment; punishment of abusers and sellers, big and small; and the interdiction of drugs flowing into the United States from abroad by air, sea, and land. Many of the bills generally labeled omnibus are money bills of some sort. The most common omnibus measures in the contemporary Congress are budget resolutions and reconciliation bills, both of which stem from the budget process. In recent Congresses (103rd, 104th, and 105th), omnibus measures have made up about 14 percent of major legislation.

The Congressional Budget and Impoundment Control Act of 1974 created an entirely new process and superimposed it on the old process by which Congress had made spending and taxing decisions. The new budget process made omnibus measures a regular part of the annual congressional workload and influenced the legislative process in other direct and indirect ways. Although a detailed examination of the budget process and its ramifications cannot be undertaken here, a discussion of the contemporary legislative process would not be complete without some discussion of the budget process. (On the budget process, see Schick 1980; Oleszek 1996; Thurber and Durst 1993.)

Congress creates and alters programs by passing authorizing legislation; the subject matter committees, such as Agriculture or Banking, report out this legislation, which authorizes the setting up of a new program (or changes in an existing one) and usually also authorizes funding up to some cap (maximum). The Constitution requires that before the federal government can spend money, it must be appropriated. This is the task of the House and Senate Appropriations Committees; every year they

---

1. Pickle is a former long-serving member of the House; Congress frequently names federal buildings after former members. Until 1995, Congress also passed many "commemoratives," bills like the one that declares August National Dairy Month.

must report out and see enacted a series of bills that appropriate money for the federal government's multitude of programs and agencies. Currently, each Appropriations Committee is organized into thirteen subcommittees, each of which reports one general appropriations bill that funds a number of government programs and agencies. For example, the Labor, Health and Human Services, and Education Subcommittee reports a bill that appropriates funds for the programs and agencies that fall under these three cabinet departments. Appropriations bills fund their programs only for one year. Were Congress to fail to pass the Labor-HHS-Education appropriations bill, many of those departments' programs as well as the administrative structure would have to shut down. (Programs such as Social Security that are funded through a mechanism other than annual appropriations would not be directly affected.)

The prospect of shutting down programs that people want and depend on is sufficiently horrendous that Congress always passes appropriations bills—though in late 1995 it did so only after a hiatus of several weeks (see the case study of the 1995 budget process in Chapter 11). Frequently, Congress cannot pass all thirteen bills by the annual deadline of October 1, the beginning of the fiscal year; in that case it passes a continuing (appropriations) resolution, referred to as a CR, that temporarily continues funding.[2] Usually continuing resolutions cover the few appropriations bills that have not yet passed and extend for only a few days or weeks. Occasionally, however, a CR encompasses half or more of the appropriations bills and extends through the full year—such a CR is truly an omnibus bill.

Not all programs are funded through annual appropriations. Some of the federal government's biggest programs are entitlement programs—programs that stipulate people who meet certain criteria are entitled to a specified benefit. Social Security, Medicare, Medicaid, government pension programs, and food stamps are all entitlement programs. Funding for many of these programs is not under the control of the Appropriations Committees. Some of the biggest—Social Security and a part of Medicare—are funded by trust funds, and some have permanent appropriations. Even in those cases, such as food stamps, where annual appropriations are required, the Appropriations Committees' discretion is highly limited. If the money appropriated runs out before the end of the year, Congress must pass a supplemental appropriations bill to fund food stamps for eligible people. Cutting spending for entitlements

2. Funding is usually set at the previous year's level or at the lower of the levels proposed by the House and Senate.

requires changing the legislation that authorized the program, and that is in the jurisdiction of the authorizing committee, not the Appropriations Committee.[3]

To provide some coherence to the process of making spending decisions, the Budget Act requires that before the appropriations bills are drafted, Congress must pass a budget resolution setting guidelines. The budget resolution specifies how much the federal government will spend in the next fiscal year, how much it expects to collect in taxes, and how large the deficit or surplus (the difference between the two) is expected to be. It also specifies how much is to be spent in each of twenty or so broad functional categories—health or agriculture, for example. The Budget Committee report accompanying the resolution may contain detailed suggestions about policy changes that would produce the overall figures. Although it may suggest that spending on particular programs be cut in order to reach the overall spending figure, its suggestions have no binding effect.

Estimating the deficit or surplus is not a routine technical exercise and may well be the source of controversy. The deficit or surplus depends on expected expenditures and revenues, both of which depend in turn on a number of economic assumptions. Tax receipts, for example, depend on the state of the economy; when the economy is growing, more people have jobs, wages are likely to be going up, and more businesses are making money, and thus people and business pay more in taxes. Federal expenditures depend on economic estimates as well; for example, when the economy is bad, more people will qualify for unemployment benefits and food stamps, so spending for such entitlement programs will go up. Congress relies on the Congressional Budget Office for its estimates. The Office of Management and Budget provides estimates for the president. In 1995 a dispute over which set of figures to use was at the center of the budget battle. Small differences in assumptions about the growth rate of the American economy over the next seven years made a huge difference in the estimate of how much needed to be cut from spending in order to achieve a balanced budget by the year 2002.

Drafting the budget resolution is the task of a Budget Committee in each chamber. Since the resolution sets overall budgetary policy and decides priorities, drafting it is too important and often too difficult a task for the committee to undertake on its own. Congressional party leaders are always involved, and the president may be as well.

---

3. Aid to Families with Dependent Children (AFDC) was an entitlement program; the 1996 welfare bill changed it from an entitlement to a block grant program that requires annual appropriations.

The legislative process on a budget resolution looks similar in many ways to the process followed on ordinary legislation. After the committees report, each chamber must pass its version. In the House the majority party leadership always brings up the resolution under a special rule that restricts amendments; usually only a limited number of comprehensive substitutes are allowed. The Budget Act limits Senate debate to fifty hours and requires that amendments be germane. Thus, a budget resolution cannot be filibustered. A conference committee is appointed to come up with a compromise between the two chambers' versions, which must then be approved by both houses. The budget resolution, however, is not legislation; it is a concurrent resolution that does not require the president's signature.

In essence, the budget resolution is a set of guidelines that Congress has agreed on to guide its own—specifically, its committees'—spending and taxing decisions for the year. The budget resolution serves as a framework within which the Appropriations Committees make their spending decisions. The conference report on the resolution divides up total spending by committee. Since the Appropriations Committees are responsible for all spending done through appropriations, they receive the largest allocation.

The resolution may—and in recent years often has—included binding instructions to other committees to bring law within their jurisdiction into conformance with the dictates of the budget resolution. For example, if the resolution specifies that so many billions of dollars be spent on agricultural programs and current law would result in more spending, the Agriculture Committee is instructed to change legislation under its jurisdiction in such a way as to save the necessary amount of money. The budget resolution instructions do not prescribe the details of the changes, only the amount of savings. Similarly, if the resolution specifies that tax revenues need to increase over what current law would bring in, the tax-writing committees—House Ways and Means and Senate Finance—will be instructed to draft a tax bill that raises a specific amount, but they will not be told how to do it—whether by raising the gasoline tax or by increasing income tax rates, for example. Again, if the budget resolution instructs the tax committees to cut taxes, the instructions consist of an amount taxes are to be cut; the report may offer suggestions as to which taxes might be cut, but these are not binding. The instructions in a budget resolution are called reconciliation instructions; they instruct the various committees to reconcile legislation under their jurisdictions with the figures in the budget resolution. These instructions usually target entitlement programs. Reconciliation instructions also specify a deadline for committee compliance.

When the budget process is used as a vehicle for making comprehensive policy change, the number of committees instructed is large. The budget resolution in 1981, which carried Reagan's economic program, instructed fifteen House and fourteen Senate committees. The 1993 resolution containing Clinton's program instructed thirteen House and twelve Senate committees. The 1995 resolution encompassing the new Republican majority's economic plan instructed twelve House and eleven Senate committees.

The instructed committees draft their legislation and then send it to the Budget Committee, which packages it into an omnibus reconciliation bill. The legislation must then win approval by each chamber. In the House special rules that tightly restrict amending activity are always used to protect these big and usually controversial packages. The Budget Act protects the reconciliation bill against a filibuster in the Senate by limiting initial floor debate to twenty hours and debate on the conference report to ten hours; in addition, only germane amendments are allowed.

Conference committees on reconciliation bills are sometimes huge. All the committees with provisions in the legislation as well as the Budget committees are represented, and the totals can run into the hundreds. The conference committee on the 1981 reconciliation bill consisted of 208 House conferees from seventeen committees and 72 senators from fourteen committees (Tiefer 1989, 798). In 1993, 164 House members from sixteen committees and 53 senators from thirteen committees served on the reconciliation bill conference committee. Generally, such conferences work in subgroups; the 1981 conference met in fifty-eight subgroups (Granat 1984, 1298). Most conferees have authority to make decisions only about the provisions their committee or subcommittee drafted. The House conference delegation for the 1997 spending reconciliation bill, for example, consisted of thirteen subgroups from eight committees, each with authority to negotiate on only a specific title or subtitle of the bill. Conferees from the Budget Committees usually have authority over the entire bill and take on the formidable task of coordination. Because reconciliation bills are so substantively and politically important, the party leadership is always involved. Speaker Gingrich, in fact, appointed Majority Leader Armey, Majority Whip Tom DeLay of Texas, and Chief Deputy Whip Hastert to the 1997 spending reconciliation bill conference; they were three of the five Republican general conferees with authority over the entire bill.

Unlike the budget resolution, the reconciliation bill is legislation, so the president can veto it. This possibility gives the president influence in the process of putting the bill together, even if Congress is controlled by the other party. Unless the congressional majority party has huge majorities in both chambers, its chances are exceedingly dim of amassing a two-thirds vote to override the president on legislation that goes to the heart of the differences between the parties. If his own party is in the majority, the president and congressional party leaders are likely to work together closely on such a major piece of legislation. (See the case studies in Chapters 10 and 11 for both circumstances.)

The budget process provides Congress with a tool for making comprehensive decisions. Before the 1974 Budget Act, Congress made spending and taxing decisions in a piecemeal and uncoordinated fashion. To pass an economic program embodying a significant change in direction such as Reagan's in 1981 or Clinton's in 1993 would have required enacting a dozen or more separate bills.

Reconciliation bills make a multitude of policy decisions through an abbreviated legislative process in which many provisions receive limited scrutiny. No committee hearings may have been held on the changes included in the legislation. With the committees operating under time constraints, many provisions may have received only perfunctory attention during committee markup; as part of a much larger package, they may have been altogether ignored during floor debate. In fact, most members may not have been aware of many of them. Yet the provisions in a reconciliation bill are very likely to become law. Simply the size of the package tends to take attention away from any but the most major provisions. In the House the bill will be considered under a special rule that prohibits most amendments. In the Senate the bill is protected from a filibuster. And a reconciliation bill is considered "must pass" legislation by the majority party.

Given these advantages, the temptation to use a reconciliation bill as a vehicle for enacting extraneous provisions that have nothing to do with implementing the reconciliation instructions is enormous. To counter that temptation, the Senate in the mid-1980s adopted the Byrd rule, named after its creator, Sen. Robert C. Byrd. The rule prohibits extraneous matter in a reconciliation bill and requires a three-fifths vote to be waived (Tiefer 1989, 891–894; Gold et al. 1992, 302–303, 326). Since what is extraneous is not self-evident, a set of rules defining what does and does not fall under the Byrd rule has developed. Application of the rule can have major policy consequences; in 1995, for example, Senate Democrats managed to knock out of the reconciliation bill big chunks of the Republicans' welfare reform legislation. The rule often adds to the strains between the House and the Senate; House members bitterly complain that a Senate rule dictates what can and cannot be included in reconciliation bill conference reports.

The Byrd rule is only one example of the way in which the budget process has superimposed onto the two chambers' rules another set of highly complex rules. In the House the result is that special rules from the Rules Committee, which can waive budget rules, become even more important in managing the business of the chamber. In the Senate another set of decisions that require a supermajority has been added. For example, the key decision in the Senate's approval of legislation implementing the General Agreement on Tariffs and Trade in 1994 was not the vote on passage, which required a simple majority. Before the Senate could vote on approval, sixty votes were needed to waive a Senate budget rule requiring that new legislation be "budget neutral." Since the GATT agreement reduced tariffs, a form of taxes, it did not comply with that rule.

Congress, the President, and Summitry

The veto, his status as head of his party, and his capacity to command media attention allow the president to play a major role in the legislative process. Many legislative proposals originate in the executive branch. Executive branch officials testify before congressional committees on most legislation; they are often present during committee markups and during conference committee deliberations. In addition, executive branch officials let committee and party leaders know through private meetings and frequent informal contacts what the president wants and will accept.

Even if the president is from the other party and has very different policy preferences, the congressional majority party must pay some attention to his wishes if it wants to enact legislation. Presidents under such conditions of divided control have become adept at veto bargaining—at threatening a veto in order to extract the maximum in terms of substantive concessions from an opposition congressional majority. Of course, if the divergence in policy preferences is very wide, the result may be stalemate rather than compromise.

In recent years the president and Congress have resorted to "summits" when normal legislative processes have been incapable of producing a bill and the costs of failing to reach an agreement have been very high. (For a similar argument, see Gilmour 1990.) Relatively formal negotiations between congressional leaders and high-ranking administration officials representing the president directly, summits have no official status; they occur when the president and the majority party leadership decide to engage in such talks. During the 1980s and 1990s, normal legislative processes often ended in stalemate because of divided control, sharp differences in policy preferences, and the tough decisions that big deficits made necessary. The deficit and the budget process, especially as revised in the mid-1980s by the Gramm-Rudman automatic spending cut provisions, often provided the sense of emergency and the statutory deadline that made inaction politically costly. After all, a budget is a statement of priorities; when resources are tight, budget decisions involve painful trade-offs.

In 1987, for example, Congress and the Reagan administration were headed toward a potentially bloody and protracted showdown. Congressional Democrats believed some tax increases were essential and had included them in their budget resolution and the reconciliation bill; Reagan was adamantly opposed. Then the stock market crashed and everyone realized a quick agreement was essential. Reagan called for a summit, congressional Democrats agreed, and a small group of high-level negotiators worked out a deal.

In 1990 the Gramm-Rudman requirement—that the deficit must be cut by a specified large amount, or a process known as sequestration will take place—meant that the costs if the president and Congress failed to reach an agreement would be very high. Sequestration would involve draconian automatic across-the-board spending cuts. Furthermore, estimates of the deficit were rising, and the economy showed signs of slowing. This situation made decisive action even more necessary.

Most independent experts agreed that a serious budget reduction package would have to include significant revenue increases. Yet in decisions about taxes, the parties saw their future electoral prospects at stake. Attempting to shake the high tax image that Republicans had successfully pinned upon them, Democrats were determined to refuse to take the initiative—and the blame—in proposing new taxes. A great many Republicans believed that their "no new taxes" stance accounted for their party's electoral success; Bush had pledged himself to that course during his 1988 campaign. As they saw it, Republicans had a great deal to lose by reneging on that promise.

Under these circumstances, normal processes were unlikely to produce results. So President Bush proposed a summit. The congressional party leaders appointed seventeen members—including chairmen and ranking minority members of the Budget, Appropriations, and tax-writing committees—as negotiators. Treasury Secretary Nicholas F. Brady, OMB head Richard G. Darman, and White House Chief of Staff John H. Sununu represented the president. The first meeting was held on May 17, 1990, and sessions continued through much of June. Estimates of the likely size of the budget deficit continued to increase, but no progress toward a plan to deal with it was made.

Finally, on September 30, the day before the beginning of the fiscal year—when a new budget must be in place to keep the government functioning—the president and congressional leaders announced that a deal had been reached. Even after Bush had conceded the need for some new revenues, differences over taxes and domestic spending cuts had continued to block progress. Eventually, the congressional negotiating group was pared down to include only the top party leaders, and it was this small group of key leaders and high-ranking administration officials that forged the agreement.

Neither Bush nor the Democratic House leadership was able to sell that agreement to their troops, and it was defeated in the House. A revised version, however, was approved soon thereafter and sequestration was avoided (Sinclair 1991).

In 1995 a budget summit between the new majority congressional Republicans and President Clinton failed to produce an agreement; but in 1997 they managed to agree on a budget deal that balanced the budget (see case studies in Chapter 11).

During the second half of the 1990s, reaching agreement on appropriations bills increasingly came to require summits. Even after the budget reached balance, President Clinton and the conservative Republicans who controlled both houses of Congress differed enough in policy preferences to prevent the normal process from being sufficient. Appropriations bills must pass every year or the government shuts down (see Chapter 11 for details). Since the president can veto appropriations bills, Congress must either satisfy him or be able to muster a two-thirds vote to override. In the partisan 1990s, the latter was never a realistic possibility for Republicans; but satisfying Clinton meant spending more for programs they disliked. Often only some of the appropriations bills could be enacted through the regular process; the rest had to be rolled into a big omnibus spending bill, the contents of which were negotiated between congressional leaders and high White House officials. In 1998, for example, eight of the thirteen appropriations bills were packaged into one omnibus bill; in 1999, five were, including the huge Labor, Health and Human Services, and Education appropriations bill.

Under difficult circumstances, a summit may offer the only hope of agreement between Congress and the president, but as a decision-making mechanism it is relatively expensive for party leaders and the institution; it not only short-circuits the normal decision-making process but also excludes most members and is therefore likely to lead to discontent.

What Is the Regular Process?

The textbook diagram of how a bill becomes a law no longer accurately describes the legislative process on major bills. In the contemporary

TABLE 5.1   Special Procedures and Practices in the House and Senate on Major
Legislation, 1987–1990, 1993–1998

Number of special procedures and practices	Percentage of major measures in which the legislative process was characterized by special procedures and practices	
	House[a]	Senate[b]
0	21	31
1	30	26
2	27	26
3 or more	22	18

[a] The enumerated special procedures and practices that the legislation may have encountered as it worked its way through the House are multiple referral, omnibus legislation, the passage of legislation as a result of a legislative-executive branch summit, the bypassing of committees, postcommittee adjustments, and consideration under a complex or closed rule.

[b] For the Senate the procedures and practices that were counted were the same as for the House except consideration under a complex or closed rule. Also counted was whether the bill ran into filibuster trouble and whether it was subject to an amending marathon (ten or more amending roll calls).

Source: Computed by the author.

Congress there are many variations; one can more accurately speak of legislative processes in the plural than of a single cut-and-dried set of steps through which all measures proceed.

While my step-by-step discussion of the legislative process makes the variety obvious, it does not yield any precise sense of the cumulative impact of these procedures and practices. That is best conveyed by a systematic analysis of the legislative process on recent major legislation. How many of the special process variations characterized the process on major legislation? How frequently did such legislation follow the old textbook process?

For each of the 255 major measures in the 100th, 101st, 103rd, 104th, and 105th Congresses, I counted the number of special procedures and practices that the legislation encountered as it worked its way through the House. The procedures and practices enumerated were multiple referral, omnibus legislation, legislation resulting from a legislative-executive branch summit, the bypassing of committees, postcommittee adjustments, and consideration under a complex or closed rule.

The House legislative process on the 255 major bills of these recent Congresses displayed at least one of these characteristics in 79 percent of the cases and two or more in 49 percent (see Table 5.1). To talk about the "regular order" in the House as the absence of these characteristics is no longer accurate, at least on major legislation.

Another perspective is provided by calculating the proportion of legislation that followed the supposedly regular process: legislation that was reported by one committee, that was not omnibus nor the result of a summit, that was not subject to postcommittee adjustments, and that was considered on the floor under an open rule. In the House the legislative process on only 8 percent of major legislation—19 out of 225 bills—in these recent Congresses meet these criteria.[4] The "regular order" is no longer the norm; on major legislation it has become the exception.

To assess the frequency of the new procedures and practices in the Senate, I counted the same characteristics as for the House, excepting, of course, the use of special rules. In the Senate these special procedures and practices are somewhat less pervasive than in the House; the legislative process on 50 percent of major bills displayed at least one special characteristic and 19 percent displayed two or more. This measure, which parallels the one constructed for the House, excludes the most notable changes in the legislative process in the Senate: the increase in floor amending activity and the more frequent use of extended debate. When a second Senate measure of special procedures and practices is created by also counting whether the bill ran into filibuster trouble or was subject to an amending marathon (ten or more amending roll calls), 69 percent of major bills display at least one and 44 percent two or more special process characteristics (see Table 5.1). In the Senate, as in the House, the legislative process on major legislation frequently no longer conforms to what we still tend to think of as the normal process.

In both chambers, then, the legislative process on major legislation has changed; such legislation is now more likely than not to traverse an unorthodox or nonstandard course. How and why this happened is the subject of the next chapter.

---

4. This figure is less than the 21 percent without any of the special process characteristics in Table 5.1 because the table includes measures that did not get to the House floor and measures considered under procedures other than rules—mostly suspension of the rules.

c h a p t e r   s i x

Why and How the Legislative Process Changed

WHY DID THE "TEXTBOOK" LEGISLATIVE PROCESS that had seemed so routinized and entrenched change extensively? In this chapter I argue that the modifications and innovations can be seen as responses to problems and opportunities that members—as individuals or collectively—confronted, problems and opportunities that arose from changes in institutional structure or challenges in the political environment.

The story is complex and its various strands intertwined in intricate ways, but three factors can be analytically isolated as key: internal reforms that changed the distribution of influence in both chambers in the 1970s; the institution of the congressional budget process, an internal-process reform with sufficiently far reaching effects to deserve separate treatment; and a political environment in the 1980s and early 1990s characterized by divided control, big deficits, and ideological hostility to the legislative goals of the congressional Democratic Party. I discuss each of these briefly and then analyze how the legislative process was affected by them.

I close the chapter with an analysis of the legislative process in the Republican Congresses of the mid- and late-1990s. How did the Republican takeover affect unorthodox lawmaking?

From Decentralization to Individualism in the Senate

In the U.S. Senate of the 1950s and before, influence was decentralized but unequally distributed, with committee chairs and other senior members, who were predominantly conservative, exercising the lion's share. It was a relatively closed and inward-looking institution. The typical senator specialized in the issues that came before his committees and participated meagerly on the floor; he was deferential to his seniors, loyal to the institution, and restrained in the use of the powers that Senate rules confer upon the individual (Matthews 1960; Sinclair 1989).

Senate rules then as now allowed unlimited debate and, in most cases, unlimited amending activity. The restraint that characterized the Senate of that period was not a function of rules; rather it depended on norms—unwritten rules of behavior—and on a political environment in which acting with restraint was relatively costless to senators.

That began to change in the late 1950s. The 1958 elections brought into the Senate a big class of northern liberal Democrats who had won competitive elections on a platform promising action; succeeding elections through the mid-1960s augmented the number of such members. These senators could not afford to wait to make their mark, as the old norms had demanded; both their policy and their reelection goals dictated immediate and extensive activism.

An activist style based on participation in a broader range of issues and on the floor as well as in committee became attractive to more and more senators as the political environment and the Washington political community changed radically in the 1960s and 1970s. New issues and an enormous growth in the number of groups active in Washington meant that senators were eagerly sought as champions of groups' causes. The news media played an increasingly important role in politics and needed credible sources to represent issue positions and to offer commentary. These developments made the role of outward-looking policy entrepreneur available to more senators. Successfully playing that role brought a senator a Washington reputation as a player, media attention, and possibly even a shot at the presidency.

Incentives to exploit fully the great powers that Senate rules confer on the individual increased immensely, and senators began to offer many more amendments on the floor and to use extended debate more often. As a result, the Senate floor became a more active decision-making arena. The proportion of legislation subject to high amending activity (ten or more amending roll calls) was tiny in the 1950s; for the 84th and 86th Congresses, it averaged 3 percent. During the 1960s and 1970s, it rose to a mean of 8 percent per Congress, and in the 1980s it averaged 15 percent (Sinclair 1989, 115).[1]

---

1. These figures are based on data for even-numbered Congresses from the 88th to the 96th Congress and for all Congresses from the 97th through the 99th.

As senators became much more willing to exploit their prerogative of extended debate, filibusters, both overt and covert, increasingly became a routine part of the legislative process in the Senate. As Table 6.1 shows, filibusters were once rare; in the 1950s a typical Congress saw one filibuster. By the 1970s more than ten filibusters occurred per Congress on average, and by the late 1980s and early 1990s filibusters were taking place at a rate of more than one a month. (See Beth 1995 for cautions about these data.) As the number of filibusters grew, so did attempts to stop them by invoking cloture; cloture votes became an ordinary part of the legislative process. While cloture was often successfully invoked, passing legislation that was at all controversial increasingly required sixty votes.

Reform and Its Legacy in the House

In the House changes in chamber and majority party rules during the 1970s transformed the distribution of influence (Dodd and Oppenheimer 1977; Sinclair 1983; Smith 1989; Rohde 1991). Even more than in the Senate, legislative influence in the House had been vested in powerful and often conservative committee leaders over whom party leaders and members had little control. Reformers, who were primarily liberal Democrats, objected to the conservative policy this system produced and to the limited opportunities for participation it afforded rank-and-file members.

Elections throughout the 1960s changed the composition of the Democratic Party in the House, increasing the number of northern Democrats, many of whom were liberal reformers, and decreasing the number of conservative southerners.

Through a series of rules changes mostly instituted between 1969 and 1975, reformers changed the distribution of influence. Powers and resources were shifted from committee chairs down to subcommittee chairs and rank-and-file members and up to the party leadership. For example, the power to appoint subcommittee chairs was taken away from the committee chair and given to the majority party members of the committee; subcommittees were ensured adequate budget and staff. Rather than securing their positions automatically through their seniority on the committee, committee chairs had to win approval by majority vote on a secret ballot of the majority party membership. Junior members gained resources, especially staff, that enormously increased their ability to participate actively in the legislative process. The Speaker, the leader of the majority party, was given the power to select the Democratic members of the Rules Committee, a greater say in the assignment of members to other committees, and new powers over the referral of bills.

TABLE 6.1   Filibusters and Cloture Votes, 82nd–105th Congresses

Congresses	Years	Filibusters[a]	Cloture votes[a]	Successful cloture votes[a]
82nd–86th	1951–60	1.0	0.4	0.0
87th–91st	1961–70	4.6	5.2	0.8
92nd–96th	1971–80	11.2	22.4	8.6
97th–99th	1981–86	16.7	23.0	10.0
100th–102nd	1987–92	26.7	39.0	15.3
103rd–105th	1993–98	28.0	48.3	13.7

[a] Entries are per Congress.

Sources: For the filibusters per Congress, "A Look at the Senate Filibuster," Special Report of the Democratic Study Group, June 13, 1994, No. 103–28, Appendix B, compiled by Congressional Research Service. For the cloture votes, Norman Ornstein, Thomas Mann, and Michael Malbin, *Vital Statistics on Congress, 1993–1994* (Washington, D.C.: Congressional Quarterly, 1994), 162. Data for the 103rd Congress are from Richard S. Beth, "Cloture in the Senate, 103rd Congress," memorandum, Congressional Research Service, June 23, 1995. Data for the 104th and 105th are from *Congressional Quarterly Almanac*, 1995–1997.

During the same period, the House adopted sunshine rules that opened the legislative process to greater public scrutiny. Recorded votes became possible—and easy to force—in the Committee of the Whole, where the amending process takes place. Most committee markup sessions and conference committee meetings were opened to the public. The greater visibility of congressional decision making increased members' incentives for activism.

These reforms had far-reaching direct and indirect effects. By reducing the power and autonomy of the committees, they made legislating more difficult for the majority party. To be sure, Democratic reformers had often been unhappy with the sort of legislation conservative-led committees had produced. By the late 1970s, however, the committee chairs and the membership of the most powerful committees were more representative of the Democratic Party than they had been earlier; Republicans and dissident Democrats had become adept at using floor amendments to make political points and confront mainstream Democrats with politically difficult votes. Compromises carefully crafted in committee were being picked apart on the floor, and floor sessions were stretching on interminably.

The number of floor amendments decided on a teller or recorded vote had risen gradually from 55 in 1955–1956 to 107 in 1969–1970. With the institution of the recorded teller, it jumped to 195 in 1971–1972, and with electronic voting it jumped again to 351 in 1973–1974 (Smith 1989,

33). During the 94th Congress (1975–1976), 372 such amendments were offered on the floor, and during the 95th, 439. In 1979 floor consideration of the budget resolution took nine days, during which fifty amendments were offered (Sinclair 1983, 180).

Democrats began to look to their party leaders, the only central leaders in the chamber, to counter these problems. The leaders responded by innovating in ways that led to alterations in the legislative process. The leadership became more involved with legislation before it reached the floor, and this involvement increasingly took the form of negotiating substantive changes in the legislation, often at the postcommittee stage, in order to produce a bill that could pass the chamber. To respond to the barrage of amendments offered on the floor, the leadership developed special rules into powerful devices for structuring floor decision making.

Budget Reform

When President Richard Nixon aggressively challenged Congress's power of the purse, Congress responded by passing the Congressional Budget and Impoundment Control Act of 1974. Presidents had been encroaching on Congress's budgetary powers for decades; lacking a mechanism for making comprehensive decisions, Congress had long used the president's budget as its point of departure for budgetary decision making and usually altered it only marginally. However, when Nixon claimed the right to impound—that is, not spend—congressionally appropriated funds, the Congress had to respond or acquiesce in a severe diminution of its powers. Nixon argued that congressional appropriations were just ceilings and that he was not required to spend any of the money Congress appropriated. In effect, he was arguing that Congress had only negative powers: Congress might be able to prevent the president from doing something by not appropriating funds, but it could not force a president to carry out a policy he opposed.

The Budget Act went far beyond devising a procedure to control impoundments: the budget process that it established provided a mechanism by which comprehensive policy making in Congress became possible. During its first few years, however, the budget process was not used in that way. In the House the battles over budget resolutions were hard fought and highly partisan; debate did turn on the political parties' different priorities, but the resolutions themselves did not call for significant policy change (Ellwood and Thurber 1981; Schick 1980).

Reconciliation instructions that mandated committees to make changes in legislation under their jurisdiction were first included in the budget resolution in 1980 (Sinclair 1983, 181–190). Frighteningly high inflation in January 1980 convinced President Jimmy Carter and the Democratic congressional party leadership that budget cuts needed to be made, and quickly. The ordinary legislative process, they decided, would take too long and be subject to delay by interests adversely affected by the cuts. Therefore, they decided to use the budget process and to include reconciliation instructions in the first budget resolution. Doing so was highly controversial (in part because the Budget Act envisioned that such instructions would be included in the second budget resolution, which in this and most other cases would be too late), and the committees subject to instructions objected vigorously. Nevertheless, the resolution with the instructions passed, and the committees did comply. To do otherwise was to defy the will of Congress as expressed in its budget resolution.

Although the policy changes required by the 1980 budget resolution were modest by later standards, the experience made clear to perceptive participants that, under certain circumstances at least, the budget process was a mechanism available to central leaders for making comprehensive policy change. David Stockman, a Republican member of the House from Michigan from 1977 to January 1981, was one of those perceptive participants. As President Ronald Reagan's first head of the Office of Management and Budget, he suggested using the budget process to enact Reagan's economic program in 1981 (Stockman 1986). The administration-supported budget resolution included instructions to committees to make substantial changes in policy; supporters forced a single vote on them as a whole and then packaged the policy changes into one massive reconciliation bill where again the key vote was whether to accept or reject them as a whole. This strategy enabled Reagan and his supporters to achieve major policy change quickly in a system resistant to such change.

The budget process has had wide-reaching effects on the legislative process. In the years since 1981, budget politics have remained at center stage. The attempt to control the big deficits Reagan's economic program created shaped the politics of the 1980s and most of the 1990s. The budget process has become the tool of choice for those attempting to bring about comprehensive policy change.

A Hostile Political Climate as a Force for Innovation: The 1980s and Early 1990s

Both the House and Senate entered the 1980s beset by problems resulting from changes in their internal distribution of influence. The highly individualistic Senate, in which each senator was accorded extraordinary latitude, was very good at agenda setting and publicizing problems, but it was less well structured for legislative decision making. The House, which had greatly increased rank-and-file members' opportunities for participation, also had problems legislating, though its central leadership had begun to develop reasonably effective responses.

The political climate of the 1980s and early 1990s exacerbated the problems of legislating, especially for the Democratic House. Ronald Reagan was a conservative, confrontational president whose policy views were very far from those of congressional Democrats, and the policy preferences of his successor, George Bush, were not much closer. In 1981 Reagan and his congressional allies ran over the Democratic House majority and enacted sweeping policy changes over futile Democratic protests. Thereafter, Reagan was never as politically strong again, but he and Bush still had the bully pulpit and the veto.

The growing ideological polarization of the parties exacerbated the conflict. Reagan's nomination had signaled the Republican Party's move to the right. The congressional party, especially the House Republican Party, had begun to change in the mid- and late-1970s. Not only were fewer moderates being elected; more hard-edged, ideological conservatives were entering the House. The elections of 1978 brought a Republican freshman from Georgia named Newt Gingrich to the House.

The Democratic Party in the 1980s became more cohesive as its southern contingent changed. Republicans won southern seats, and the southern Democrats that remained depended for reelection on the votes of African Americans. The Republican Party's increasing conservatism also made ideological differences among Democrats seem smaller.

The voting cohesion of House Democrats began to increase after the 1982 elections, and in the late 1980s and early 1990s it reached levels unprecedented in the post–World War II era. For the period 1951 through 1970, House Democrats' average party unity score was 78 percent; it fell to 74 percent for the period 1971 to 1982.[2] After the 1982 elections the scores began rising and averaged 86 percent for the 1983–1994 period. During this same period, the proportion of party votes also increased, averaging 56 percent compared with 37 percent during the 1971–1982 period. During the 103rd Congress, a majority of Democrats opposed a majority of Republicans on 64 percent of House recorded votes (Rohde 1991; *Congressional Quarterly Almanac,* various years).

---

2. Party votes are recorded votes on which a majority of Democrats voted against a majority of Republicans. A member's party unity score is the percentage of party votes on which he or she voted with a majority of his or her party colleagues.

During the 1980s, then, an increasingly cohesive House Democratic majority faced a hostile president, a Republican Senate, and a more aggressive and conservative Republican minority.

After 1981 big deficits became chronic and severely restricted feasible policy options. Democrats often found themselves in the position of fighting to protect past policy successes. Not infrequently the decisions that had to be made, if not carefully managed, had the potential of pitting Democratic members against each other.

Partisan conflict and stalemate in Washington fed public cynicism about government's ability to handle effectively the problems facing the country; many people concluded that government could not do anything right. Passing legislation that majority Democrats considered satisfactory became very difficult in such a climate. Even enacting legislation to keep the government going was hard, both because of the ideological gulf between congressional Democrats and Republican presidents and because the legislation frequently required making unpalatable decisions. This tough climate forced further innovation in the legislative process, especially in the House.

How Internal Reform and a Hostile Climate Spawned Unorthodox Lawmaking

Internal reforms, the hostile political climate, and other lesser changes in the environment altered the context in which members of Congress functioned. As they and their leaders sought to advance their goals within this altered context, they changed the legislative process. Sometimes changes were brought about by formal revisions in chamber rules; more frequently, they were the result of alterations in practices.

Multiple Referral

As our society and economy evolve over time, the issues at the center of controversy change. In the 1950s and early 1960s, for example, environmental protection was an obscure issue, and congressional attempts to deal with it mostly entailed programs to help municipalities build water treatment plants; by the 1970s the environment had become a highly salient issue, and Congress was considering ambitious legislation to protect endangered species and to force auto makers and other polluters to clean up the air. As new issues arise and old ones change, the fit between the prominent issues on the congressional agenda and the committee system becomes increasingly poor. Yet Congress, especially the House, has great difficulty in realigning committee jurisdictions. Taking away jurisdiction from a committee reduces its clout; both committee members and affected interest groups that have established good working relationships with the committee will fight the change. Since committee membership is a considerably more important basis of members' influence in the House than in the Senate, realigning jurisdictions so that they fit better with the issues of the day is harder in the House than in the Senate.

By the early 1970s committee jurisdictions that had last been significantly overhauled in 1946 were seriously outmoded; jurisdiction over a number of key issues—energy, the environment, and health, for example—was spread over a number of committees, leading to a lack of coordination and numerous turf fights. The House attempted to reform its committee jurisdictions in the mid-1970s but largely failed (Davidson and Oleszek 1977). The Senate's attempt at committee reform in the late 1970s was considerably more successful (Davidson 1981).

Unable to realign committee jurisdictions and driven by reform-minded members' desire to increase opportunities for broad participation in the legislative process, the House in 1975 changed its rules to allow multiple referral of legislation (Davidson and Oleszek 1992).[3] In the first Congress with multiple referral, 1975–1976, 6 percent of the measures introduced were multiply referred. Over time and driven by the same forces that led to its institution, multiply referred legislation became an increasingly prominent part of the House workload (see Table 6.2). On average a little more than 10 percent of measures were multiply referred during the four Congresses between 1977 and 1984; the frequency rose to 14 percent in the 99th Congress and averaged 18 percent in the 100th and 101st Congresses (Young and Cooper 1993, 214).

For major legislation, the increase has been steeper. The congressional agenda of major legislation included almost 9 percent multiply referred legislation in the 94th Congress, a figure very close to that for all measures. Since then, however, multiply referred measures have made up a considerably greater proportion of major legislation than of all legislation. In the late 1980s and 1990s, about 30 percent of major measures were mul-

---

3. Actually, even before then, something quite similar to multiple referral occurred under specialized circumstances; when legislation referred to a committee other than Ways and Means contained a revenue component, that section would be sent to the tax committee. In the 91st Congress (1969–1970), for example, three bills primarily under the jurisdiction of a committee other than Ways and Means were also referred to Ways and Means for consideration of their revenue sections; thus, the Interstate and Foreign Commerce Committee was mostly responsible for the Airport Development Act, but the trust fund and tax provisions were handled by Ways and Means.

TABLE 6.2   Multiple Referral in the House and Senate, 94th–105th Congresses

		House		Senate	
Congress	Years	Percentage of all measures	Percentage of major legislation	Percentage of all measures	Percentage of major legislation[a]
94th	1975–76	6.0	8.6		5.2
95th	1977–78	10.3			
96th	1979–80	11.7		6.4	
97th	1981–82	9.6	13.7	5.0	5.6
98th	1983–84	11.6		4.4	
99th	1985–86	14.0		3.0	
100th	1987–88	17.5	33.3		6.5
101st	1989–90	18.2	30.0		7.0
103rd	1993–94		27.8		14.5
104th	1995–96		50.9		11.1
105th	1997–98		26.2		10.0

[a] Includes cases of multiple committee consideration of legislation that was not formally multiply referred.

Sources: The data on the House for all measures are from Young and Cooper (1993, 214). The data on the Senate for all measures are from Davidson (1989, 381). Other data were compiled by the author. Major legislation is defined by the list of major legislation in the *CQ Weekly*, augmented by those measures on which key votes occurred, again according to *CQ Weekly*.

tiply referred. The 104th Congress is an exception; despite a rule change intended to rein in multiple referral, 51 percent of major measures were referred to more than one committee in the 104th Congress.

Multiple referral of legislation has always been possible in the Senate through unanimous consent. The Senate, however, did manage to realign its committee jurisdictions during the 1970s, and because senators can more easily influence legislation outside the committee setting than can House members, they have less incentive to insist on a referral (Fenno 1973; Sinclair 1989). As a consequence, the referral of legislation to more than one committee continues to be considerably less frequent in the Senate. Several committees do sometimes consider different bills on the same topic, a procedure that can create complications much like those formal multiple referral can produce.

Roger Davidson found that from the late 1970s through the mid-1980s on average less than 5 percent of all Senate measures were multiply referred and that, if there was a trend, it was toward a decrease (Davidson 1989, 381). Major measures, however, show a mild increasing trend toward multiple committee consideration from the late 1980s to the 1990s (see Table 6.2). In an interview with the author, an informed observer suggested that the frequency of multiple referral in the House was pressuring the Senate to include more committees in the process formally so that the substantive expertise and political support of these committees' leaders would be available in conference with the House.

Committees as Shapers of Legislation

By reducing the power of committee chairs and increasing the opportunities and incentives for rank-and-file members to participate in the legislative process, the House reforms of the 1970s diminished the capacity of committees to pass their legislation without change. No longer were bills protected by a powerful chair with the weapons to retaliate against members who challenged his legislation in committee or on the floor or by voting rules that prevented most recorded votes on floor amendments. Junior committee members and members not on the committee now had the staff and the access to information that made their participation feasible. The increased prevalence of multiple referral lessened committee autonomy; committee leaders were not always capable of resolving the conflicts among their committees, yet unresolved intercommittee conflicts endangered legislation on the floor. The reformers had given Democratic majority party leaders some new tools, and, as the problems the reforms had wrought became increasingly evident, the now more ideologically homogeneous Democrats began to expect their leaders to use those tools to engineer passage of legislation broadly supported by the Democratic membership.

To respond to their members' demands, the Democratic leadership became more involved in the legislative process in the period before legislation reached the floor. A bill's substance is by far the most important determinant of its fate on the floor. As it became more difficult for the committee or committees of jurisdiction to write a bill that could pass on the floor, the party leaders stepped in more often to help.

Party leaders, of course, may involve themselves informally on legislation during committee consideration; anecdotal and interview evidence indicates that such intervention is much more frequent than it used to be (Sinclair 1995). That kind of involvement is, however, impossible to document systematically across time. Substantive adjustments to legislation after it is reported—whether engineered by the party leadership or others—can be counted with more precision.[4]

---

4. I ascertained the presence or absence of a postcommittee adjustment and whether it was directed by the party leadership by doing a case study of each of the major measures for the selected Congresses. The case studies relied primarily on the *CQ Weekly* and the *Congressional Quarterly Almanac*. Thus, instances not ascertainable from the public record could have been missed; however, when I had independent information from interviews or participant-observation available, they confirmed the coding done on the basis of the written record.

Postcommittee adjustments were rare in the prereform era. In the 91st Congress there was no such instance in the House on the fifty-four major measures, though in one case the leadership was involved in making an adjustment of this kind after a veto. Committees were quite successful on the floor, lessening the need for tinkering after they had finished their work. Even when committees lost on the floor and when that loss was no big surprise, leaders seem to have made no attempt to head off the floor defeat by substantive adjustments in the legislation. Presumably the committee leaders had done what they could and would in committee, and the party leaders lacked the tools to get involved.

In the 94th Congress there were two clear instances of postcommittee adjustments to major measures; both cases involved the new budget process. In 1975 and again in 1976 it became clear that the budget resolution as reported by the Budget Committee would not pass. In each case the party leadership stepped in and crafted an amendment to the budget resolution to ensure passage in a form acceptable to most Democrats.

In the 1980s and early 1990s the hostile political climate made passing legislation Democrats wanted difficult. Big deficits made it harder for committee leaders to forge broadly acceptable deals; a climate of scarcity begets zero-sum politics in which one group's gain is perceived as a loss by other groups and fewer "sweeteners" to induce support are available. As committee Democrats tried to craft a bill that was passable yet as close as possible to their preferred policy position, they could easily misjudge what was passable. Furthermore, changes in the political environment after the committee had reported—in the salience of the issue or in the public's response to presidential rhetoric—could alter what would pass. Leadership counts of members' voting intentions often showed not enough support for the committee-reported bill. Therefore, major legislation frequently required substantive alterations. As important legislation increasingly involved a number of committees, the compromises that needed to be made among the committees to bring a passable bill to the floor were often beyond the capacity of committee leaders to negotiate. In such a climate postcommittee adjustments, almost always directed by the party leadership, became almost routine (see Table 6.3).

The increased frequency with which committees are bypassed is a result of the same forces—namely, (1) internal reforms that decreased the power and autonomy of committees and empowered the party leaders and (2) the hostile political climate that exacerbated the difficulties the reforms had produced. To be sure, not every instance of the bypassing of committees is directed by the leadership; occasionally a discharge petition is successful. Most often, however, when committees are bypassed, it is the party leadership that made the decision, though not necessarily over the

TABLE 6.3　The Changing Role of Committees in the Legislative Process, 91st–105th Congresses

Congress	Years	Percentage of major legislation in which the committee with jurisdiction was bypassed		Percentage of major legislation subject to postcommittee adjustment	
		House	Senate	House	Senate
91st	1969–70	2	4	0	2
94th	1975–76	2	3	4	2
97th	1981–82	8	4	23	22
100th	1987–88	21	18	37	22
101st	1989–90	18	11	39	35
103rd	1993–94	6	13	29	36
104th	1995–96	13	28	48	60
105th	1997–98	10	13	35	28

Source: Compiled by the author.

committee's opposition. Sometimes a committee is bypassed with its members' full concurrence simply to speed the process—when identical legislation has passed in the previous Congress, for example.

On the fifty-four major measures in the 91st Congress (1969–1970), the committee was never actually bypassed in the House, though in one case the committee reported only because of a threat of discharge. (That case, an organized crime control bill forced out of a reluctant Judiciary Committee, is counted as a bypass in Table 6.3.) In the 94th Congress the committee was bypassed in one case; the leadership undertook the drafting of an internal reform measure. As Table 6.3 shows, bypassing the committee became considerably more frequent in the 1980s. The circumstances varied widely, but in most cases the decision to bypass the committee was a majority party leadership decision. In the 103rd Congress the frequency decreases; in the 104th it increases again, but the relatively low figure is somewhat deceiving, as I discussed in Chapter 2; although most items in the Contract with America went through the formal committee process, they were actually drafted elsewhere.

When the party leadership decides to bypass a committee, it does so in order to move legislation. Since bypassing committee is a violation of committee prerogatives and likely to make some members unhappy, especially in the House, leaders would prefer to avoid doing so. Therefore, House leaders will bypass a committee only as a last resort and thus are more likely to do so when the political context makes legislating particularly difficult. With the same party (the Democrats) controlling Congress and the presidency in 1993–1994, legislating became a little less difficult for the House, and House leaders had less need to use costly tactics—thus the decline in the 103rd Congress shown in Table 6.3.

If internal reforms had unintended consequences that made legislating more difficult for the House, the Senate's individualism run rampant made the House's problems look picayune. Furthermore, the Senate, unlike the House, did not give its central leadership new tools for dealing with the problems.

In the Senate as in the House, one response was an increase in postcommittee adjustments to legislation. They were rare in the late 1960s and 1970s; the 91st and 94th Congresses saw one case each. In the 1980s and 1990s postcommittee adjustments became much more frequent. The Senate majority leader often engineered or at least oversaw the working out of postcommittee changes in legislation, but committee leaders and even individual senators sometimes took on the task, reflecting the wide dispersion of power in the Senate.

Although the frequency of postcommittee adjustments declined appreciably in the 103rd Congress in the House, in the Senate it crept up a bit. For the majority-rule House, united control made legislating somewhat easier; at least amassing large margins to dissuade the president from vetoing the legislation was no longer necessary. The Senate, in contrast, still needed sixty votes to pass most controversial legislation. With the return of divided control in the 104th, postcommittee adjustments became more frequent again in both chambers.

In the Senate the frequency with which committees are bypassed has also increased. Committees were seldom bypassed on major legislation before the mid-1980s; the 91st, 94th, and 97th Congresses each saw two cases. The frequency increased substantially with the 100th Congress, remained well above its previous level in the 101st and the 103rd Congresses, and reached a new high in the 104th.

Special Rules in the House

In the prereform era most legislation was brought to the House floor under a simple open rule that allowed all germane amendments. Tax bills and often other legislation from the Ways and Means Committee were considered under a closed rule that allowed no amendments (except those offered by the committee itself); such legislation was regarded as too complex and too politically tempting a target to allow floor amendments. In the 91st Congress (1969–1970), for example, 80 percent of the major legislation was considered under simple open rules; 16 percent— primarily bills reported by the Ways and Means Committee—came to the floor under closed rules. Only two measures were considered under rules with provisions more complex than simply allowing all germane amendments or barring all amendments.

The reforms made legislation much more vulnerable to alteration on the floor. With rank-and-file members having greater incentives and resources for offering amendments on the floor, the number of amendments offered and pushed to a roll call vote shot up. Committee bills were more frequently picked apart on the floor, members were often forced to go on the record on votes hard to explain to constituents back home, and floor sessions stretched on late into the night.

The reformers had given the Democratic leadership the power to name the Democratic members and the chair of the Rules Committee and had thereby made the committee an arm of the leadership. In the late 1970s some Democrats began to pressure their leaders to use special rules to bring floor proceedings under control. Forty Democrats wrote Speaker Thomas P. O'Neill Jr., D-Mass., in 1979 asking that he make more use of restrictive rules in order to curtail frequent late-night sessions (Smith 1989, 40–41).

As Table 6.4 shows, as late as 1977–1978 most special rules were still open rules; only 15 percent restricted amendments in some way. As Democratic members began to comprehend the costs of the wide-open amending process fostered by the reforms and to demand that their leaders do something about it, the frequency of restrictive rules increased. In the hostile climate of the 1980s and early 1990s, restrictive rules were used more and more often. Holding together compromises and protecting members from political heat became more difficult and more essential; and leaders, in response to their members' demands, developed special rules into powerful devices for shaping the choices members face on the floor. By 1993–1994, 70 percent of special rules restricted amendments to some extent.

When only major measures are examined, the trend is even stronger. The frequency of open rules dropped steeply between the 1970s and the early 1980s and again between the early and the late 1980s. By the late 1980s almost three-quarters of major measures were considered under restrictive rules.

The power and flexibility of special rules make them a useful tool under a broad variety of circumstances. Both the uncertainty that the 1970s reforms begot and the problems that majority Democrats faced in legislating during the adverse political climate of the 1980s and early 1990s stimulated an increase in the use of complex and restrictive rules (Bach and Smith 1988; Sinclair 1983, 1995). The election of a Democratic

TABLE 6.4   Change in the Character of Special Rules in the House, 91st–105th Congresses

Congress	Years	Percentage of all rules that were restrictive[a]	Percentage of major legislation considered under restrictive rules
91st	1969–70	—	16
94th	1975–76	—	9
95th	1977–78	15	26
96th	1979–80	25	
97th	1981–82	25	32
98th	1983–84	32	
99th	1985–86	43	
100th	1987–88	46	72
101st	1989–90	55	72
102nd	1991–92	66	
103rd	1993–94	70	82
104th	1995–96	54	77
105th	1997–98	60	78

[a] This includes all rules for initial consideration of legislation, except rules on appropriations bills, which only waive points of order. Restrictive rules include closed rules, modified closed rules, and modified open rules. These rules are defined in Chapter 2, p. 22.

Sources: Data on all rules were compiled by Donald Wolfensberger, minority counsel, Committee on Rules, from the Rules Committee calendars and surveys of activities. The 104th and 105th Congress data are from *Survey of Activities of the House Committee on Rules, 104th Congress and 105th Congress*. Data on major measures were compiled by the author.

president in 1992 presented congressional Democrats with a great legislative opportunity, but it also put them under pressure to deliver under difficult circumstances. The Democratic leadership responded by intensifying its employment of restrictive rules during the 103rd Congress.

The new Republican majority in the 104th Congress had promised to pass an ambitious agenda, much of it in the first 100 days. Before the election, however, House Republicans, including prominently their leadership, had vehemently denounced restrictive rules and promised not to use them. The proportion of all rules that were restrictive did go down in the 104th, though Democrats claimed Republicans manipulated the figures by considering under open rules some uncontroversial legislation that should have been considered under the suspension procedure. Major legislation was mostly considered under restrictive rules; the usefulness of such rules for promoting the Republicans' legislative objectives outweighed any damage from the inevitable charges of hypocrisy that their use provoked. In the 105th Congress, when the Republican margin of control had narrowed, the use of restrictive rules on all legislation rose and that on major legislation remained high.

The Senate Floor: Amending Activity and Extended Debate

The Senate, unlike the House, has not developed effective tools for coping with the consequences of alterations in its internal distribution of influence and challenges from its political environment. The attractiveness to modern senators of rules that give the individual so much power and the difficulty of changing Senate rules make developing such tools extraordinarily difficult. Since a two-thirds vote is required to cut off debate on a proposal to change Senate rules, an oversized coalition for change must be constructed. To be effective, the tools would have to give more control to the majority party leadership as they did in the House, but minority party senators certainly have no reason to do so, and even many majority party senators are likely to be ambivalent.

The rules changes the Senate was able to make were modest. Perhaps most important, the Budget Act imposed limits on debate on budget resolutions and reconciliation bills, preventing filibusters on these important measures. In 1975 the number of votes required to invoke cloture was lowered from two-thirds of those present and voting to three-fifths of the full membership—usually sixty. (Cloture on changes in Senate rules was exempted and still requires a two-thirds vote.) In response to the postcloture filibuster developed in the 1970s, rules concerning delaying tactics in order after cloture were tightened. In 1986 floor consideration after cloture was limited to a total of thirty hours.

None of the new rules placed limits on the amendments senators can offer on the floor, and a senator's right to offer unlimited amendments to almost any bill proved as useful to senators in the 1980s and 1990s as it had in the 1970s. The political climate of the 1970s may have been more conducive to policy entrepreneurship, and floor amendments may have been more frequently used as tools toward that end. But amendments also proved to be useful tools in the more ideological and partisan struggles of the 1980s and 1990s.

During the contentious 1980s and 1990s, major legislation was likely to encounter a barrage of floor amendments. On average, 35 percent of major measures that reached the Senate floor in the 103rd through 105th Congresses (1993–1998) were subject to amending marathons (ten or more amendments offered and pushed to a recorded vote).

Senators continued to increase their use of extended debate during the 1980s and early 1990s. The rules changes may have made imposing

TABLE 6.5   Extended Debate–Related Problems on Major Legislation, 91st–105th Congresses

Congress	Years	Percentage of major legislation[a]
91st	1969–70	10
97th	1981–82	24
100th	1987–88	27
101st	1989–90	30
103rd	1993–94	51
104th	1995–96	52
105th	1997–98	53

[a] Percentage of major legislation that was subject to a filibuster that encountered a problem related to extended debate (for example, filibuster, threat of filibuster, hold) discernible from the public record.

Source: Compiled by the author.

cloture easier, but they did not reduce the incentives to use extended debate. Rampant individualism combined with the highly charged political climate to put an increasing share of major legislation under at least a threat of a filibuster. In the 1990s, the filibuster increasingly became a partisan tool. By the 103rd Congress (1993–1994), half of major measures experienced some filibuster-related problem discernible from the public record, and the 104th and 105th Congresses maintained the same high level (see Table 6.5). Passing major legislation in the Senate has come to require sixty votes.

Omnibus Legislation and the Budget Process

Omnibus legislation—legislation of great substantive scope that often involves many committees—increased as a proportion of the congressional agenda of major legislation from none in the 91st Congress (1969–1970), to 8 percent in the 94th (1975–1976), and to 20 percent in the 97th (1981–1982) and 100th (1987–1988). In the 101st, the first Congress during George Bush's presidency, the proportion decreased to 8 percent, but this figure included some of the most important legislation of 1989–1990. In the 1990s (103rd–105th Congresses), on average 14 percent of major measures were omnibus.

During the 1980s, the Democratic majority party leadership sometimes decided to package legislation into omnibus measures as part of a strategy to counter ideologically hostile Republican presidents, especially Ronald Reagan, who was so skillful at using the media to his advantage.

Measures the president very much wanted could sometimes be packaged with others that congressional Democrats favored but the president opposed, thus forcing the president to accept legislative provisions that, were they sent to him in freestanding form, he would veto. By packaging disparate and individually modest provisions on salient issues such as trade, drugs, or crime into an omnibus bill, Democrats sought to compete with the White House for media attention and public credit. During the 103rd Congress, congressional leaders no longer needed to coerce the president into signing their legislation, but omnibus measures remained useful for raising the visibility of popular legislation, and the device continued to be employed in that way. When the Republicans took control of Congress, they used omnibus legislation for similar purposes.

Many omnibus measures are budget related. Budget resolutions, reconciliation bills, and massive continuing resolutions have constituted the preponderance of omnibus measures since the passage of the Budget Act in 1974. In both the 94th and the 101st Congresses, for example, all of the omnibus measures were budget related. The budget-related measures, however, were much more important pieces of legislation in the 101st than in the 94th. The Budget Act made omnibus measures a regular part of the congressional agenda, but changes in the political environment made budget measures the focus of controversy. In the 1980s the budget process moved to the center of the legislative process, and it has remained there. The Reagan administration's use of the budget process in 1981 to redirect government policy made its potential clear; since then it has remained the tool of choice for comprehensive policy change and was used for that purpose by the Clinton administration in 1993 and by the new Republican majority in 1995.

The budget process's centrality stemmed even more, however, from the impact of the big budget deficits of the 1980s and 1990s. During the 1970s, the budget resolutions did not include reconciliation instructions (that is, instructions to committees to make changes in law); the budget process, by and large, accommodated what the committees wanted to do rather than constrained them. In 1980, as I discussed in Chapter 5, the president and congressional Democratic leaders, in response to an economic crisis, used the budget process to make spending cuts; reconciliation instructions were included in the budget resolution for the first time. Then in 1981 the Reagan administration and its congressional allies not only used the budget process to make radical cuts in domestic spending; they also enacted a huge tax cut. The deficits that resulted from that tax cut shaped American politics and kept the budget process at the center of the legislative process. Even after deficits turned into surpluses in the late 1990s, the partisan and interbranch battles over priorities continued to be fought out in the context of the budget process.

From the mid-1980s to the late-1990s, efforts to do something about the deficit dominated political debate, if not always legislative enactments. The decisions made in the budget resolution and in the reconciliation bill that it usually required became the crucial legislative decisions. Decisions on other legislative issues were made within the context of scarce resources and, as discretionary domestic spending shrank, the trade-offs that had to be made among programs became increasingly tough. The Gramm-Rudman legislation, the stated aim of which was to force Congress to balance the budget, complicated the process by adding targets and deadlines that, if missed, would result in horrendous automatic spending cuts.

The politics of big deficits thus made unpalatable policy decisions necessary. The deep policy divisions first between Republican presidents and congressional Democrats and, after 1994, between President Clinton and congressional Republicans made reaching agreement between the branches on such decisions excruciatingly difficult. The 1980s and 1990s saw a succession of high visibility, high stakes showdowns between the branches and the parties on budget measures. Reconciliation bills, like other omnibus measures, were sometimes used to try to force on an opposition party president provisions he opposed; such attempts, of course, raised the level of conflict. The existence of the budget process at least made it possible to wrap unpopular spending cuts and sometimes tax increases into one big package—often sweetened with provisions that members wanted—and get a single vote on the package as a whole. The congressional leadership frequently could persuade its members to pass such a package because defeating it would be devastating for the party's reputation; passing the components individually would have been impossible.

Summits

In the 1980s and 1990s the sharp differences in policy preferences between presidents and opposition party majorities in the Congress and the tough decisions that had to be made sometimes stalemated normal processes. When normal processes, even supplemented by the increasingly active role of majority party leaders, were incapable of producing legislation, the president and Congress had to find another way; the costs of failing to reach an agreement on budget issues were just too high, especially after Gramm-Rudman with its automatic spending cuts went into effect in the mid-1980s. The new device was the summit, relatively formal negotiations between congressional leaders and high-ranking administration officials representing the president directly. Because summits take place only when the stakes are very high, congressional party leaders have always represented their members in such talks; members are not willing to rely on committee leaders to make such decisions on behalf of the party membership as a whole.

Actually, the first instance of major legislation emerging from a process similar in some respects to the summits of the late-1980s and 1990s was the 1980 (FY1981) budget resolution and reconciliation bill during the Carter administration. The announcement on February 22, 1980, that the consumer price index had increased at an 18 percent annual rate in January created a crisis atmosphere. In early March an unprecedented series of meetings between the Carter administration and the Democratic congressional leadership took place for the purpose of discussing budget cuts. The budget resolution approved by Congress closely followed the agreement that had been reached in those meetings (Sinclair 1983).

In the mid-1980s attempts at summit negotiations were made several times but with limited success. The 1983 deal to reestablish the fiscal soundness of the Social Security system emerged from a process that shows some similarities to the summits as well (Gilmour 1990, 248–250). A commission had been appointed to develop a solution, but the deal was really worked out behind the scenes by a few commission members who directly spoke for President Reagan and Speaker O'Neill.

During the 100th and 101st Congresses (1987–1990), four summits took place. Three concerned budget issues. In the fall of 1987, the stock market crashed; in response, Reagan administration officials met with the congressional leadership and worked out a deal that shaped the 1987 reconciliation bill and the full-year continuing resolution. The deal also determined the major outlines of the following year's budget resolution (FY1989). In the spring of 1989, the new Bush administration and the congressional leadership worked out a more modest deal to avert Gramm-Rudman across-the-board cuts; this agreement shaped the 1989 (FY1990) budget resolution and the 1989 reconciliation bill, though it by no means settled all the major issues, especially on reconciliation. The need for action and the inability of normal processes to produce agreement again led to a summit on budget issues in 1990. The highly intense issue of aid to the Nicaraguan contras was the subject of the fourth summit. In 1989 the Democratic leadership met with Bush administration representatives to work out a final agreement on contra aid. (For details on these cases, see Sinclair 1995.)

An emergency and severe time pressure may create the conditions for a summit as they did in 1980, but usually when the congressional majority and the president are of the same party, normal processes supplemented by informal consultation and negotiations will suffice. Thus there were no summits during the 103rd Congress. Normal processes are more likely to fail when the president's and the congressional majority's policy and electoral goals are in conflict, as they tend to be under divided government, when the presidency is controlled by one party and the Congress by another. With the return of divided control after the 1994 elections, the president and Congress found themselves again resorting to summits. The budget summit of 1995–1996 failed to produce an agreement; however, in 1997, Clinton and the congressional Republicans did manage to work out a deal to balance the budget. Increasingly, differences on appropriations bills also came to be negotiated in an end-of-the-fiscal-year summit between administration officials and congressional leaders (see Chapter 11).

Unorthodox Lawmaking in the Republican Congress

The 1994 elections brought enormous and unexpected political change to Congress, especially to the House of Representatives. Republicans won majorities in both chambers, taking control of the House for the first time in forty years by picking up fifty-three seats. During the campaign, House Republicans had promised to change the way Congress works if the voters would give them control. In fact, the rules changes that constitute the reforms of the 1970s were in many cases changes in Democratic party rules, not changes in the rules of the House itself. Much of the weakening of committees and their chairs and the strengthening of the party leadership was the result of new Democratic Caucus rules concerning committee assignments and the designation of committee and subcommittee chairs.

One might thus expect that a change in party control would have brought with it major alterations in how the House functions. Yet the data on special procedures and practices presented in this chapter tend to show continuity and sometimes even an acceleration—especially in the 104th Congress—in existing trends rather than a change in direction. An analysis of why this is so illuminates the relationship between the congressional process and the broader political process in which it is embedded.

On the first day of the 104th Congress, House Republicans did, in fact, make some significant changes in House rules. Modest committee jurisdiction reform was accomplished by shifting some of the Energy and Commerce Committee's immense jurisdiction to other committees; three minor committees were eliminated; and committee staffs were cut by a third. By House rule, committee chairs were subjected to a limit of three terms; proxy votes, which absent committee members could give to any other committee member to cast for them but most often gave to the chair, were banned; and sunshine rules were modestly strengthened, making it harder to close a committee meeting.

Term limits, staff cuts, and the abolition of proxy voting potentially weakened committee chairs. However, because Republican party rules pertained, the new Republican committee chairs were in some ways actually stronger than their Democratic predecessors. They controlled the entire majority staff of the committee and had more control over the choice of subcommittee chairs and over the assignment of members to subcommittees.

During the 1980s and early 1990s, House Republicans had in many instances imitated House Democrats by adopting rules that decreased the autonomy of their committee leaders and strengthened their party leadership. Their committee leaders (ranking minority members when the party was in the minority, committee chairs when Republicans became the majority), after being nominated by the Committee on Committees, were made subject to a secret ballot ratification vote in the Republican Conference, the organization of all House Republicans; the Republicans' top leader had been given the power to nominate Republican members of Rules and more say on the party committee that makes committee assignments. Thus, rules strengthening Republican party leaders were, by and large, not new at the beginning of the 104th Congress, nor did they give Republican leaders powers that Democratic party leaders had not possessed.

Political circumstances, not rules changes, made Newt Gingrich a powerful Speaker. Gingrich, in the eyes of most Republicans and the media, was the miracle maker; he was seen as responsible for the unexpected Republican victory in 1994. Gingrich had worked and schemed to build a majority for many years (Connelly and Pitney 1994); he had recruited many of the House challengers who won and had helped them with fund raising and campaign advice. The Contract with America was Gingrich's idea, and he had orchestrated its realization.

Consequently, the 1994 election results gave Gingrich enormous prestige. They also provided him with a membership that was ideologically homogeneous and determined to enact major policy change. The huge freshman class—seventy-three strong—consisted largely of true believers, deeply committed to cutting the size and scope of government and to balancing the budget; with the sophomores, who were very similar in outlook, they made up over half of the Republican House membership. These members and a considerable number of more senior Republicans believed themselves to be mandated to make such policy change. Even moderate Republicans strongly agreed that, for the party to maintain its majority, Republicans had to deliver on the promises they had made in the Contract.

The combination of an extraordinarily ambitious agenda, a new majority united behind the agenda, and a leader with enormous stature made the exercise of strong leadership both necessary and possible. Without strong central direction, passing the agenda would have been impossible. Without a membership united in its commitment to swift and drastic policy change, no Speaker could have exercised such strong, central direction of the legislative process.

Relying on his immense prestige with House Republicans, Gingrich, in the days after the 1994 elections, exercised power well beyond that specified in Republican Conference rules. He designated Republicans to serve as committee chairs, bypassing seniority in several instances. According to the rules, the party committee on committees nominates chairs and the Conference approves them. Gingrich preempted that process, assuming correctly that his stature would prevent anyone from challenging his choices.

The 104th Congress saw enormous party leadership involvement and oversight on major legislation; committee leaders were clearly subordinate to party leaders on Contract with America bills and on much of the major legislation that went into the Republicans' attempt to balance the budget (see Chapter 11). Because most senior Republicans had signed the Contract, Gingrich had a strong tool for persuading committee leaders to report legislation without making major changes and to do so quickly; he reminded them: "We promised to do it in 100 days; we must deliver." In early 1995, and later when balancing the budget was at issue, the chairs knew that the leadership was buttressed by the freshmen's strong support.

The attempt to deliver on the ambitious promises House Republicans had made took the full set of procedural tools available to the majority party leadership. The need for speed and flexibility, and occasionally the political delicacy of the issues involved, dictated that the leaders sometimes bypass committee. The leadership made extensive use of member task forces on legislative issues ranging from agriculture policy to gun control to immigration reform. By and large, committees were not bypassed on the issues task forces worked on, but the task forces did have the purpose and the effect of keeping the pressure on committees to report in a timely fashion legislation that was satisfactory to the party majority.

Even though political circumstances made committee leaders unusually responsive to the wishes of the party leadership and the party membership, party leaders frequently found it necessary to make post-committee adjustments in legislation. Multiple referral, the need for speed, and the ambitiousness of the agenda all contributed to producing circumstances where the legislation as reported had to be altered in order to engineer passage in a form that would accomplish the party's objectives.

As developed by Democratic leaders in the 1980s and early 1990s, special rules had become powerful and flexible tools for the leadership. Given the task Republicans had set themselves, their leaders could hardly eschew using restrictive rules, despite their preelection promise to use predominantly open rules. In working to pass their ambitious agenda, House Republican leaders continued the creative use of restrictive rules.

The extraordinary political circumstances that allowed such hyper-aggressive use of the full set of leadership tools, including the tools of unorthodox lawmaking, waned even before the end of the 104th Congress. The 105th Congress saw leaders retreat a bit from the deep substantive involvement on almost all major legislation that had characterized their role in the 104th. The extremely high rate of postcommittee adjustment in the 104th of 48 percent declined to a more "normal" 35 percent in the 105th Congress; task forces were employed less frequently. The reversion, however, was to a legislative process still heavily characterized by the practices and procedures I have labeled unorthodox lawmaking. In their attempts to satisfy the party's members by passing the legislation they favored, House party leaders continued to make use of the tools of unorthodox lawmaking. Even Speaker Hastert, who promised a return to "regular order" when he assumed the speakership in 1999, found himself frequently drawn into legislative substance and having to either bypass committees or make postcommittee adjustments. His extremely narrow margin in the 106th Congress gave him no choice. Just passing the essential appropriations bills took a herculean effort. When the first appropriations bill, the usually easy to pass agriculture bill, came to the floor, deficit hawk Tom Coburn, R-Okla., upset by the spending level, bogged the process down by offering amendment after amendment. Because Coburn was backed by enough of his fellow conservatives to deprive the GOP of its fragile majority, the leadership had to step in. Under leadership direction, postcommittee adjustments cutting funding were drafted for this and later appropriations bills and offered as amendments on the floor (Taylor 1999a, 1999b). Hastert also bypassed committee when political circumstances dictated and used strategic restrictive rules extensively, as the patients' bill of rights case study shows (see Chapter 8).

If passing the Republicans' agenda in the majority-rule House was a big task, getting it through the Senate was an even more difficult, and sometimes impossible, endeavor. Majority Leader Bob Dole and his successor Trent Lott used all the special procedures available to them. In the 104th Congress especially, committees were frequently bypassed, and great effort went into postcommittee adjustments to bills in the attempt to craft legislation that could amass the sixty votes Senate passage usually requires.

Having had the filibuster wielded against them so effectively in the 103rd Congress, Democrats, now in the minority, made full use of their prerogatives under Senate rules; major legislation frequently encountered extended debate–related problems. The minority Democrats became increasingly adept at using extended debate and the Senate's loose amending rules in combination to get their issues onto the Senate agenda. By threatening or actually offering their bills as often nongermane amendments to whatever legislation the majority leader brought to the floor and using extended debate to block a quick end to debate, Democrats forced Republicans to consider a number of issues they would rather have avoided—most prominently the minimum wage, tobacco taxes, campaign finance reform, and managed care (see Chapter 8).

The Republican majority responded with procedural strategies of its own. Majority Leader Lott attempted to impose cloture immediately upon bringing a bill to the floor because after cloture all amendments must be germane. When cloture failed, he simply pulled the bill from the floor to deprive Democrats of an opportunity to debate and vote on their amendments. Lott also "filled the amendment tree," that is, he used his right of first recognition to offer amendments in all the parliamentarily permissible slots, thus barring Democrats from offering their amendments. Democratic cohesion on cloture votes, however, limited the effectiveness of such majority party strategies; so long as the minority party can muster forty-one votes, the majority party may be able to prevent the minority from getting votes on its bills but it cannot pass its own. The result has most often been gridlock.

Even when Republicans successfully got their agenda through the House and the Senate, they still had to worry about President Clinton if their bills were actually to become law. As Democrats had when facing a hostile Republican president, Republicans made use of omnibus bills to try to force the president to accept provisions he disliked by linking them to must-pass legislation or to provisions he favored. The strategy, however, produced mixed success at best (see Chapter 11). Increasingly the Republican leadership and the president had to resort to summits to reach agreement.

The Evolution of Unorthodox Lawmaking:
A Summary

In this chapter I have sketched the story of how changes in internal structure and in the political environment created problems for and presented opportunities to members of Congress—as individuals and collectively—and how members' responses led to modifications and innovations in the legislative process. Changes in the internal distribution of influence in both the House and the Senate provided opportunities to individual members to participate more fully in the legislative process. However, the high rate of activity and the uncertainty that resulted when members took advantage of their new opportunities created problems for the chambers and their majority parties; legislating became more difficult.

The adverse political climate of the 1980s exacerbated the problems of legislating, especially for congressional Democrats, who were the majority party in the House throughout the 1980s and early 1990s. Party leaders, responding to their members' demands for legislative success, sought ways of coping with the problems. They began to use omnibus legislation more frequently; summits were developed as a last-resort means of reaching agreements between Congress and the president.

In the House, party leaders involved themselves in the legislative process on major legislation earlier and more deeply, often negotiating compromises after the committee or committees had reported legislation so as to ensure the legislation's passage on the floor. Special rules from the Rules Committee were developed into powerful tools for controlling floor consideration and sometimes for shaping floor outcomes.

The Senate, in contrast, failed to develop ways of coping effectively with the problems created by internal reforms and the political environment. The enormous opportunities for influence that full use of the Senate's rules gave each senator were just too valuable to senators as individuals; senators were unwilling to curtail their power. Senate leaders also increased their involvement in the legislative process, seeking to put together deals that made legislation passable; but they did so without enhanced tools or resources. Consequently, legislating remains problematic in the Senate.

The change in party control of Congress as a result of the 1994 elections did not disrupt the trend toward unorthodox lawmaking for two reasons. First, key conditions did not change: internal rules were not altered very much (certainly, strong, autonomous committees were not resurrected); the budget process continued to dominate congressional decision making; and the congressional majority faced a hostile, opposition-party president. Second, the frequent employment of these special procedures and practices continued because, whatever their origins, they have become flexible tools useful to members and leaders under a variety of circumstances.

chapter seven

National Service Legislation: (Mildly) Unorthodox Lawmaking

THE LEGISLATIVE PROCESS in the contemporary Congress is better conceptualized as plural rather than singular; there are now many paths from introduction of a bill to enactment. This chapter and the next two illustrate some of the variety through case studies of the 1993 national service bill, managed care reform legislation (the "patients' bill of rights") in 1999, and an omnibus drug bill in 1988. The process in these three cases ranges from mildly to extraordinarily unorthodox. The process by which national service became law in 1993 is similar in many respects to the old standard process, though with some unorthodox elements; the legislative process on the patients' bill of rights in 1999 was much less like the textbook process; the 1988 drug bill became law through a radically unorthodox "designer" process. Examining the process on specific legislation also illuminates how and when the various special procedures and practices are employed and with what effects. Often majority party leaders use procedures under their control to solve political problems, sometimes problems created by individual members' or by the minority party's exploitation of the special procedures that they can employ.

Why National Service? Origins and Prospects

A national service program under which young people would perform needed services in communities across the nation and, in return, receive financial assistance for their education was a central element of newly elected President Bill Clinton's agenda in 1993. He had highlighted the proposal during the 1992 campaign; in a press conference the day after the election, he listed it as one of his priorities along with health care and economic recovery. He called for a "season of service" in his inaugural address, and, in his first address to a joint session of Congress on February 17, 1993, he urged the program's swift enactment.

As Clinton and his advisers saw it, a correctly structured national service program could accomplish several important objectives beyond the obvious. Needed services of all sorts—from teaching children to refurbishing park land to bringing meals to shut-in senior citizens—would get performed. Young people would earn financial aid for college. In addition, however, Clinton and other national service advocates in the administration believed the program could give young people from all parts of American society the opportunity to work with and get to know each other, thus fostering understanding across racial and class divides and, like the Peace Corps has done, foster in these young people an ethic of service (Waldman 1995, 24–29, passim).

On April 30, 1993, the Clinton administration unveiled its bill, and on May 6 it was introduced in both houses of Congress. Passing the legislation was clearly important to the new administration and to the majority congressional Democrats, who after twelve years of divided control needed to show they could govern. Democratic Party leaders did not expect any real problems; the idea of national service was broadly popular, and the bill neatly fit into the jurisdiction of only one committee in each house, making for a simpler process than on much major legislation. Passing the legislation, however, proved to be a more complicated undertaking than its supporters anticipated; the zero-sum budget game that big deficits had induced pitted popular programs against each other for funding, and the highly partisan climate encouraged Republicans to oppose the program so as to deprive the Clinton administration of a victory.

Committee Action

After a day of hearings held jointly by the Subcommittee on Select Education and Civil Rights and the Subcommittee on Human Resources of the House Education and Labor Committee, the full committee met to mark up the legislation. There it ran into a blizzard of Republican amendments. Attempting to split Democratic support, Republicans argued that money for the new program would come at the expense of other education programs such as Pell grants and work study; since eligibility for the latter but not the former was based on need, the result would be switching

funds from poor to middle-class students. This was an argument that res-
onated with the liberal Democrats who made up much of the Democratic
membership of the Education and Labor Committee. Thus, the biggest
test came on an amendment by Rep. Bill Goodling, R-Pa., the committee's
ranking minority member, to means-test national service; under the
amendment only the financially needy could receive the educational
awards. The administration strongly opposed the amendment because it
would negate one of the major goals of the program. With committee
chair William Ford, D-Mich., George Miller, D-Calif., another influential
liberal on the committee, and the administration working against it, the
Goodling amendment was defeated on a 12–29 vote.

On June 16, 1993, after a single day of markup, the Education and
Labor Committee reported the bill, HR2010, by a voice vote. The Republican attacks, however, had put supporters on notice that this legislation
would not get a free ride on the House floor.

The Senate Labor and Human Resources Committee also marked up
the legislation on June 16. Sen. Nancy Landon Kassebaum of Kansas,
ranking minority member of the committee, attacked the program, saying
it took away resources from other education programs. Still, the bill was
reported out on a 14–3 vote; Senators Hatch and Thurmond voted with
Kassebaum, but a number of other conservative Republicans supported
the bill.

The Special Rule and House Floor Action

In the House the next step toward passage was obtaining a rule for
floor consideration. Although the national service bill was important legislation (as its swift movement through committee indicated), it had to
compete for floor time with other major legislation, including the must-
pass appropriations bills. On June 29, 1993, the Rules Committee granted
a rule for general debate only; the next day a Rules Committee member
announced on the floor that the rule regulating amending activity would
require amendments to be printed in the *Congressional Record* at least a day
before they were offered.

General debate on national service took place on July 13. By a
239–159 vote, the House adopted the rule; Democrats supported the rule
unanimously, and all but three Republicans voted against it. Despite the
generous three hours of general debate the rule provided, Republicans
complained about the separation of general debate and the amending
process, about the preprinting requirement the second rule would
impose, and about the bill itself.

On July 14 the Rules Committee on a party-line vote reported out the rule governing the amending process. It stipulated that, to be in order, an amendment had to be printed in the *Congressional Record* by July 20. Thus, members had been given three weeks altogether to prepare their amendments. Nevertheless, when the rule came to a vote on July 21, most Republicans voted against it; it passed on a 261–164 vote.

The decision on the character of the special rule has become an important part of legislative strategy. Legislation in this issue domain has traditionally been considered under an open rule. Neither the substance nor the politics of this particular bill justified a truly restrictive rule; it was certainly not in enough political trouble to warrant such a move. The Rules Committee and the party leadership, however, could and did help the bill's supporters by requiring the preprinting of amendments. Supporters thus could plan their strategy without worrying about an unanticipated amendment that might wreak havoc with the bill. Eventually, eighteen amendments would be introduced. The rule also specified that Chairman Ford could offer a group of amendments that would be voted on as a package.

Chairman Ford offered his "nondivisible en bloc amendments," and after a short debate they were adopted on a voice vote. Included were some modifications he had worked out with members of the committee minority and a number of the amendments proposed by House members not on the committee. By rolling these noncontroversial changes into a package, Ford saved floor time and bolstered support for the bill; the members whose amendments were incorporated in the bill had, as a result, an added incentive to support the legislation.

Republicans' arguments that the program would consist of "make work" and that it would add to the bureaucracy did not worry supporters. Some Republicans, however, focused on the contention that the program took from the poor to give to the better-off. Representative Armey called it "a welfare program for the aspiring yuppies of America," and Representative Goodling intoned, "Immoral is the only term I can use, because it is Robin Hood in reverse" (Waldman 1995, 187–188). This argument could split the Democratic coalition. On the floor the supporters of the bill countered by pointing out the benefits that diversity in the program could yield.

The most important work, however, had already been done. Because they knew which amendments would be offered, supporters—including the White House—had been able to mount an effective information and persuasion effort before the bill hit the floor. As an important part of their campaign to pass the bill, the White House and congressional proponents made sure that members were aware of the broad range of groups that supported it; the informational packets they distributed included letters of endorsement from the National Governors Association, the Girl Scouts, police and firefighters' unions, major companies such as Dow Chemical and the Ford Motor Company, and the Red Cross (headed by Elizabeth Dole, the wife of bill opponent Bob Dole, the Senate's minority leader at the time). Most persuasive with liberals, who were a special target, was a letter from Marian Wright Edelman, the highly respected head of the Children's Defense Fund, a liberal advocacy group; she endorsed the program as it stood, without means-testing.

Amendments identical to those advocated by Republicans in committee—for means-testing and for fully funding other education programs first—were defeated on largely party-line votes. Other Republican amendments were defeated or amended to make them acceptable to the bill's supporters. One amendment passed over supporters' objections, but it was of a technical nature and relatively minor.

One Republican amendment confronted supporters with a serious problem. Arguing that those who defended the country and perhaps risked their lives doing so deserved more than civilian volunteers, Rep. Bob Stump, R-Ariz., proposed reducing the education benefit to 80 percent of that provided by the GI bill. The ranking minority member of the Veterans' Affairs Committee further argued that equal benefits would make recruiting for the all-volunteer army much harder.

The administration adamantly opposed the Stump amendment. Clinton had already compromised on the size of the educational benefit. A whip count of Democratic members' voting intentions, however, persuaded the Democratic leadership that the Stump amendment could not be defeated on an up-or-down vote. The veterans' groups that supported Stump were too powerful a lobby. An administration proposal to compromise on 95 percent would also not fly, Majority Whip David Bonior, D-Mich., determined; a more significant compromise would have to be made.

By July 28, when the House returned to consideration of national service, a deal had been worked out. Working through G. V. "Sonny" Montgomery of Mississippi, the Democratic chairman of the Veterans' Affairs Committee, Ford had gotten Stump to agree to 90 percent. As Ford said on the floor:

> I am pleased to have had the help of the chairman of the Committee on Veterans' Affairs and the ranking member of the Committee on Veterans' Affairs who are working with us to try to resolve this matter in a satisfactory way. I understand that language has been worked out and is at the desk, and I am prepared to accept the language that was worked out and is at the desk.

> Mr. Chairman, if the gentleman will ask for unanimous consent to modify his
> amendment by the language at the desk, we will accept the gentleman's
> amendment. (*Congressional Record,* July 28, 1993, H5392)

The Stump amendment as modified was accepted by voice vote.

Later the same day the House passed the bill. Members had cast
eleven recorded votes on amendments and had decided a number of others by voice votes. After rejecting Goodling's motion to recommit the bill
by voice, the House voted for passage 275–152; twenty-six Republicans
supported it, five Democrats voted against it. The result was a victory for
the administration and for House Democrats, especially for Education
and Labor Committee Democrats and the party leadership. They had
passed a major Clinton initiative largely intact.

Senate Floor Action

On July 15, 1993, the Senate agreed by unanimous consent to take up
S919, the national service bill reported a month earlier by the Labor and
Human Resources Committee, immediately after disposing of a bill to
revise the Hatch Act. On July 20 debate began. As in the House, opponents argued that the new program would take money away from existing
education programs. Sen. Pete V. Domenici, R-N.M., offered an amendment requiring full funding for a number of existing programs before
national service could receive any funds; it was tabled and thus killed on a
largely party-line vote of 55–44. Senator Kassebaum offered two amendments altering and scaling back the program; both were rejected on near
party-line votes.

On July 22 debate took an unexpected and dramatic turn when Senator Helms offered an amendment to extend a congressional design patent
for the insignia of the United Daughters of the Confederacy; the insignia
included the Confederate flag. Even though the amendment had
absolutely nothing to do with national service, it was in order because Senate rules do not require amendments to most legislation to be germane.
Carol Moseley-Braun, D-Ill., the Senate's only African American, moved to
table the Helms amendment, but her motion failed on a 48–52 vote, with
twelve Democrats joining all but four Republicans in voting against her.
Vowing to filibuster "until this room freezes over" to reverse the vote, Senator Moseley-Braun gave a passionate speech:

> The issue is whether or not Americans such as myself who believe in the
> promise of this country . . . will have to suffer the indignity of being
> reminded time and time again that at one point in this country's history we
> were human chattel. . . . We were property. We could be traded, bought and

sold. [The Confederate flag] is something that has no place in our modern times . . . no place in this body . . . no place in our society. (Quoted from Zuckman 1993, 1960)

Other senators rose to support Moseley-Braun. When Sen. Howell Heflin, D-Ala., said he would switch his vote, it was clear the tide had turned. A conservative southerner whose ancestors had fought for the Confederacy, Heflin made clear that he would not knowingly contribute to divisions between the races. By a 76–24 vote, the Senate agreed to reconsider its initial vote and then voted 75–25 to table and thus kill the Helms amendment. The Senate then returned to debating national service and voted down several more Republican amendments.

On the same day, July 22, Senate Republicans decided to filibuster national service (Waldman 1995, 201–203). They clearly lacked the votes to change the legislation significantly via amendments, but by their attacks they had made the legislation sufficiently vulnerable, they believed, to maintain a filibuster. The word quickly spread; senators continued to debate and to attempt to amend the bill, but everyone knew a filibuster was on. That evening Majority Leader Mitchell and Minority Leader Dole put the situation on the record with this exchange:

> Mitchell: I would like, if I might at this moment, to inquire of the Republican leader whether under the circumstances we will be permitted to get a final vote on the bill or whether under the current circumstances it will be necessary for us to file a cloture motion to terminate debate.
>
> Dole: I think if I were majority leader, I would suggest maybe filing a cloture motion. (*Congressional Record,* quoted from Waldman 1995, 212)

Mitchell filed a cloture petition that night.

Mitchell pulled the bill off the floor and negotiations began. Republicans said they were most concerned about the program's costs; the original bill authorized $394 million in fiscal 1994 and unspecified sums for the next four years. Labor Committee chair Edward Kennedy offered to decrease the authorization to three years, to scale back the fiscal 1994 authorization to $300 million, and to specify figures for the two subsequent years—$500 million for fiscal 1995 and $700 million for fiscal 1996. Republicans responded that a two-year authorization was the maximum they would support. The administration called that unacceptable, pointing out that, given a six-month start-up period, a two-year authorization would make it impossible to guarantee participants their full two years of service. On July 26 Mitchell filed a second cloture motion on the bill, and on July 28 he filed two motions to invoke cloture on the Kennedy substitute amendment.

Continuing negotiations could not break the impasse, and on July 29 Mitchell moved to close debate on the Kennedy substitute amendment. The motion failed on a 59–41 vote; only three Republicans had joined all the Democrats in voting to cut off debate, leaving national service supporters one vote short.[1]

Senate Republicans had won the battle but their cohesion was loosening. Moderate Republicans were under increasing pressure to defect. The Kennedy substitute had alleviated many of the concerns on which they had based their opposition. The blocking of national service had become a big news story, and Republicans were being blamed. The White House had worked hard to persuade the media to pay attention and to adopt their spin (Waldman 1995, 214–215, 223–225). Headlines such as "Petty Politics on National Service" and "Senate GOP Stalls National Service Bill" began to appear. After cloture failed, moderate Republicans who had voted to support the filibuster found themselves under direct press attack at home. The largest paper in Oregon headlined an editorial "Oregon's Obstinate Obstructionists: Hatfield and Packwood Engage in Filibuster Abuse." The Philadelphia *Inquirer* wrote, "Sen. Arlen Specter chose his party over his principles yesterday" (Waldman 1995, 237–238). Knowing he no longer had the votes to maintain the filibuster, Dole met with Mitchell and agreed on a unanimous consent agreement for bringing the bill to a vote.

On July 30 Mitchell presented the unanimous consent agreement to the Senate. It directed that consideration of S919 resume immediately (interrupting consideration of an appropriations bill), that the listed amendments be the only first-degree amendments in order, and that at 10 a.m. on Tuesday, August 3, the Senate vote on passage. Dole rose to endorse the agreement, saying: "I think we have a satisfactory arrangement. Let me just make the record clear, we did not have the votes to prevent cloture. We had five of our colleagues who would have voted for cloture today, and we would have been one vote short. . . . I still hope before they finish the debate this afternoon there can be some adjustment on funding" (*Congressional Record,* July 30, 1993, S9938).

Although the unanimous consent agreement made fifteen amendments—and amendments to them—in order, only three were pushed to a roll call, and all were defeated. On August 3 the bill as modified by the Kennedy substitute passed the Senate 58–41; fifty-one Democrats and

---

1. Under normal procedures the vote would have occurred on July 30 because the rules require a day to elapse between the day the cloture petition is filed and the day of the vote. However, reflecting the curious combination of conflict and accommodation that characterizes the contemporary Senate, Mitchell asked and received unanimous consent for the vote to take place on July 29.

seven Republicans voted in favor, thirty-seven Republicans and four Democrats opposed the bill.

The Final Steps

Congressional Democrats rushed the bill to conference, hoping to finish the process before the summer recess, scheduled to begin at the end of the week. Although the legislation had been considered by only one committee in each chamber, Senate conferees were appointed from two committees: sixteen from the Committee on Labor and Human Resources and three from the Committee on Governmental Affairs. The thirty House conferees were appointed from six committees. Amendments to the legislation had extended its scope.

Despite the conference committee's relatively large size and diverse makeup, agreement was quickly reached. The Senate's three-year $1.5 billion framework was kept; supporters feared another filibuster were they to move appreciably toward the House's higher funding level. Informal negotiations preceded the formal meeting of the conference committee, so the formal meeting on August 5 required only about fifteen minutes.

The House approved the conference report the next day on a 275–152 vote. Time ran out on the Senate; it was not until September 8, after the recess, that the Senate voted 57–40 to adopt the conference report. The president signed into law the National Service Trust Act of 1993 on September 21, a little less than five months after he unveiled his bill. (See Table 7.1 for a chronology of House, Senate, and postpassage action.)

The Legislative Process on National Service Legislation: A Little Bit Unorthodox

The legislative process by which the national service bill became law differed from the textbook process only moderately. The legislation had high priority for the president and the Democratic leadership. Since it was basically a widely popular idea and it fell into the jurisdiction of only one committee in each chamber, no big problems were expected. The leaders saw no need to come up with a special legislative process to ensure the bill's passage.

By and large, the special procedures the leaders employed were responses to problems that arose as the bill made its way through the chambers. In the House postcommittee adjustments were made to facilitate

TABLE 7.1   National Service Trust Act of 1993: A Chronology

Date	House Action	Date	Senate Action	Date	Postpassage Action
			Clinton administration unveils its bill on April 30, 1993.		
5/6	HR2010 introduced in the House; referred to the Committee on Education and Labor.	5/6	S919 introduced in the Senate; referred to the Committee on Labor and Human Resources.		
5/19, 5/20, 5/25	Committee and its subcommittees hold hearings.	5/11, 5/18, 6/8	Committee and its subcommittees hold hearings.		
6/16	Education and Labor Committee marks up HR2010 and orders it reported.	6/16	Committee on Labor and Human Resources marks up S919 and orders it reported.		
6/29	Rules Committee holds hearing and grants rule for general debate only.				
7/13	House approves rule and completes general debate.				
7/14	Rules Committee grants modified open rule for further consideration; requires preprinting of amendments.	7/15	Senate agrees by unanimous consent to take up S919 on July 20.		
7/21	House approves second rule and begins amending process. Chairman Ford offers modified en bloc amendments, and they are approved. The amending process proceeds; *Democratic leaders realize they cannot defeat the Stump amendment.* Leadership pulls bill from floor.	7/20	Senate begins consideration of S919.		
		7/22	Helms offers nongermane amendment; Moseley-Braun moves to table amendment but Senate rejects motion. Moseley-Braun threatens to filibuster; Senate reverses itself and votes to table (and thus kill) the Helms amendment. *Republicans decide to filibuster S919.* Mitchell files cloture petition and pulls bill from Senate floor.		
	Negotiations continue over the Stump amendment.				

7/28   HR2010 again considered on the House floor. Stump modified amendment (compromise version of the Stump amendment) agreed to by voice vote. House passes measure as amended.

Negotiations begin; Kennedy proposes a compromise version.

7/26   Mitchell files a second cloture petition.

7/28   Senate resumes consideration of S919. Kennedy offers his compromise as an amendment. Mitchell files two cloture petitions to close debate on the Kennedy amendment.

7/29   Senate votes on motion to close debate on the Kennedy amendment; the motion fails 59–41.

Mitchell and Dole negotiate.

7/30   Senate accepts Mitchell's unanimous consent request (which he negotiated with Dole) for consideration of S919.

8/3   Senate passes bill as modified by the Kennedy amendment.

8/3   Senate conferees named.

8/4   House conferees named.

8/5   Conferees agree to file conference report.

8/6   House agrees to conference report.

9/8   Senate agrees to conference report.

9/21   President signs bill, and the National Service Trust Act of 1993 becomes law.

Note: Official actions are in roman type; behind-the-scenes, unofficial actions are in italics.

passage; the committee chairman built some added support by offering a number of amendments as a package on the floor, a tactic made possible by the rule. A more major change was the compromise version of the Stump amendment, which the leadership determined had to be accepted for the bill to pass without greater change.

In the Senate that body's unique rules, and senators' willingness to exploit them fully, left their mark on the process and on the resulting legislation. The nongermane Helms amendment had the potential to derail the bill had the vote approving it not been reversed. The majority party was forced to make significant postcommittee concessions because it could not muster sixty votes to overcome a Republican filibuster of the original bill. Although the Republican leadership tried, after Senator Kennedy's compromise was offered, the minority party could not maintain its filibuster; under pressure from the press in their home states, moderate Republicans broke ranks, and the compromise was approved. Public opinion, actual and anticipated, influences senators' willingness to use extended debate to hold up specific legislation.

Senate rules and practices influenced conference deliberations as well. Because supporters feared another filibuster, the conference agreement simply incorporated the concessions that Senate supporters had made in the Kennedy substitute.

chapter eight

The "Patients' Bill of Rights": Unorthodox Lawmaking in a Highly Partisan Environment

DURING THE 1990s, Americans were increasingly receiving their health care through some sort of managed care plan. As managed care became more pervasive, concerns and complaints that cost control was trumping good medical care also grew and, with them, calls for government regulation. President Clinton in his 1998 State of the Union address had advocated passage of a "patients' bill of rights" regulating managed care plans; Democrats and Republicans in Congress introduced bills, and the House passed a Republican leadership bill that Democrats argued was much too weak. Despite Democratic efforts, no bill came to a vote in the Senate and no legislation was enacted. That set the scene for an even more intense effort in 1999 to pass legislation, to gain political advantage for trying to do so, or—even more desirable but less likely—to do both.

Agenda Setting

In 1999 the president and Democratic leaders in both chambers put patients' bill of rights legislation at the top of their agenda. Congressional Democrats had highlighted the issue during their 1998 election campaigns, and, in a feat not accomplished since 1934, the president's party had gained seats in a midterm election. Senate Minority Leader Tom Daschle introduced his party's bill on January 19 as S6, making it the Senate Democrats' top priority. House Democrats put it high on their "families first" agenda, and the president advocated passage during his State of the Union address. On March 3, when Clinton and congressional Democrats held a joint news conference to publicize their agenda for the 106th Congress, the patients' bill of rights was prominently featured.

Because public opinion polls showed increased support for action, Republicans also assumed that managed care regulation would be on the congressional agenda. When Majority Leader Trent Lott presented his party's agenda on the floor of the Senate on January 19, he mentioned the issue as one on which action would occur, but it was not among the Republicans' top five priorities, which were embodied in S1 through S5. With their antiregulatory philosophy of government and their close alliance with business, most congressional Republicans preferred little to no new regulation; yet, for those whose constituents demanded action, doing nothing would be dangerous. If legislation were to pass, Republicans wanted to both shape it and gain credit with the public. Furthermore, physicians, usually a reliable Republican constituency, were clamoring for action; they believed managed care had taken too many medical decisions away from doctors and put them into the hands of insurance companies. Thus the issue was a difficult one for the Republican party.

On January 22, Lott introduced a bill co-sponsored by forty-eight Republican senators. A year before he had asked Majority Whip Don Nickles to put together a task force to draft a Republican bill. Although Republicans as the majority party controlled the committees, Lott resorted to a within-party task force, which allowed inclusion of all the key Republican actors—and the exclusion of Democrats. The task force of nine included the chairs of the two committees with jurisdiction but also Bill Frist of Tennessee, the only doctor in the Senate, moderate Susan M. Collins of Maine, and conservatives Dan Coats of Indiana, Rick Santorum of Pennsylvania, and Phil Gramm. By using a task force Republicans were able to develop their bill with less public scrutiny than the regular committee process entails. The task force came up with a bill that included some patient protection provisions—but not a right to sue—and "access" provisions, primarily tax breaks aimed at helping the uninsured buy insurance. The bill was referred to the Health, Education, Labor and Pensions Committee.

On March 17, the Senate Health, Education, Labor and Pensions Committee (HELP) met to mark up S326, a managed care bill introduced by its chairman Jim Jeffords, R-Vt., and based on the patient protection provisions of the task force bill. Committee Democrats, who believed the Republican bill was much too weak, offered S6, their bill, as a substitute, but it was rejected by a 10–8 party-line vote. This set the tenor for the contentious two-day markup; eighteen Democratic amendments were defeated on party-line votes before the committee approved the Republican bill on a strict party-line vote.

Pre-Floor Partisan Maneuvering in the Senate

The Democrats' strategy on managed care called for making the issue as visible as possible. With Democrats lacking control of both chambers, only strong public interest could provide the leverage to get their proposal on the congressional agenda and perhaps even pass it. If the public strongly supported the Democrats' patients' bill of rights, Republicans might be pressured into voting for it or at least be made to pay an electoral price for killing it. To rouse public opinion, Democrats needed media coverage. Their activities promoting the Democratic agenda had been aimed at garnering media attention. So were Democratic reactions to the Senate Republicans' bill. President Clinton criticized it as falling "far short of the legislation the American people deserve" (Foerstel 1999a, 701); Ted Kennedy, ranking Democrat of HELP, called it a "bill of wrongs, not of rights" (Foerstel 1999a, 702).

Beyond raising an issue's visibility, such a PR campaign is also aimed at framing the debate so as to advantage one's position. From a policy perspective, Democrats objected to the narrow scope of the Republican bill—it covered only a fraction of the people in managed care; and they faulted it for not allowing patients to sue their health care providers when care was denied. Democrats argued that the fear of suits was an important guarantor of good behavior on the part of providers. To simplify and dramatize a complex set of arguments, Democrats honed their message to two basic points: health care decisions should be made by doctors on a medical basis, not by insurance companies on a financial basis, and HMOs, like everyone else, should be held accountable for mistakes they make. When the bill was introduced, Ted Kennedy sounded these themes:

> Mr. President, today, we renew the battle in Congress to enact a strong Patients' Bill of Rights to protect American families from abuses by HMOs and managed care health plans that too often put profits over patients' needs.
>
> Our Patients' Bill of Rights will protect families against the arbitrary and self-serving decisions that can rob average citizens of their savings and their peace of mind, and often their health and their very lives. Doctors and patients should be making medical decisions, not insurance company accountants. Too often, managed care is mismanaged care. (*Congressional Record,* Jan. 19, 1999, S366)

Republicans and interest group opponents of managed care regulation responded by trying to frame the debate to their advantage. The Democratic bill, they claimed, would raise costs and make trial lawyers rich without improving health care. The insurance and employer groups opposed to managed care regulations also attempted to shift the debate from patients' rights to help, through tax incentives, for the uninsured. Blue Cross/Blue Shield had run a series of ads hammering at that point (Foerstel 1999b, 1079).

Lott, intending to bring to the floor a package that included the "access" tax breaks, told the Finance Committee, which had jurisdiction over those provisions, to produce legislation. Democrats opposed many of the access provisions, convinced they would not help ordinary Americans and were just a giveaway to the rich. Furthermore, they saw the access provisions as a smokescreen put up to distract attention from the core issues of patient protection. Thus united Republican support was needed on this closely divided committee. However, moderate Republican John H. Chafee of Rhode Island would not go along, and the committee could not get a majority to report out the bill. Despite increased partisanship in the Senate, individualism still poses a problem for Senate leaders. Senators have the resources to go their own way and many are still willing to do so, even if it means opposing a high-priority proposal of their own party.

Democrats were eager for Senate floor debate. Republicans, in contrast, were in no hurry. Lott continued to promise floor consideration some time in the future. The Democratic leadership pushed aggressively for an agreement to bring the legislation to the floor but bridled at the conditions Lott was demanding.

Given Senate rules, Lott knew he could not simply deny Democrats a vote altogether. But, because the legislation confronted both his members as individuals and the party with political perils, Lott's aim was to kill the Democratic legislation, by passing the Republican bill if necessary, and to do so as quietly as possible. "What the Republicans want," explained a high-ranking Democratic aide, "is basically to have a vote on the two versions—the Republican and the Democratic—and then go on and just get it over with, and that would give them the ability to say they voted for one and it would keep much attention from focusing on it." To that end, Lott was insisting that Democrats limit themselves to five amendments and, the aide continued, "that he see the amendments before we offer them so he could in effect veto amendments." The Republican leadership wanted to protect its members from politically difficult votes. As Majority Whip Don Nickles later explained, "I don't want our members to go through a lot of votes that can be misconstrued for political purposes" (*Washington Post,* June 24, 1999, A8). Furthermore, Lott was demanding that Democrats promise not to revive the issue during the remainder of the Congress.

Lott's conditions were unacceptable to Democrats. After all, as a Democratic leadership staffer said, "We don't have any illusions that we can pass our bill, but we at least want a full debate. We want to be able to define the issues." To do so, Democrats wanted to be free to offer and debate at least twenty amendments.

Extended discussions between Daschle and Lott made no progress, and Democrats decided to ratchet up the pressure. According to an aide, Democrats gave Republicans "two weeks' notice that June was going to be patients' bill of rights month." Senate Democrats staged a series of "special orders" on the floor of the Senate in which senators engaged in lengthy discussion of the need for and virtues of their bill. The Democrats' aim was to catch the attention not just of the faithful but tiny C-SPAN2 audience but of the news media. Stories about their effort did begin to appear. Daschle put the Republican leadership on notice that starting Monday, June 21, Democrats would offer their patients' bill of rights legislation as an amendment to anything brought to the floor.

Lott countered by bringing up the agriculture appropriations bill; endangering the passage of funding legislation for agricultural programs would be politically tough for Daschle, a farm state senator. Democrats nevertheless proceeded with their plan, and Lott, blasting Democrats for hurting farmers, temporarily withdrew the agriculture bill. The following day, the Senate voted 53–47 to table the Democratic patients' bill of rights amendment. Democrats then threatened to offer their proposal piecemeal as a series of amendments. Forcing their party members to cast a long series of tough votes was exactly what Republican leaders wanted to avoid, so stalemate again ensued.

"It looks like they're acting on behalf of trial lawyers and stepping over the corpses of American farmers," Lott charged, attempting to make the strategy as costly as possible for Democrats (*Washington Post,* June 24, 1999, A8). Lott also urged Republican farm state senators to talk to their local media, emphasizing the same point. The Democrats held fast. "We'll get the votes," said Minority Leader Daschle. "It's either that or we'll sit on the Senate floor looking at each other" (*Washington Post,* June 24, 1999, A8).

Lott then filed cloture petitions on four appropriations bills. He knew that none were likely to get the necessary sixty votes but believed forcing votes would highlight the Democrats' obstructionism. An aide explained: "The other side has decided to block everything. Essentially, they think the way to win back the Congress is to make us look like a do-nothing Congress, and Lott at least wants to make sure that the media and the Beltway understand that that's what the Democrats are doing, if in fact there is a train wreck on appropriations, it's the Dems' fault." On Monday, June 28, all four cloture motions were defeated on party-line votes.

The Unanimous Consent Agreement

The next day, Lott and Daschle announced they had reached an agreement for debating the patients' bill of rights legislation. The leaders had been negotiating throughout this period and, having determined their relative strengths, had figured out what they could and couldn't get. Lott took the floor on June 29 to announce the agreement.

> Mr. President, let me say first Senator Daschle and I have labored long and hard to come to an agreement on a unanimous-consent procedure to deal with the Patients' Bill of Rights issue, appropriations bills, and nominations, and it still takes an awful lot of good faith. We have to work together. We have to have some trust. We have to give the benefit of the doubt to the leaders. . . .
>
> I ask unanimous consent that the majority leader or his designee introduce the underlying health care bill and it be placed on the calendar by 12 noon on Thursday, July 8, and the bill become the pending business at 1 p.m. on Monday, July 12, 1999, with a vote occurring on final passage at the close of business on Thursday, July 15, and the bill be subject to the following agreement:
>
> That the bill be limited to 3 hours of debate, to be equally divided in the usual form, that all amendments in order to the bill be relevant to the subject . . . , and all first degree amendments be offered in an alternating fashion with Senator Daschle to offer the initial first degree amendment and all first- and second-degree amendments be limited to 100 minutes each, to be equally divided in the usual form. I further ask consent that second-degree amendments be limited to one second-degree amendment per side, per party, with no motions to commit or recommit in order, or any other act with regard to the amendments in order, and that just prior to third reading of the bill, it be in order for the majority leader or his designee to offer a final amendment, with no second-degree amendments in order. (*Congressional Record*, June 29, 1999, S7811)

Minority Leader Daschle praised the agreement:

> Mr. President, I want to publicly commend the majority leader for the effort he has made over the last several days to find a way to resolve this impasse. I believe this is a win-win. . . . I am grateful to him and have, once again, enjoyed the opportunity to resolve what has been a very significant procedural difficulty for us all. . . .
>
> I believe this is a good agreement any way one looks at it. It provides us with the opportunity to have a good debate. It provides us with the opportunity to have a series of amendments. It certainly provides us with the focus that we have been looking for with regard to the Patients' Bill of Rights. This is a very good agreement, agreed to, I think, with the direct involvement of a lot of people. So we are grateful. (*Congressional Record*, June 29, 1999, S7813)

Daschle and other Democrats undertook to make sure informal agreements reached behind closed doors were made part of the record. Thus Daschle said:

> The majority leader mentioned a couple of other matters, one having to do with his desire to work full days. He has assured me we will work 9- to 12-hour days that week we come back because he recognizes the importance of giving this issue a full opportunity for debate. I appreciate his commitment in that regard. (*Congressional Record,* June 29, 1999, S7813)

"The presumption is that this flexible process will allow a sufficient number of amendments to come to the floor," Democratic Whip Harry Reid of Nevada reiterated. He sought public assurances from Lott "that it will not be a process where one or two amendments are brought up and then through a series of extended second-degree amendments delayed." Lott replied that such obstructionist tactics would not be possible under the agreement (*Congressional Record,* June 29, 1999, S7813).

Democrats thus had obtained a four-day debate on their issue, under ground rules that assured them the opportunity to offer and get votes on most if not all of their amendments. In this case, Democrats wanted the time limits on general debate and on individual amendments so that Republicans could not use procedural means to run out the clock and thereby block a debate and vote on the provisions Democrats wanted to highlight. In return, Republicans got a specified time for the end of the debate and an informal promise from Daschle that, if the issue were indeed fully aired, he would not bring it up again.

Also included in the unanimous consent agreement was a promise to vote on a number of nominations, most notably that of Larry Summers as treasury secretary. In retaliation for the Democrats' tactics, some Republicans had put a hold on the Summers nomination. The adverse reaction of the stock market had, however, made the hold more of a liability than an asset to Republican bargaining, so Lott was happy to include it in the deal.

As the bill headed to floor debate, the PR war intensified. Democrats set up near the Senate floor their "intensive communication unit" (ICU)—named to garner media attention. The ICU was staffed by experienced press aides. Democratic senators could walk off the floor and participate in news interviews via rapid satellite feed, radio, or Internet. Although Republicans would have preferred to keep the issue in the background, they too had a "war room" and attempted to get press attention to their perspective, especially to their claim that the Democratic plan would raise costs and thus decrease coverage.

Republicans were aided by a number of influential interest groups with a major stake in the outcome. Since 1998 health plans and business groups had spent millions fighting managed care regulation legislation, and they participated aggressively in the 1999 battle, even running TV ads. During the first two weeks of July 1999, $1 million was spent on TV ads by the Health Benefits Coalition, which includes the Business Roundtable, the National Federation of Independent Business, the U.S. Chamber of Commerce and other business and industry groups (Foerstel 1999c, 1718–1719). "Make me pay more for health insurance and then expect my vote? Forget it!" a tough looking construction worker said in one frequently run ad.

The AFL-CIO and the American Medical Association, both of which supported the Democrats' plan, also ran some ads, though their budgets were considerably smaller. Democrats nevertheless benefited from their broad support and made that an important part of their message strategy. The Democratic bill, said Edward Kennedy,

> is supported by a broad and diverse coalition of doctors, nurses, patients, and advocates for children, women, and working families, including the American Medical Association, the Consortium of Citizens with Disabilities, the American Cancer Society, the American Heart Association, the National Alliance for the Mentally Ill, the National Partnership for Women and Families, the National Association of Children's Hospitals, and the AFL-CIO, to name just a few of the more than 180 groups endorsing our bill. (*Congressional Record*, Jan. 19, 1999, S366)

Senate Floor Consideration

Senate rules had prevented Lott from barring the patients' bill of rights issue from ever getting to the floor or from simply disposing of it in one quick vote once on the floor. They did not, however, deprive him entirely of procedural tools that could affect consideration. On July 8 Lott revealed a part of the Republican strategy when he introduced the Democrats' bill to use as the base bill. By making the Democrats' version the bill that would be amended, Lott sought to prevent Democrats from offering the most popular provisions of their measure piecemeal as amendments and forcing Republicans to take a series of hard votes. Pointing out that the Democrats had asked to have their bill made the main vehicle, a Lott spokesman deadpanned, "We offered the Democratic bill to make them defend their own legislation" (*Roll Call*, July 12, 1999, 38). Democrats responded by introducing the Republican bill as a complete substitute, which they could then amend. The two bills were debated simultaneously, with alternate amendments offered to each (*CQ Weekly*, July 17, 1999, 1717).

Ordinarily on a major bill, the bill's sponsor, usually the committee or subcommittee chair, manages and so plays the most prominent role in floor debate. In this case, Republican strategy called for highlighting senators who would put the most sympathetic and credible face on the Republicans' effort. Only a few weeks before, in the wake of the Columbine High School shooting, Republicans had taken a public drubbing on the Senate floor on gun control legislation; the fact that their point man was a National Rifle Association board member had only made matters worse for the party. On managed care, having Dr. Bill Frist and Susan Collins play prominent roles was intended to counter Democratic claims that the Republicans were insensitive to women's health needs and to the opinions of doctors.

Tactical use of floor amendments constituted the crux of the Republican strategy. The leadership task force chaired by Republican Whip Nickles exhaustively surveyed Republican senators on the full range of topics that Democratic amendments addressed (Evans 1999, 15). Using this information, the task force drafted a narrower amendment on the same topic whenever an amendment Democrats planned to offer would put Republicans in a difficult position. Thus, Republicans could vote for the narrower Republican version and against the Democratic version and still argue that they had supported the popular position at issue.

Sen. Charles S. Robb, a Virginia Democrat facing a tough reelection battle in 2000, led off by offering the Democrats' least controversial amendment; it allowed women to designate an obstetrician or gynecologist as their primary care physician and gave doctors, not the managed care plan, the right to determine the length of the hospital stay after a mastectomy. On a 48–52 vote with only three Republicans defecting, Republicans defeated the amendment. The next day Maine Republican Olympia Snowe offered a similar but narrower amendment, and it passed on a straight party line vote. That set the tone for the rest of the floor consideration. Democratic amendments were defeated; Republican amendments on similar topics but often with much weaker provisions won.

The unanimous consent agreement specified that the majority could offer the last amendment, which could not then be amended. The Republicans combined their patient protection provisions with the tax incentives intended to make health insurance more affordable. The Finance Committee had never managed to get a majority for these access provisions, so Lott bypassed the committee. The package passed on a 53–47 vote. The legislation did not allow suits against HMOs and covered only 44 million of the 160 million people in managed care plans. All Democrats voted against it. The Clinton administration blasted the Republican bill and threatened a veto.

Although trounced on the Senate floor, Democrats believed that they had won the public relations battle. For both parties, the fight had been as much over party image as over legislation. Although Republicans had managed to provide their members with cover—with an explanation for tough votes—Democrats had managed to force the issue to the floor and, for a short time at least, to the top of the news.

Drafting Legislation in the House

Meanwhile, the House Republicans' struggle over how to address the issue continued. Like their party colleagues in the Senate, they were caught between the imperatives of their political beliefs and the wishes of some of their strongest interest group supporters, on the one hand, and the fear that opposing such a popular cause could be electoral poison, on the other. In addition, the Republican margin in the House was razor thin, and several House Republicans with medical backgrounds held strong views about the need for regulation.

During 1998 Republicans Charles Norwood, a dentist from Georgia, and Greg Ganske, a medical doctor from Iowa, had worked with the Republican leadership on the issue, and they were willing to do so again in 1999; however, they were less sure a satisfactory bill could be agreed on and made clear that, if necessary, they would cross the aisle on the issue. To make the point, Norwood introduced his own strong bill on January 6, 1999. The next day, in a memo to his colleagues, Majority Leader Armey, acknowledging that the GOP would have to confront the issue, wrote that the party needed to "seize the initiative" and pass legislation that "protects patients from genuine HMO abuses" (Carey 1999a, 129–130).

Three committees share jurisdiction over the issue in the House: Commerce, Education and the Workforce, and Ways and Means. Thomas Bliley, chair of the Commerce Committee, asked Norwood, Ganske, and Tom Coburn, another doctor, all of whom were committee members, to craft a compromise bill that could command some bipartisan support. Ganske left the working group over policy and strategy differences, but on May 14 Norwood and Coburn delivered their proposal to Bliley and, several days later, met with Commerce members of both parties to promote the plan. The plan allowed people to sue their health plans for punitive damages in state court, a provision opposed by Republican leaders but strongly supported by Democrats.

On June 10, Speaker Hastert met with the chairs of the committees and subcommittees involved in the issue. Unhappy with the direction Commerce was taking, Hastert handed primary jurisdiction over the issue, and especially over the liability provision, to the Education and the Work-force Committee. Hastert justified his move on the basis that the Education and the Workforce Committee oversees the Employment and Retirement Security Act, which would have to be amended on the liability issue, but most observers believed that the real motive was ideological, not juris-dictional. Education Committee chair Bill Goodling opposed any increase in patients' right to sue, just as Hastert and Armey did, while Bliley seemed prepared to accept an increase.

On June 16 the Subcommittee on Employer-Employee Relations of the Education and the Workforce Committee approved a package of eight modest managed care reform bills. The subcommittee chair, John Boeh-ner, a strong ally of business, adamantly opposed the right to sue and it was not included.

Getting a Bill to the House Floor

Through the early months of 1999, House Democrats had joined President Clinton and Senate Democrats in a joint effort to raise the visi-bility of the issue and pressure the Republicans toward action. In concert with Families USA, an advocacy group in favor of a strong bill, Democrats launched an Internet petition calling on Congress to pass a patients' bill of rights. During the May recess they held a series of events in districts around the country to highlight the petition and the issue (Lipinski 1999, 15–16). A big rally in Philadelphia featured President Clinton.

House minorities lack the procedural tools for forcing their issues onto the agenda that Senate minorities have. Yet a determined majority, even if it is composed mostly of members of the minority party, can bring a measure to the floor using a discharge petition. Signing a discharge peti-tion is considered an affront to the committee of jurisdiction and to the majority party leadership, but for success it only requires 218 votes. In June, John Dingell, ranking Democrat on Commerce and the party's point man on managed care, began to threaten to go that route.

Ratcheting up the pressure further, on June 25 President Clinton gave a major speech advocating action on the patients' bill of rights. On June 23 Dingell had filed a petition to discharge from the Rules Commit-tee a resolution he had introduced that provided for consideration of S358, his managed care reform bill, and by June 25 the discharge petition had 180 signatures.

Education and the Workforce Committee leaders, though under intense pressure from the Republican leadership to act, could not put together a majority to pass Boehner's bill or to defeat Norwood's, which he intended to offer as an amendment during full committee markup. Twice, scheduled meetings had to be canceled for fear of defeat. Although supposedly no longer having jurisdiction over much of the issue, the Commerce Committee continued to work on a broad bill through staff and, more importantly, through negotiations between Bliley and Dingell. On July 27, however, the two committee leaders declared their negotiations dead (Foerstel 1999d, 1862).

When he became Speaker at the beginning of 1999, Dennis Hastert had promised the House he would restore "regular order" and allow committees to work their will on legislation. But with the committees unable to produce the sort of bill he wanted and the danger of a successful discharge petition looming, Hastert appointed a task force of subcommittee chairs to draft a Republican bill that could pass the House. Bill Thomas, R-Calif., chair of the Ways and Means Subcommittee on Health and an opponent of expanded liability, was designated task force chair.

Convinced that their own leadership had sunk the Dingell-Bliley talks and unhappy with the composition of the task force, Republican rebels began to work with Democrats and even threatened to sign the discharge petition. On July 28 Norwood and Dingell announced a tentative agreement on a bipartisan package. When the final compromise bill, HR2723, was introduced on August 5, it had twenty-one Republican co-sponsors, more than enough to pass the bill if all Democrats voted in favor.

Although Hastert had promised a vote before the August recess, disarray within the Republican camp forced him to postpone it. The task force found it difficult to come up with a bill that both moderate and conservative Republicans could support. Finally, on September 9, Tom Coburn and John Shadegg, R-Ariz., introduced their bill, but without the blessing from Hastert they had expected. Their bill gave up too much ground on the right to sue in the view of Hastert and many of the other members of the task force. The vote that had been promised for September was postponed again and set for the week of October 4.

On September 28 the Speaker endorsed a medical tax-break bill sponsored by James Talent, R-Mo., and John Shadegg. Industry groups had for much of the year been pushing for tax breaks to help people afford insurance; they hoped to shift the debate from restrictions on managed care providers to increased access to insurance, thus providing cover for members to vote against any increase in the right to sue. Republicans had been supportive of the notion, and the House leadership saw the bill as part of a strategy that might derail the Norwood-Dingell legislation. The Talent-Shadegg bill was named the Access to Care for the Uninsured Act.

The Republican task force finally managed to come up with a patient protection bill that they hoped would command a GOP consensus, and

Hastert announced his support on October 5. A revised version of the Coburn-Shadegg bill fine-tuned by Porter Goss, R-Fla., Bill Thomas, and James Greenwood, R-Pa., it would allow suits in both federal and state courts but under a more restricted set of circumstances and with more conditions and limitations than the Norwood-Dingell bill. Ironically, the bill the Republican leadership endorsed actually expanded the right to sue more than the bill they had rejected earlier; the political momentum Norwood-Dingell had developed forced the Republican leaders to support provisions they disliked in the hopes of heading off what they considered an even worse outcome.

The Special Rule

On October 6, as promised, the Republican leadership brought the rule for considering managed care reform to the floor. The rule specified that HR2990, the tax bill, would be considered first; no amendments would be allowed, but one motion to recommit, through which Democrats could attempt to amend the bill, was in order. Next HR2723, the Norwood-Dingell bill, would be considered. Three hours of general debate were divided equally among the three committees with jurisdiction. The only amendments in order were three substitutes—the plan endorsed by the Republican leadership; another, narrower proposal sponsored by Amo Houghton, R-N.Y., and Lindsey Graham, R-S.C.; and the very modest Boehner proposal, which did not allow lawsuits. The rule specified:

> Each amendment may be offered only in the order printed in the report, may be offered only by a Member designated in the report, shall be considered as read, shall be debatable for the time specified in the report equally divided and controlled by the proponent and an opponent, and shall not be subject to amendment. . . . The adoption of an amendment in the nature of a substitute shall constitute the conclusion of consideration of the bill for amendment. (*Congressional Record*, Oct. 6, 1999, H9421)

This last sentence simply reiterates that the House is following its normal procedures: when language in a bill has been amended, it may not be amended again; so if a substitute, which, in effect, amends everything in a bill, is adopted, then no more amendments are in order. The leadership had other choices; it could have used a king- or queen-of-the-hill rule, which does allow votes on a number of substitutes (see Chapter 2). In this case, however, the normal procedure gave the Republican leadership a strategic advantage and explains why the majority party leaders were willing to use the Norwood-Dingell bill, which they strongly opposed, as the base bill. If any of the Republican substitutes could get a majority, Norwood-Dingell would be dead without members having to go on record against it. Finally, the rule specified that, if both the tax bill and some form of the managed care bill passed, they would be combined into one bill without a separate vote and sent to the Senate as a package.

Democrats indignantly opposed the rule. The Rules Committee had refused to allow Norwood-Dingell supporters to offer an amendment with revenue offsets to pay for the cost of the bill. Democrats believed the amendment was barred simply to give Republicans a basis for attacking the Norwood-Dingell bill. "To force Members to be fiscally irresponsible as a Republican ploy to win what they cannot win through honest debate is shameful," Rules Committee member and Democratic Caucus chair Martin Frost charged (*Congressional Record*, Oct. 6, 1999, H9422). Norwood-Dingell supporters objected even more strongly to combining the two bills. President Clinton and most Democrats opposed many of the provisions in the tax bill as giveaways to special interests. Therefore, combining the two bills would make a difficult conference even harder; it was, in effect, a poison pill, they charged.

House Floor Consideration

The House approved the rule on a nearly party line vote; on this procedural issue, the Republican supporters of Norwood-Dingell voted with their party colleagues. Defecting from your party on procedural votes is considered a greater offense than defecting on substantive issues, and the Republican rebels were unwilling to accept the leadership and peer disapproval doing so would bring. The access bill was debated and approved, again on nearly party line votes; five Republican supporters of Norwood-Dingell, including Norwood and Ganske, voted against passage of the bill, but eleven Democrats supported it and it passed 227–205.

The next day, the House took up the patients' bill of rights legislation. Supporters of Norwood-Dingell argued that the protections in their bill were necessary and just; "HMOs and foreign diplomats are the only people who are above the law. That should end," they claimed (*Congressional Record*, Oct. 7, 1999, H9587). They described the problems with the current system: "I am worried about . . . that mother today who took her child to the pediatrician and the doctor says her child needs to be hospitalized and the insurance industry 2,000 miles away says, no, we cannot do that" (H9600). They pointed to the more than 300 groups, including most of the medical groups, that supported their bill. Opponents argued that allowing suits would just raise costs and enrich trial lawyers without raising the quality of health care and that increased costs would mean fewer people could afford health insurance.

> [T]heir bill is poison for our health care system today. . . . Expanding lawsuits against employer-based health plans means expanding lawsuits against employers. If employers are exposed to lawsuits, they are going to stop providing coverage to their employees. (*Congressional Record,* Oct. 7, 1999, H9554)
>
> The same plaintiff lawyers who took on the tobacco companies and are taking on the gun manufacturers are lining up for the biggest pot since tobacco, the HMOs. And when they sue, they will not just sue the HMO, they will sue everybody in sight, including the employer. (H9555)
>
> Norwood-Dingell . . . will take billions and billions of dollars out of treatment rooms and put it into courtrooms. (H9556)

The task for the supporters of Norwood-Dingell was twofold: they needed enough votes to pass their legislation, and, more immediately, they needed to hold support for all of the Republican substitutes under a majority. In Democratic Caucus meetings, Minority Leader Gephardt emphasized the need for unity in opposition to Republican substitutes. The broad interest-group coalition supporting Norwood-Dingell, which included liberal and labor groups, the AMA, other medical groups, and the trial lawyers, sent their lobbyists to the Hill to reiterate the point.

The Boehner substitute came to a vote first and was soundly defeated 145–284. The big test for Norwood-Dingell proponents came next with a vote on the Republican leadership–supported Goss-Coburn-Shadegg substitute. In arguing against the substitute and for his bill, Charlie Norwood said:

> Mr. Chairman, this is the painful part. It is not any fun going against our friends. And the gentleman from Oklahoma (Mr. Coburn) is my friend. . . . My colleagues, what this really is all about is about two very strong American principles. It is about the right to choose in this country and choose our own doctor, and it is about the right to ask people to be responsible for their actions. We do that all the time, and it is time that we ask the insurance industry to be responsible for its actions. (*Congressional Record,* Oct. 7, 1999, H9600)

Speaker Hastert closed debate for the supporters of the substitute, arguing:

> As we debate these bills and these options before us today, there are a lot of similarities. People getting the access, people being able to get into emergency care, getting to their caregiver, their pediatrician, or their Ob-Gyn so that they can take care of them. They are all the same. . . . The difference in these bills is to some a fine line, but the difference in these bills is how far we go, how far that we give license to the trial lawyers, how far that we take the

incentive away from corporations and employers to provide health care for their employees. (H9601)

The substitute went down to defeat on a 193–238 vote, with 29 Republicans (and 2 Democrats) crossing party lines. The Republicans who voted against their leadership's substitute were largely but not exclusively moderates, many but not all from the northeast.

The debate and vote on the Houghton substitute was anticlimax; it was defeated 160–269. Norwood-Dingell had survived against all its challengers; now it needed a majority vote to pass. That on the passage vote it received a majority was not surprise, but the size of the majority was: 275 members, including 68 Republicans, voted for the bill; 149 Republicans and 2 Democrats opposed it. On this vote, the 29 Republican defectors were joined by an ideologically and regionally more disparate group, many of whom were likely responding to constituency sentiment. For example, although only two of fourteen Florida Republicans joined the core supporters of Norwood-Dingell in voting against the Republican leadership's substitute, nine voted for passage.

Although Republican House leaders did not concede defeat, they realized that their chances of prevailing on the floor were poor. To avoid doing more damage to party unity than necessary, Speaker Hastert did not deploy the aggressive whip system run by Tom DeLay but relied on an informal whip team made up of the sponsors of the Goss-Coburn-Shadegg bill, committee chairs, and deans of state delegations. They attempted to persuade members to stick with the leadership, but gently (Koszczuk 1999, 2356).

The insurance industry and employer groups opposed to the bill worked the vote aggressively. Yet that well-organized, affluent coalition failed in the House. TV ads, letter writing campaigns, and phone calls arranging for supportive constituents to talk to their members did not sway a third of the Republicans. These members concluded that their constituents wanted the bill, so it would be dangerous for them not to support it. As Indiana Republican Mark E. Souder, a conservative member of the class of 1994, said, "There's only so much you can do when 80 percent of the people want HMO reform" (Koszczuk 1999, 2356).

Yet the bill was far from becoming law. Given the U.S. legislative process, the proponents still had a harder task ahead than the opponents. Since the Senate and House bills were so different, the conference was bound to be difficult and give opponents, including the majority leaderships in both House and Senate, many opportunities to kill the bill. "You don't see too many crossbreeds between a Chihuahua and a Great Dane," an opponent and likely conferee said (Carey 1999b, 2357).

In appointing conferees in November 1999, Speaker Hastert used his prerogatives to diminish the bill's chances even further; he refused to appoint any of the active Republican supporters of the bill to the conference committee; in fact, only one Republican conferee had voted for passage. Even Charles Norwood, chief sponsor, was denied appointment, despite a House rule admonishing the Speaker to appoint the sponsor of major amendments adopted by the House. So long as a majority supports the Speaker, there is no way of enforcing this rule. (See Table 8.1 for a chronology of the managed care reform legislation.)

That is where the story stood as of this writing. What happened in 2000 and why?

Unorthodox Lawmaking in a Highly Partisan Environment

The battle over managed care reform illustrates the difficulties of lawmaking in a highly partisan environment, especially when control of the government is divided. The fight over the patients' bill of rights was largely partisan, though it depended on the support of a small but crucial number of Republicans for success in the House. From the perspective of the congressional majority party, it was a fight to prevent the minority Democrats from stealing agenda control from the Republican majority in order to pass an initiative strongly opposed by most majority party members. From the Democrats' perspective, it was a battle by the president, strongly supported by his fellow partisans in Congress, to force a recalcitrant majority party to consider a central issue on the president's agenda, one with strong public support. Although electoral concerns were certainly at issue, it was also a substantive legislative fight, with both sides convinced their position represented good public policy.

Given divided government and the differences in the parties' legislative preferences on the issue, it was inevitable that much of the war would be fought through a PR battle. In this case, the Democrats, who had a popular issue but lacked control over the congressional agenda, mounted an elaborate and sophisticated campaign to raise the issue's visibility. They knew they had to mobilize public pressure to induce the majority Republicans to consider their bills, and they had the president with his bully pulpit.

In both chambers, the majority party leaderships resorted to unorthodox lawmaking to counter the Democratic initiative and to attempt to pass a Republican bill instead. Multiple referral and the flexibility it gives the

TABLE 8.1 Patients' Bill of Rights: A Chronology

Date	House Action	Date	Senate Action	Date	Postpassage Action
		1998/ early 1999	*Republican task force drafts Republican bill.*		
1/6	Norwood introduces HR216; it is referred to the Commerce Committee and also to the Committee on Education and the Workforce.	1/19	Minority Leader Tom Daschle introduces S6, the Democratic Party's bill.		
	Bliley, chairman of the Commerce Committee, asks committee members Norwood, Ganske, and Coburn to craft a compromise bill.	1/22	Majority Leader Lott introduces a bill cosponsored by 48 Republican senators and drafted by a party task force.		
		1/28	Jim Jeffords, chair of Senate Health, Education, Labor and Pensions Committee (HELP), introduces S326, a bill based on the patient protection provisions of the task force bill.		

Date	Event	Date	Event
3/17, 3/18	HELP marks up and reports S326. *Lott and Daschle negotiate over conditions for floor consideration.*	5/14	*Norwood and Coburn deliver their proposal to Bliley.*
		6/10	Speaker Hastert gives primary jurisdiction over the issue and especially over the liability provision to the Education and the Workforce Committee.
6/22	Democrats offer their patients' bill of rights as an amendment to the agriculture appropriations bill; Lott motion to table (kill) amendment approved 53–47. *Lott and Daschle negotiate over conditions for floor consideration.*	6/16	The Subcommittee on Employer-Employee Relations of the Education and the Workforce Committee approves a package of eight modest managed care bills.
		June	Education and the Workforce Committee unable to get a majority to report out these bills and to defeat Norwood bill. Democrats begin circulating discharge petition.

TABLE 8.1 Patients' Bill of Rights: A Chronology *(Continued)*

Date	House Action	Date	Senate Action	Date	Postpassage Action
		6/28	*Lott and Daschle reach agreement on a UCA.*		
		6/29	Lott announces UCA on Senate floor.		
July	*Hastert appoints a task force of subcommittee chairmen to draft a Republican bill.*	7/12– 7/15	Bill debated and amended on the floor.		
		7/15	Republican substitute accepted and bill passed 53–47.		
7/28	*Norwood and Dingell announce they have reached a bipartisan compromise.*				
8/5	Norwood-Dingell bill (HR2723) introduced.				
9/28	*Speaker endorses HR2990, the Talent–Shadegg sponsored Access to Care for the Uninsured Act.*				

Date	Action
10/5	*Speaker endorses the Goss-Coburn-Shadegg bill, the Republican task force patient protections bill.*
10/6	House approves rule for consideration of HR2990 and HR2723. House debates and passes HR2990 227–205.
10/7	House debates HR2723 and Republican substitutes. Goss-Coburn-Shadegg substitute defeated 193–238. Norwood-Dingell bill (HR2723) passes 275–151.
10/14	Senate asks for conference.
10/15	Senate conferees appointed.
11/3	House conferees appointed.

Note: Official actions are in roman type; behind-the-scenes, unofficial actions are in italics.

Speaker allowed Speaker Hastert to shift primary responsibility from a committee that, from his perspective, was proceeding in the wrong direction to one that was more likely to draft satisfactory legislation. When the contentiousness of the issue stymied that committee as well, Hastert bypassed committee altogether and entrusted the drafting of the bill to a partisan task force. At the leadership's behest, the Rules Committee drafted a special rule that gave the leadership position the advantage. Yet the majority party was on the defensive throughout the battle. The Republicans' extremely narrow margin made a seldom successful special procedure a realistic threat in the 106th Congress; supporters of strong managed care reform used the discharge procedure to force the majority leadership to bring the issue to the floor. The Democrats, who were united in favor of a strong bill, and the minority of Republicans who also favored a strong bill together made up a majority of the House. Despite the majority party's control of floor procedure, the support coalition held together on the House floor and passed the strong bill. Electoral concerns, in part stimulated by the Democrats' PR offensive, motivated a number of Republicans who had not been supporters of the strong bill to vote for it on final passage.

Senate minorities have a much greater capacity to affect their chamber's agenda than House minorities do. Senate Democrats employed the Senate's permissive debate and amending rules to force the majority leader to bring their legislation to the floor. The majority countered with a creative use of the permissive amending rules as well and prevailed on the floor. Yet Democrats believed they had won the PR battle and set the stage for ultimate success.

chapter nine

The Omnibus Drug Bill:
A "Designer" Legislative Process

IN LATE APRIL 1988 Speaker of the House Jim Wright decided Congress should pass comprehensive antidrug legislation. The drug problem was becoming an increasingly salient issue in the early months of 1988 as Jesse Jackson, running for the Democratic presidential nomination, focused attention on it and struck a chord with audiences of all sorts. Responding to public concern, members of both chambers were introducing bills and offering amendments aimed at the drug problem. Thus, Wright saw an opportunity to accomplish something useful, and he knew that he had to act quickly if the Democratic party leadership wanted to control the legislative process on the issue. On a hot-button issue such as drugs, some proposals that are draconian, unworkable, or both are always offered; strong and early involvement would allow the leaders to exert a measure of quality control. Furthermore, in a presidential election year and with an opposition party president in the White House, Speaker Wright wanted the Democratic Party to receive credit for passing antidrug legislation.

Speaker Wright decided Congress should pass an omnibus bill. The drug problem is multifaceted; members and experts alike agreed that education, treatment, interdiction, prosecution, and punishment were all necessary parts of an effective antidrug strategy, even if they disagreed about how much emphasis should be given to the various approaches. In addition, the Speaker knew that an omnibus bill would garner much more media attention than would a series of narrower bills and thus yield more credit. In 1985, the Speaker explained, the Democratic House had passed a series of antidrug bills; Republicans, who then controlled the Senate, put the bills together into one package in the Senate, called it the

Republican drug initiative, and got all the press attention. That, he said, had taught Democrats a lesson.

Passing an omnibus bill would not be easy. Many committees would have to be involved, and time was short; less than half a year remained till adjournment, and much other business needed to get done. Furthermore, while almost everyone in Congress—Democrats and Republicans, liberals and conservatives—wanted to pass a drug bill, many of the specific provisions would be highly contentious.

Putting Together the House Bill

The procedure the Speaker chose was designed to ameliorate these problems. Wright asked Majority Leader Tom Foley to oversee the process of putting together a bill and to do it in concert with Minority Leader Bob Michel, R-Ill. The need for speed and the subject matter dictated a bipartisan effort. Partisanship would slow the process down. What is more, a fierce partisan battle between Democrats advocating more money for education and treatment and Republicans supporting more severe punishment of users and dealers would not benefit the Democrats' image with the electorate. Passing a balanced bill would.

On May 2 Wright, Foley, and Majority Whip Tony Coelho, D-Calif., met with the chairs of eleven committees—ten with relevant jurisdiction and the Select Committee on Narcotics Abuse and Control (which, as a select committee, could not report legislation)—to discuss what might be included in the bill. The Speaker asked the chairs to make it a bipartisan effort. "I don't want a bidding war," he said. He told them that the target date for reporting out their legislation was June 21, and they promised to comply.

On May 9 Speaker Wright announced the initiative at his daily press conference, explaining both the procedure to be used and the deadline. His primary purpose, of course, was to publicize the effort. A not unwelcome by-product of making the deadline public was to increase the pressure on the committees to produce their legislation in a timely fashion.

By mid-June committees began to report their legislation, and by the end of the month, all the committees with jurisdiction had reported. The issue had continued to increase in saliency; on June 15 Vice President George Bush, who by then had wrapped up the Republican nomination for president, appeared on Capitol Hill with Republican House leaders as they unveiled their drug legislation, a package put together by the Republican Leadership Task Force on Drugs, chaired by Bill McCollum, R-Fla. Republicans, too, wanted credit for the legislation. Furthermore, in the

Democrats' eagerness to pass a bill, they saw opportunities to enact provisions they favored. Republicans worked in the committees with mixed success to incorporate their provisions into the legislation reported. Some Republican amendments provoked sharply partisan battles within committees; others found bipartisan support. In the end all of the committees reported their legislation on a bipartisan vote.

Taken together, the legislation reported by the ten committees constituted a comprehensive attack on the drug problem; interdiction, education, treatment, and penalties were each addressed from a number of different angles. There were many widely ranging provisions—making it more difficult for drug kingpins to launder money (reported by the Banking Committee), establishing new drug awareness and education initiatives (reported by Education and Labor), authorizing more money for Coast Guard drug interdiction (reported by Merchant Marine and Fisheries), increasing penalties for drug offenses and devising controls to prevent the flow of solvents used to refine cocaine (reported by Judiciary), and creating programs for treatment and rehabilitation (reported by Energy and Commerce).

It was Majority Leader Foley's job to take these provisions, and the myriad others in the ten measures reported, and meld them into a coherent whole. From the beginning of the process, Tom Foley and senior leadership staff had monitored the committees. They had worked to spot problems and to try to work them out and had pushed the participants to move quickly and settle their disputes expeditiously. Periodic meetings of the chairs had been held to keep the pressure on. To maintain as much bipartisanship as possible, Foley had conferred regularly with Minority Leader Michel.

In putting together the bill to take to the floor, Foley faced two sorts of problems: jurisdictional and political. One of the problems, an aide explained, is that "a lot of committees did each other's work." In other words, they invaded each other's jurisdiction. The Ways and Means Committee complained that six major provisions drafted by other committees trespassed on its jurisdiction. For example, the Merchant Marine and Fisheries Committee had drafted an "innocent owner" provision to limit the ability of the Customs Service and the Coast Guard to seize boats on which small amounts of drugs were found if the owner of the vessel knew nothing about the drugs; because Ways and Means has oversight jurisdiction over the Customs Service, it considered this an invasion of its turf. A number of committees complained that the Judiciary Committee had overstepped its bounds. "[The committees have] been told to work it out by the deadline, or we'll do it for them or work it out on the floor," a leadership aide asserted.

The second problem was how to handle numerous highly contentious issues, many of which were not simply partisan but split Democrats as well. The Democratic leadership had hoped to take a broad consensus vehicle to the floor and handle "the controversial stuff" through floor amendments. The legislation reported by the committees made that largely though not completely possible.

By the time the committees had finished their work, the issues that would provoke the most heated conflict had become clear. A Republican proposal on "user accountability" that would deny federal benefits of various sorts to those convicted of drug use was voted down on a largely party-line vote in the Education and Labor Committee; a different version was approved by the Judiciary Committee. Judiciary turned down a provision allowing the death penalty for drug kingpins, another Republican priority, but adopted one requiring a seven-day waiting period to complete the purchase of a handgun. The adamant opposition of the powerful National Rifle Association (NRA) to a waiting period ensured a battle on that provision.

Designing the Rule

The process of putting together the legislative vehicle to take to the floor merged into that of crafting the rule for floor consideration. Despite intense lobbying by the NRA, the seven-day waiting period was left in the omnibus bill. Amendments to weaken it, however, would be made in order by the rule. A number of the jurisdictional problems were solved by removing the offending provisions from the base bill but allowing them to be offered as amendments on the floor; the Judiciary Committee's user accountability and drug czar provisions were handled in this way. Foley and Michel, in lengthy negotiations, decided which of the hot-button amendments would be allowed on the floor. Foley agreed to votes on the Republicans' top priority amendments—on user accountability, the death penalty, and the exclusionary rule—in return for their limiting the number of amendments they would offer.

Liberal Democrats particularly would have preferred a rule that disallowed Republican amendments on those hot-button issues; such votes confronted members with a choice between "trashing the Constitution" by voting for punitive provisions contrary to the Bill of Rights and casting a vote very hard to explain to constituents right before an election, they believed. However, the price of Republican cooperation was allowing votes on some of these controversial amendments, and the Democratic leadership knew that it could not pass a rule that barred such votes. Too many of its own members would defect. The Democratic leadership gave liberal members opportunities to attempt to counter Republican amendments they believed pernicious; eight amendments aimed at ameliorating the Republicans' death penalty amendment were made in order.

At about 11 p.m. on August 10, after three days of deliberation, the Rules Committee reported out a rule for consideration of HR5210, the Omnibus Drug Initiative. Members had proposed over 150 amendments; the Rules Committee, under leadership guidance, decided to allow thirty-five—nineteen to be offered by Republicans, sixteen by Democrats.

A long and complex rule, it carefully structured floor consideration. After three hours of general debate equally divided between the majority and minority leaders, the thirty-five amendments were to be debated under varying time limits adding up in total to another twelve and a half hours of debate. In the words of the rule:

> No amendment to the bill shall be in order except the amendments specified in the report of the Committee on Rules accompanying this resolution, or those amendments offered by the majority leader in the manner specified herein. The amendments printed in the report of the Committee on Rules shall be considered only in the order and in the manner specified in the report. . . . Each amendment may only be offered by the Member designated for such amendment in the report of the Committee on Rules, or his designee. . . . Debate on each of said amendments shall not exceed the time specified in this resolution or in the report of the Committee on Rules, to be equally divided and controlled by the proponent and a Member opposed thereto. . . . No amendment shall be subject to amendment, except as specified in the report of the Committee on Rules. (*Congressional Record*, Aug. 11, 1988, H6846)

Two pairs of amendments were to be considered under a king-of-the-hill procedure. A death penalty amendment by Rep. George W. Gekas, R-Pa., and a life imprisonment alternative by Rep. Charles B. Rangel, D-N.Y., were paired. The Gekas amendment was given the advantaged last position; the Democratic leadership did not believe this was a winnable fight. Two amendments on establishing a drug czar were to be brought up under the same procedure; in this case the version offered by the chair of the Government Operations Committee was to be voted on after the Republican alternative and thus adopted should both receive a majority.

House Floor Action

On August 11 the House approved the rule on a vote of 363 to 41. The leaders had succeeded in crafting a rule that most members considered fair but that nevertheless structured and limited debate. Although swift by congressional standards, the process had dragged on long enough that consideration of the bill could not be completed before the August recess. To cement the agreements that had been reached, the Democratic leaders decided to bring up the rule before the recess; especially in an election year, members at home campaigning might be tempted to toughen their stance.

The House took up the drug bill when it returned from its August recess and, after six days of consideration, approved it on a 375–30 vote. The Gekas death penalty amendment passed, but so did some of the mitigating amendments. The relatively moderate Judiciary Committee version of the user accountability amendment was approved, as was the Republicans' exclusionary rule amendment. The seven-day waiting period was struck from the bill, but Democrats defeated a Republican attempt to delete the innocent owner provisions. The Democrats' drug czar amendment prevailed.

Putting Together the Senate Bill

If the legislative process in the House deviated from the textbook model in a number of important respects, the legislative process in the Senate on the drug bill bore almost no relationship to the textbook model. In response to the growing saliency of the issue, both of the Senate parties formed working groups and charged them with formulating a package of antidrug proposals. Individual senators, taking advantage of the Senate's permissive rules on amendments, had been offering their own proposals on the floor; on June 10 Sen. Alfonse M. D'Amato, R-N.Y., proposed legislation allowing the death penalty for drug kingpins, and it passed on a 65–29 vote. He had threatened to attach the death penalty measure as an amendment to the defense authorization bill and, in return for withdrawing it, was given a floor vote on the freestanding measure.

The Senate Democratic working group, chaired by Senators Nunn and Moynihan, unveiled its proposals in the last week of June. The Senate Republican task force followed on July 7. Both packages were comprehensive, covering the same broad range from education to interdiction as the House measure. The two parties' packages differed, however, not only in details but also in emphasis. The Democrats focused 60 percent of the resources on reducing the demand for drugs through education and treatment, while the Senate Republicans, like their House colleagues, proposed strict user accountability provisions and the death penalty for drug kingpins.

If the normal process had been followed, and these proposals had been sent to the committees with jurisdiction, antidrug legislation almost certainly would not have been enacted in 1988. Given the many committees that would have had to be involved and the number and contentiousness of the issues, the time left before the 100th Congress adjourned permanently was just too short. Yet most senators wanted to pass a bill. They not only wanted to respond to public demand; they also knew that, if the House passed legislation and the Senate did not, they would look terrible.

To solve the problem, the joint party leadership—Majority Leader Byrd and Minority Leader Dole—decided to forgo committee consideration altogether and appoint a bipartisan working group to negotiate a bill. This group of about twenty senators, most of whom had worked on their party's task force, "had literally hundreds of hours of meetings," as Sen. Warren Rudman, R-N.H., one of its most active members, reported (*Congressional Record*, Oct. 12, 1988, S15636). Other senators with an interest in any aspect of the problem were invited to present their proposals to the working group. After several months of tough negotiations, the group produced a consensus core bill. Included were the provisions on which this politically diverse group managed to reach full agreement. Several highly controversial issues were left to be decided on the floor.

Getting the Bill to the Senate Floor

On October 3, 1988, Senator Nunn introduced S2852, the core bill, on behalf of the bipartisan working group and the joint leadership. Because of its scope and importance but also because it would likely be one of the last major bills to clear during the 100th Congress, S2852 immediately attracted scores of amendments. If all these and possibly other amendments were debated on the floor, time would run out, and all the hard work would be for naught. To get the bill to a passage vote, a unanimous consent agreement (UCA) limiting debate would have to be negotiated. Yet to get all senators to agree, senators' rights had to be preserved.

Democratic leader Byrd and Republican leader Dole agreed on a complex procedure that they hoped would yield such an agreement. Amendments would be classified into three categories: those on which the working group could agree, mostly noncontroversial ones; a limited number of highly contentious amendments that would be debated and voted on individually on the floor; and an intermediate group for which some other procedure would have to be worked out. Byrd and Dole sent the most active members of the working group back to work, examining and classifying the 100 or so amendments that had been filed.

Over the course of several days of intensive meetings, the working group identified more than thirty amendments on which they could agree. Eight amendments—on the death penalty, user accountability, and other contentious issues—warranted individual floor debate, the working group decided. Another eighteen or so amendments—later called the purgatory group—fell into neither of these categories: they were too controversial for the working group to accept but not important enough to warrant scarce floor time.

The unanimous consent agreement that Byrd and Dole presented to their membership on October 12 specified that the first group of amendments would be packaged together and jointly offered by the two leaders and the co-chairs of the working group. Together with the original bill developed by the working group, these amendments would constitute the new core bill. There would be a single vote up or down on this package.

The eight hot-button amendments would be debated under specific time limits; any amendments to those amendments would have to be germane. The fate of the purgatory amendments, Byrd and Dole agreed and the UCA specified, would be determined by a special four-person task force they set up. The task force—Nunn, Moynihan, Rudman, and Gramm—would review the amendments, giving their sponsors an opportunity to defend them. If the four agreed on the amendment, it would go into the package; if not, Byrd and Dole would act as a court of appeal. The amendments turned down by both the task force and the leaders could not be offered.

"[A] single objection, of course, will mean we have no agreement, and a single objection may mean that we will have no drug bill," Majority Leader Byrd said pointedly as he presented the UCA on the floor (*Congressional Record*, Oct. 12, 1988, S15633). William Armstrong, R-Colo., complained vehemently about the restraint on senators' rights. He argued that the Senate had set up its own Rules Committee and that it was "a bad practice and a bad precedent," but in the end he did not object (Lawrence 1988a, 2978). Unwilling to be responsible for the demise of the bill, he and other senators who disliked the UCA delayed it for a day but ultimately acceded.

The UCA made it possible for the Senate to complete the bill after two days of debate and only nine roll call votes. On October 14 the Senate passed the bill 87–3.

Reconciling House-Senate Differences:
The Initial Phase

Well before Senate passage, House and Senate majority party leaders had begun discussing how to resolve the differences between the chambers. By a September 22 meeting to coordinate the two chambers' end-of-the-session schedules and to discuss problem legislation, the leaders had begun to conclude that sending the legislation to conference would kill it. Given the number of issues and the number of committees involved, a conference would not be able to produce a compromise bill in the limited time left before adjournment. A less formal process would have to be used.

To be ready to start working out agreements between the chambers as soon as the Senate passed its bill, the House leadership began preparations. On Thursday, October 13, the Speaker and Majority Leader Foley met with the committee and subcommittee chairs involved. They informed the chairs that the Senate expected to finish the bill late Friday and urged them to begin working out their differences with their Senate counterparts over the weekend. The chairs complained about the Senate process: "Who do we talk to? There's a 'core group' over in the Senate who are putting the bill together. It doesn't necessarily include the committee people," groused one. "There's no one to talk to," lamented another, reflecting the consensus view. The leaders commiserated with their members and tried to soothe them. "We can't solve [the Senate's] process problems," the Speaker responded to the chairs' complaints. "After the Senate gets a bill, they will have to talk," the majority leader pointed out. Both the Speaker and the majority leader urged the chairs to focus on getting an agreement. "If you're leaving town this weekend, designate a staff person to start the process," the Speaker said. "Please have your staff monitor Senate action and keep in touch with leadership staff," prompted the majority leader.

When the Senate passed its bill about 4 p.m. on Friday, the two chambers' leadership staffs were ready. At 5 p.m. the House and Senate Democratic leadership staffs met to figure out the differences between the two bills and to identify where the problems were likely to be. The House leadership staff distributed the Senate package to all relevant House committees "so they [the staff] could spend the weekend looking over the differences between the two bills." A number of the most contentious issues fell into the jurisdiction of the Judiciary Committees; their House and Senate staffs worked Saturday afternoon and all day Sunday to get a head start.

Monday and Tuesday were devoted to negotiations at the staff level. "One of the problems," a leadership staffer explained, "is that we [in the

House] are doing it by committee, and the Senate is doing it by subject matter." House committee staff did not know with whom to deal on the Senate side. House leadership staffers identified for the House committee staffs the Senate staff aides working on issues within their jurisdictions. Shifting groups of staffers worked through their sections of the bill, clarifying differences, trying to resolve minor ones, and identifying "member issues"—those important and politically delicate enough that members would have to resolve them.

By Wednesday morning staffers had done what they could do; the minor and the easy issues had been resolved. Members had also been meeting with their counterparts from the other chamber, trying to reach agreements on the more difficult issues. The Senate's unorthodox procedure continued to annoy the House chairs, who complained to their party leadership about senators who did not show up for scheduled meetings, and about others who lacked expertise because they did not serve on the committee of jurisdiction. At a 2 p.m. meeting of the House Democratic leadership and the chairs, many also charged that getting agreements to stick was a problem. "It is all independent contractors over there [in the Senate]. If you come to an agreement with one of them, others may not go along," a powerful chair complained. "Our staff negotiated with Orrin Hatch's staff for several hours," another chair recounted. And then in came the staffs of Gramm and Sen. John Danforth, R-Mo., who said, "Hatch can't speak for the Republicans on that; we refuse to accept anything that has been done." Called to assess progress, the meeting made clear that substantial headway had been made but that reaching an overall agreement would require a more assertive leadership role.

At 4 p.m. the top Democratic and Republican party leaders of the House and Senate met in the Speaker's Capitol office and agreed upon a procedure for resolving the remaining differences. Byrd and Dole designated Nunn and Rudman as lead negotiators for the Senate. Foley and Michel would mediate for the House. Sections of the bill on which there were unresolved problems would be taken up one by one, the members involved called in, and a compromise worked out. Staff drew up a schedule; the process was to begin at 6 p.m. and continue the following day until all outstanding differences had been ironed out.

The marathon meeting began in a large room on the House side of the Capitol. When their issues were called up, House members and some senators briefly stated their case. Many of the affected senators were represented by staff or were consulted by phone by Nunn and Rudman. The two senators and Foley were the most active participants, Michel often having business elsewhere. They pressed members to compromise and sometimes suggested provisions or even legislative language to that end.

Some problems were resolved entirely; on others agreement was reached in principle, and the affected members were sent off to work out the details; on still others, no progress was made, but the members were exhorted to go back and try again.

By late Thursday afternoon, October 20, this process had accomplished what it could. Many differences had been resolved. However, others, which had seemingly been resolved, emerged again as tentative agreements fell apart. The time pressure under which members negotiated sometimes led to disagreements about what actually had been agreed to; the process of transforming verbal agreements into legislative language sometimes revealed disagreement; and sometimes negotiators found they could not sell a deal they had made to their interested colleagues. On still other disagreements, the opponents refused to give any ground. Late in the day the issue of random drug testing of transportation workers, an issue on which House and Senate were adamant and split, came up again. Foley in jest suggested trial by combat. Not long after, Dole came in and, after being briefed, concluded that the testing issue was "one of those issues that will have to go to the 'Supreme Court'" of top leaders. "Is it the only one?" he asked hopefully. No, Nunn told him, there are seven or eight such issues.

Resolving the Tough Ones: The "Supreme Court" Decides

At 7 p.m. in the Speaker's office, the "Supreme Court" gathered: Speaker Wright, House Majority Leader Foley, House Minority Leader Michel, Senate Majority Leader Byrd, Senate Minority Leader Dole, and Senators Nunn and Rudman. An amendment by Senator Helms, lifting diplomatic immunity for diplomats who deal in drugs, drive drunk, or commit a violent crime, was the first order of business. The Reagan administration opposed the amendment, as did many House Foreign Affairs Committee members; the senators were not willing to fight for it, and it was tentatively dropped. The related issues of drug testing and tough new certification standards for labs that do drug tests were discussed. Representative Dingell, chair of the committee that had drafted the certification provisions, came by to report that some seemingly hopeful talks had gotten nowhere. Finally, the leaders decided to drop the provisions altogether.

Senate Democrats "had problems" with the House's user accountability provision; they believed it unworkable. Dropping that provision was not, however, a viable option; both chambers had voted for a version, and there was too much support for it, especially in the House. After lengthy discussion a compromise was worked out between the House and Senate versions that included the Senate's provision making the denial of benefits discretionary for the judge. The innocent owner provision was still a problem; the Customs Service, Rudman reported, was strongly opposed to the change: "they keep coming back at us like the Mongolian hordes." Working from the various proposals that had been made on the issue, the leadership group came up with a hybrid compromise: if someone is caught with a small amount, forfeiture of the boat or other vehicle could occur only if the owner displayed "willful blindness"; on the other hand, if someone is caught with a large amount, the owner must show that he did everything reasonable to prevent the use of his boat or vehicle for the purpose of drug running.

A nongermane provision in the Senate bill, a far-reaching proposal on child pornography and obscenity, proved to be the single most difficult issue. Language allowing the federal government to seize property used to commit or promote the commission of an obscenity offense was so broad, opponents claimed, that innocent retailers might have their bookstores or video rental businesses seized because a federal prosecutor determined that a book or video in the store's inventory was "obscene" (Lawrence 1988b, 3032). Judiciary Committee negotiators believed they had reached an agreement to drop the obscenity language late October 19. However, when the Moral Majority, a Christian Right group, learned of the deal and began to put pressure on members, the agreement fell apart. Thus, this provision fell to the top leaders to resolve as well.

Florida representatives Bill McCollum and E. Clay Shaw Jr., Republican Judiciary Committee members deeply involved in the issue, stopped by the leadership meeting; although they had not been invited, their presence provided the leaders with an opportunity to pressure them. Foley began by saying he had heard disturbing rumors that Republicans planned to violate any agreement reached and to try to defeat the previous question on the rule; their aim, he believed, was to make obscenity a major political issue right before the election. McCollum explained that the provision was a hot political issue with church groups and Women For, a conservative women's group. He conceded that "some guys would like to defeat the previous question." Minority Leader Michel quickly spoke up, saying he knew nothing about such a plan.

The leaders, Democratic and Republican, argued at length that the obscenity language as written was badly flawed and probably unconstitutional. McCollum and Shaw, to a large extent, indicated they agreed with their substantive arguments but that "the political forces behind this are too strong for any of us to stop"; if the obscenity language were dropped from the bill there was nothing they could do to stop right-wing members from trying to defeat the previous question and, in fact, they would have to join in the attempt. After considerable pressure from the combined leaders—with Democrats letting Republicans take the lead—McCollum and Shaw did agree to rewrite the language to decrease the draconian effect of the forfeitures on people who do not produce but sell or show "obscene" materials. McCollum promised to work out the details of the language with his House and Senate Democratic counterparts.

By the next morning the obscenity provisions were still a problem; Judiciary Committee members were working on language but had not yet come to an agreement; the chair of House Judiciary still wanted to drop the provision entirely, a course of action House party leaders were convinced could not be sold to their members or sustained on the floor. Only days before the election few Democrats would be willing to cast a vote that an opponent could characterize as pro-obscenity. A usually reliable Democrat warned Foley on the floor that a deal on the obscenity provision had to be worked out; if it came to a vote, he would have to vote with the revolters. The innocent owner provision was causing problems again as well. Because he had been out of town, New Jersey Democrat Bill Hughes, chair of the House Judiciary subcommittee with jurisdiction, had not been a party to the most recent negotiations and objected strenuously to some aspects of the agreement reached by the leaders.

After spending much of the day working on other legislation, most importantly a tax bill, the Speaker, Foley, Majority Whip Coelho, Byrd, Michel, and Dole met for a final time at 5:30 p.m. on October 21. Foley, who had continued his task of monitoring, reported on the six or so problems that remained. Hughes was called in, and an agreement on the innocent owner provision was reached. A number of other issues were discussed, in several cases ones that had seemingly been resolved earlier. This time everyone knew there would be no tomorrow, and final decisions were made, sometimes after checking by phone with the administration or affected members.

The obscenity provision remained unresolved. Hughes and McCollum were called in and reported that they had agreed on "85 percent" but were at loggerheads on the remaining issues. Foley had a staff aide call Senator Rudman, hoping he could persuade McCollum to compromise. He was being besieged by the religious right, McCollum claimed, and could not give in any more than he already had. After a long discussion, Hughes suggested a compromise by which the stringent forfeiture provisions would apply only to those "engaged in the business" of selling pornography, thus exempting the inadvertent store owner. Under intense pressure from everyone in the room, with Rudman taking the

TABLE 9.1 Omnibus Drug Initiative Act of 1988: A Chronology

Date	House Action	Date	Senate Action	Date	Postpassage Action
April	*Speaker Wright decides Congress should pass drug bill; asks Majority Leader Foley to oversee process of putting together a bill.*				
5/2	*Democratic leaders meet with chairs of eleven committees to discuss what to include.*				
5/9	*Wright announces initiative at his press conference.*				
5/9–late June	*Committees work on legislative language; Foley rides herd.*	June	*Party working groups craft drug proposals.*		
Mid-June–August 11	*Foley works with committees to put bill together; works with Minority Leader Michel on rule for its consideration.*	July	*Majority Leader Byrd and Minority Leader Dole appoint a bipartisan working group to negotiate a bill.*		
		July–September	*Bipartisan working group negotiates.*		
8/10	Rules Committee grants rule for consideration of omnibus drug initiative.				
8/11	Foley introduces HR5210, the Omnibus Drug Initiative Act of 1988; House agrees to rule.				
9/7–9/8, 9/14–9/16	House considers HR5210.				
9/22	House passes HR5210.				

10/3   Senator Nunn, leading Democrat on the working group, introduces S2852, the core bill agreed on by the working group; S2852 is placed directly on the Senate's legislative calendar.

Unanimous consent agreement for considering S2852 is negotiated by the working group leaders and the party leadership.

10/12   Senate accepts unanimous consent agreement.

10/13   Senate considers S2852.

10/14   Senate considers and passes bill: it strikes all after the enacting clause of HR5210 and inserts in lieu thereof the text of S2852; then passes HR5210 as amended.

10/14–10/21   *House and Senate members and leaders negotiate informally and reach an agreement.*

10/21   House concurs in the Senate amendment (Senate bill) with an amendment (bill negotiated between the chambers). Senate agrees to House amendment to Senate amendment.

11/18   President signs Omnibus Drug Initiative Act of 1988 and it becomes law.

Note: Official actions are in roman type; behind-the-scenes, unofficial actions are in italics.

lead, McCollum agreed to take the compromise proposal to the members threatening to try to defeat the previous question and "see if I can sell it."

At 9:50 p.m. Hughes and McCollum found the Speaker in the House dining room having a quick dinner and reported they had a deal. Even then, getting McCollum's religious right colleagues to sign off on the exact wording took more time. The tax bill was finally ready for floor consideration at 10 p.m. Negotiations on that bill had been going on simultaneously with those on the drug bill and the party leaders, especially the Speaker and Dole, had to divide their time between the two. At 11 p.m. the Speaker, Foley, and Michel left the floor of the House and went to the Speaker's ceremonial office to place the traditional call to the president, informing him that Congress was about to adjourn. Although the leaders usually make the call after adjournment, they decided the president would really rather not be called in the middle of the night.

The tax bill was completed and the drug bill called up on the House floor about midnight. At 1:20 a.m. the House cleared the drug bill on a 346–11 vote. The House actually voted to agree to Foley's motion to concur in the Senate amendment to HR5210 with an amendment—this "amendment" being the product of the lengthy negotiations. At 3:15 a.m. the Senate concurred in the House amendment by voice vote, thus clearing the Omnibus Drug Initiative Act of 1988 for the president. Both chambers adjourned sine die immediately after their vote, thereby bringing the weary 100th Congress to an end. (See Table 9.1 for a chronology of House, Senate, and postpassage action.)

The 1988 omnibus drug bill was enacted through a "designer" process; abandoning the orthodox, leaders by plan and by improvisation devised a process to cope with the specific problems this piece of legislation presented. Little about this process—from the majority leader's supervisory role in the House, to the bypassing of committees and use of task forces to craft legislation in the Senate, to the informal multistage process culminating in the "Supreme Court" of top party leaders to resolve differences between the chambers—would have been familiar to members who served in the Congress of the 1970s or even the Congress of the early 1980s.

Unorthodox Lawmaking in the House and Senate: Lessons from Three Cases

The legislative process in the U.S. Congress is much more varied than it used to be; as the three cases in Chapters 7, 8, and 9 illustrate, the path from introduction to enactment (or legislative death) can differ radically from one bill to another.

The net impact of the new procedures and practices differs substantially for the House and the Senate, as these cases also suggest. In the House the procedures by and large are under the control of majority leaders who use them to further the legislative goals of their members by facilitating the passage of legislation. On balance, the majority party leadership in the House has gained considerable control over the legislative process and is often now able to tailor the process to the problems specific legislation raises.

In contrast, because of senators' willingness to push their prerogatives to the limit, passing legislation in the Senate requires that all interested senators be accommodated or supermajorities mustered. In trying to promote the passage of legislation his members need and want, the Senate majority leader often becomes a key negotiator. In working out postcommittee adjustments to legislation and in other negotiations, he does not, however, operate from a position of strength; unlike the House Speaker, the Senate majority leader has few tools for facilitating the passage of legislation. Because of his scheduling responsibilities and his central location in the chamber's information network, the Senate majority leader is often more likely than anyone else to be able to put together an agreement on highly contentious legislation. That does give him some leverage, but only with those senators who want legislation. On the 1988 drug bill the Senate party leaders in concert were able to exert extraordinary control over the process because most senators ardently desired legislation and none wanted to be responsible for killing the bill. On national service, the majority leader's leverage was much more limited. Furthermore, as the managed care case illustrates, the increased and increasingly sophisticated use of the Senate's permissive rules by the minority party has eroded the majority leader's already tenuous control over the Senate floor agenda.

chapter ten

The Budget Process as an Instrument for Policy Change: Clinton's Economic Program

Dᴜʀɪɴɢ ᴛʜᴇ 1992 ᴄᴀᴍᴘᴀɪɢɴ, candidate Bill Clinton advocated making major changes in the direction and priorities of the federal government. In 1993 the problem confronting President Clinton and the congressional Democratic leadership was how to get such comprehensive —and sometimes painful—policy change through Congress. The usual difficulties of enacting major policy change would be exacerbated, they knew, by the highly charged partisan atmosphere and the growing ideological gulf between the parties. Two years later the new Republican congressional majorities faced the same problem in even starker terms; in their Contract with America House Republicans were advocating considerably more far-reaching changes in policy direction, they confronted an opposition-party president, their margin was narrower, and the atmosphere had become even more intensely partisan.

In both cases, as this and the next chapter show, the procedural solution to the problem was the congressional budget process. Through the budget process many changes in policy can be made in one piece of legislation rather than in a number of separate bills, so fewer battles have to be won. By custom, budget measures are considered on the House floor under tight rules restricting the number of amendments that may be offered, thus further reducing the number of fights that must be waged.

I thank Edward Artinian and Chatham House Publishers, Inc., for permission to reprint in this chapter in considerably rewritten form parts of pages 102–109 from my essay "Trying to Govern Positively in a Negative Era: Clinton and the 103rd Congress," in *The Clinton Presidency: First Appraisals,* edited by Colin Campbell and Bert Rockman, published in 1996.

Senate rules prohibit extended debate on budget measures, a huge advantage to those endeavoring to enact legislation. The deadlines in the Congressional Budget and Impoundment Control Act of 1974 (hereafter the Budget Act) exert a pressure to action that can also work to the advantage of those attempting to pass a bill.

The congressional budget process is, however, a complex process even when it is not used to attempt to enact comprehensive policy change. Its deadlines can present problems as well as exerting salutary pressure for action. Successful completion of the budget process depends upon supervision and coordination by the congressional majority party leadership; when the process is used to make major policy change, leadership involvement must be continuous and intense. Adroit use of the full set of procedural strategies that the new legislative process makes available to leaders is necessary but, as the next chapter shows, still does not guarantee success.

Budget Policy Making and Politics: The Context in 1993

Because the economy was the 1992 campaign's dominant issue, the success of Bill Clinton and the Democratic Congress in enacting an effective economic program became a key test of whether the Democratic Party could govern.[1] Democrats had been out of the White House for twelve years, and Jimmy Carter, the last Democratic president, was remembered as ineffective. Could a Democratic president provide effective leadership, and would congressional Democrats, accustomed to going it alone, work cooperatively with the new president?

As a newly elected president who had run on the issue, Clinton set the economic policy agenda. The approach Clinton had outlined during the campaign was complex: it involved an immediate stimulus to jumpstart a sluggish economy, major long-term investment spending in areas such as education and infrastructure, and deficit reduction through tax increases on the wealthy and spending cuts in less essential programs. The news media, however, painted the election as primarily a public call for deficit reduction, in part because of Ross Perot's surprisingly strong showing in the 1992 presidential election. A sizable number of congressional Democrats, including many of the large freshman class, believed they would be judged in terms of how much they cut spending and reduced

---

1. At the beginning of the 103rd Congress, there were 258 Democrats, 176 Republicans, and 1 Independent in the House; the Senate consisted of 57 Democrats and 43 Republicans.

the deficit. In contrast, Democrats from core Democratic districts tended to emphasize the economic stimulus and investment spending.

On February 17, in his first address to a joint session of Congress, Clinton outlined an economic program containing the three basic elements: economic stimulus, investment spending, and deficit reduction. In response to the political climate and strong economic growth in the fourth quarter of 1992, the direct spending part of the stimulus program was reduced to $16.3 billion. The revenue component included tax increases for corporations, the wealthy, and upper-income Social Security recipients, and it contained a broad-based energy tax (the Btu tax).

Congressional Democrats, by and large, reacted favorably, though they knew passing the package would not be easy given its ambitiousness. Republicans immediately went on the attack, blasting the proposal for being tax heavy (Hager 1993, 355–359). Opposition to any new taxes has become a core tenet of Republican ideology, and many congressional Republicans believed George Bush's reneging on his "no new taxes" campaign pledge had cost him reelection to the presidency in 1992. Understandably, the public never wants to pay more taxes, and, in a period of pervasive distrust of government, no politician will damage his reelection prospects by opposing them.

The lack of incentives for Republicans to support Clinton's economic program made it clear from the beginning that Democrats would have to pass it on their own. Representative Armey, a Republican leader in the House, expressed his party's hard-line opposition: "They wanted to lead, now they've got to live with the accountability. Why should we give them cover?" (Fessler 1993, 380).

Although the stimulus package would be enacted as a supplemental appropriations bill, most of the rest of the program would be enacted through the budget process. That would require Congress to pass a budget resolution with instructions to the substantive committees to bring law in their areas of jurisdiction into conformity with the budget resolution and then enact a massive reconciliation bill incorporating all the necessary changes.

Committing to the Clinton Plan: Crafting and Passing the Budget Resolution

On March 10 the House Budget Committee approved a budget resolution that closely followed Clinton's plan. However, the Congressional Budget Office's estimate of how much deficit reduction the Clinton plan accomplished had showed a shortfall of about $66 billion from the administration's estimate and, to get the support of "deficit hawk" Democrats, Democratic Budget Committee leaders had had to add $63 billion in spending cuts to the resolution. With this change committee Democrats held firm and voted down every Republican amendment, frequently on straight party-line votes. The committee approved the resolution on a vote of 27 to 16 with every Democrat supporting it and every Republican opposed.

Two days later the Senate Budget Committee approved a similar resolution on a 12–9 party-line vote. Despite the Senate committee's much narrower partisan margin, Senate Democrats maintained sufficient unity to vote down every Republican attempt to alter the resolution.

The House Democratic leadership brought the budget resolution to the floor on March 17. Such early consideration was the result of a problem that developed with the stimulus package. Republicans' attacks made many Democrats nervous about voting for spending increases before they voted for spending cuts. To alleviate those members' concerns and ensure their votes, Clinton and the congressional leadership decided on a schedule change: action on the budget resolution would be accelerated, and it would be brought to the floor before the stimulus package.

On March 17 a rule for general debate on the budget resolution was approved. This rule, which provided for ten hours of general debate, allowed the House to begin consideration while the rule covering the amending process was still being worked out. The next day the second rule was brought to the floor and approved by a strictly party-line vote. That rule allowed votes only on four comprehensive substitutes; crucially, no narrow amendments aimed at particular unpopular provisions were allowed. The substitutes were not amendable and were to be voted on in the order specified using the king-of-the-hill procedure, under which the last one approved prevails. A substitute by Rep. John R. Kasich, R-Ohio, then ranking minority member on the Budget Committee, was placed first; it proposed deeper spending cuts and no tax increases. Another Republican substitute, offered by Gerald B. H. Solomon of New York, was placed second; the Solomon substitute added to the draconian spending cuts in the Kasich proposal some of the tax increases in the Democrats' plan to achieve much deeper deficit reduction. The Black Caucus substitute, placed third in order, was a liberal plan that increased taxes more and made greater cuts in defense spending in order to make fewer domestic spending cuts. Last, in the advantaged position, was the "substitute consisting of the text of the concurrent resolution as reported by the Budget Committee"—that is, the Democratic leadership's proposal.

The House voted down all three substitutes by wide margins; even the Kasich substitute garnered only 135 votes; about a quarter of Republicans voted against it. Only nineteen Republicans (and one Democrat) voted for the Solomon substitute, showing again the central place that opposition to all new taxes had come to occupy in Republican Party doctrine. The Black Caucus substitute attracted eighty-seven votes. The budget resolution was then approved by a vote of 243 to 183; no Republicans voted for it, only eleven Democrats voted in opposition.

In the Senate Democratic leaders had to pass the budget resolution without the help of a restrictive rule to protect their members from tough votes. To keep the plan intact, Democrats had to vote down a plethora of amendments, most offered by Republicans to cause Democrats maximum pain. Thus, Republicans forced votes on amendments to delete the tax increase on high-income Social Security recipients, to reduce or delete the new energy taxes, to exempt certain small businesses from the increase in corporate taxes, and to cut Congress's own operating funds by 25 percent. Democrats stuck together and voted down every substantive change Republicans attempted to make. To make it a little easier on their members, Democratic leaders offered a number of "sense of the Senate" resolutions, which allow senators to go on the record but have no binding effect. Senator Kennedy, for example, offered an amendment to express the sense of the Senate that the Btu tax should not apply to fuel used for home heating. On March 25, after six days of floor debate and forty-five roll calls, the Senate approved by a 54–45 vote a budget resolution very similar to the one that passed the House; no Republican supported the economic blueprint, and all but two Democrats voted for it. Because budget resolutions are considered under special Budget Act rules that limit debate, Republicans could stretch out the process and make Democrats take a series of tough votes, but they could not block action.

The differences between the House and Senate versions were not large, and the conference committee quickly came to an agreement. The House on March 31 and the Senate on April 1 approved the conference report. The votes were largely along party lines and almost identical to the initial passage votes. (See Table 10.1 for a chronology of action on the budget resolution and on the reconciliation bill that followed.)

Delivering on Promised
Policy Change: Reconciliation

Passing a budget resolution that reflected Clinton's priorities was an important first step; the crucial next step of enacting a reconciliation bill would, Democrats knew, be much harder. The budget resolution is a blueprint for future congressional decisions. It does not become law and does not actually make any changes in policy; the detail about policy that it, or the report accompanying it, may contain is just advice to committees. To enact into law policy changes meeting the budget resolution's deficit reduction targets, Congress must pass a reconciliation bill. In the Senate particularly, Democratic leaders had persuaded some of their members to vote for the resolution and against Republicans' attempts to change it by reminding them that the policy detail in the resolution was not binding. Once work on the reconciliation bill began, that argument could no longer be made. As Minority Leader Dole put it, "We start shooting with real bullets from here on" (*Congressional Quarterly Almanac* 1993, 106).

The political climate had also become more difficult for Democrats. Although the scheduling change had facilitated easy passage of the stimulus package in the House, a Republican filibuster in the Senate eventually killed it. Republicans had won the media battle, successfully portraying the stimulus bill as wasteful spending on pork barrel projects. The consequent lack of public demand for the bill allowed Republicans to kill it without great fear that they would pay an electoral price (Sinclair 1996).

Reconciliation in the House

The 1993 budget resolution contained instructions to thirteen House committees and twelve Senate committees to make changes in law under their jurisdiction so as to meet specific deficit reduction targets assigned to them. By Budget Act rules the committees are free to ignore any specific recommendations for policy change contained in the budget resolution or the report accompanying it, but they are bound to meet the total amount of savings assigned to them. For example, the tax-writing committees could ignore any budget resolution recommendations about what sorts of taxes to raise; they were required only to make changes in law sufficient to produce their deficit reduction figure. In its policy recommendations the 1993 budget resolution largely followed Clinton's economic program. Only if the resolution's recommendations were followed at least in broad outline could the end result of the process be considered a victory for the president and his supporters.

The Btu tax was shaping up as a particular problem. The administration favored it because it was a broad-based tax on all energy sources and thus seemed fair and because it would improve air quality by promoting more efficient use of energy. The tax's broad reach, however, proved to be a serious problem: a broad range of interests were roused to lobby against the tax. The big umbrella business organizations, such as the National Association of Manufacturers and the U.S. Chamber of Commerce, opposed it; many affected industries—for example, the oil industry,

TABLE 10.1   1993 Budget Process: A Chronology

		Budget Resolution			
Date	House Action	Date	Senate Action	Date	Postpassage Action
President Clinton outlines economic program in an address to a joint session of Congress on February 17, 1993.					
2/23–3/5	House Budget Committee holds hearings.				
3/10	House Budget Committee marks up the budget resolution, H.Con.Res. 64, and orders it reported.	3/12	Senate Budget Committee marks up the budget resolution, S.Con.Res. 18, and orders it reported.		
	House Democratic leadership negotiates postcommittee adjustments.				
3/16	Rules Committee grants rule for general debate only.				
3/17	House approves rule and completes general debate. Rules Committee grants second rule allowing votes on four substitutes.				
3/18	House approves rule, considers resolution for amendments, and passes resolution, 243–183.	3/25	Senate passes budget resolution, 54–45.	3/25	House and Senate name conferees.
				3/31	Conferees agree to file a conference report. House approves conference report, 240–184.
				4/1	Senate approves conference report, 55–45.
					Budget resolution, having been approved by both chambers, is now in effect.

			Reconciliation Bill		
Date	House Action	Date	Senate Action	Date	Postpassage Action
3/31– 5/13	House committees instructed by reconciliation instructions in budget resolution hold hearings and mark up their recommendations.				
5/6	Budget reconciliation recommendations are ordered reported by the Banking, Finance, and Urban Affairs Committee.				
5/11	Budget reconciliation recommendations are ordered reported by the Energy and Commerce Committee and the Veterans' Affairs Committee.				
5/12	Budget reconciliation recommendations are ordered reported by the Armed Services, Education and Labor, Merchant Marine and Fisheries, and Natural Resources committees.	6/9– 6/18	Senate committees instructed by reconciliation instructions in budget resolution consider and mark up their recommendations.		
5/13	Budget reconciliation recommendations are ordered reported by the Agriculture, Ways and Means, Post Office and Civil Service (with a provision approved by Foreign Affairs), and Public Works and Transportation committees.	6/9	Budget reconciliation recommendations are ordered reported by the Energy and Natural Resources, Banking, Housing and Urban Affairs, and Governmental Affairs committees.		
5/20	Budget Committee marks up reconciliation bill, HR2264, and orders it reported.	6/10	Budget reconciliation recommendations are ordered reported by the Armed Services, Veterans' Affairs, Judiciary, Foreign Relations, Environment and Public Works, and Labor and Human Resources committees.		

TABLE 10.1 (Continued)

			Reconciliation Bill		
Date	House Action	Date	Senate Action	Date	Postpassage Action
5/26	*Majority Leader negotiates postcommittee changes in bill to pick up support.*				
	Rules Committee grants rule with self-executing provision and allows only the Kasich substitute.	6/15	Budget reconciliation recommendations are ordered reported by the Commerce, Science and Transportation Committee.		
5/27	House adopts rule. House considers and passes reconciliation bill, 219–213.	6/18	Budget reconciliation recommendations are ordered reported by the Finance Committee.		
		6/22–	Budget Committee orders		
		6/24	reported the reconciliation bill, S1134. Senate begins consideration of bill.	6/24	Senate conferees are named.
				7/14	House conferees are named.
				7/15	Additional House conferees are named.
		6/25	Senate considers and passes bill, 50–49 (with the vice president voting 'yea').	8/3	Conferees agree to file conference report.
				8/5	House considers and approves conference report 218–216.
				8/6	Senate considers and approves conference report 51–50 (with the vice president voting 'yea').
				8/10	President Clinton signs HR2264, the Omnibus Budget Act of 1993, and it becomes law.

Note: Official actions are in roman type; behind-the-scenes, unofficial actions are in italics.

which was especially heavily taxed by the plan, and the aluminum industry, which is a heavy energy user—worked feverishly to get changes or kill
the Btu tax altogether.

The House Ways and Means Committee and the Senate Finance
Committee were responsible for by far the single biggest chunk of deficit
reduction; not only do these committees write tax legislation, but they also
have jurisdiction over Medicare, from which the Clinton plan proposed
extracting a significant amount of savings. Because the Constitution specifies that tax legislation must originate in the House, the Ways and Means
Committee began work first. Its chairman, Rep. Dan Rostenkowski, D-Ill.,
vowed to produce legislation close to Clinton's proposal. To put together
a coalition that could withstand Republicans' continuing attacks on the
Clinton plan, he met behind closed doors with committee Democrats,
working out agreements that brought them on board. Much of the negotiation concerned the Btu tax; members sought to protect their regions and
crucial industries in their districts. A number of exemptions were written
into the legislation. The chairman made it clear that Democrats who were
accommodated were then expected to support the bill actively. On May 6,
when committee markup began, Democrats immediately voted to work on
the bill in closed session; Rostenkowski knew that holding his coalition
together would be easier away from the press and the legion of interested
lobbyists. Democrats voted down every Republican amendment and, on
May 13, approved the legislation on a 24—14 party-line vote.

The legislation that Rostenkowski had put together and that the committee approved largely followed Clinton's blueprint. It raised income
taxes on the rich and on high-income Social Security recipients; it
included a Btu tax (though one with some exemptions); it increased the
earned-income tax credit for the working poor; and it extracted significant savings from Medicare. To lessen the opposition of business and thus
gain the votes of conservative Democrats, Rostenkowski significantly cut
the increase in the corporate tax rate that Clinton had proposed.

All thirteen House committees met their May 14 deadline for reporting and met the deficit reduction targets assigned to them; although a
multitude of smaller compromises were made to get the necessary majorities, the major features of Clinton's economic program were preserved.
The Budget Committee packaged the provisions from all the committees
into one bill and ordered it reported on May 20.

Clinton and the Democratic leadership faced a formidable task in
passing the bill. Ambitious deficit reduction targets had been met, which
meant that inevitably many committees had made unpopular decisions.
Not only would Democrats have to pass the legislation without any help
from Republicans, they would have to contend with the Republicans' loud

and repeated charge that the program consisted mostly of taxes on the middle class.

The job of passing the bill in the House became immeasurably harder when, on May 20, Sen. David Boren, D-Okla., an ally of his home state's gas and oil interests, and three colleagues (two moderate Republicans and another conservative oil-state Democrat) proposed an alternative reconciliation package that eliminated the Btu tax and imposed a cap on entitlement spending. A few days later Boren formally announced that he would vote against the Btu tax in the Senate Finance Committee, which would have to approve the tax law changes. Since the party ratio on the committee was only eleven Democrats to nine Republicans, his opposition made the survival of the Btu tax, and even of the broader package, appear doubtful. House Democrats were leery of voting for the unpopular Btu tax only to see it die in the Senate. "We don't want to be in a position of walking the plank and then have them go over and make a compromise in the Senate," Rep. Charles Wilson, D-Texas, explained (Hager and Cloud 1993a, 1278). Boren's high-profile opposition also gave impetus to a push by conservative House Democrats for a cap on entitlement spending, which was in Boren's plan as well.

A deal on the entitlement cap, intimations of changes in the Btu tax in the Senate, adept procedural strategy, and an intense lobbying campaign by the House Democratic leadership and the administration produced a close win on the House floor.

Majority Leader Richard A. Gephardt of Missouri brokered a compromise on entitlements that satisfied conservatives without alienating liberals. Throughout the budget process two deficit hawk Democrats—Charles W. Stenholm of Texas and Timothy J. Penny of Minnesota—had advocated placing a tight cap on entitlement spending; they wanted a mechanism by which, if such spending exceeded the cap, cuts would automatically occur. This was a proposal that neither the White House nor Democratic leaders liked. Stenholm had been pressuring the Speaker to allow him to offer such an amendment on the floor, threatening to lead a revolt by conservative Democrats against the rule if his amendment were barred. When shortly before floor action was planned, Democrats still lacked enough votes to pass the rule, the Speaker instructed the majority leader to try to work out a deal. Less than twenty-four hours before the floor vote, an agreement was reached: rather than automatic cuts if the entitlement cap were exceeded, either the president would have to propose a way of paying for the overspending or he would have to raise the cap. Congress would have to vote on whatever the president proposed.

The administration got some energy-state Democrats back on board by acknowledging what was becoming inevitable: the Btu tax would be altered in the Senate.

The House leadership brought the bill to the floor under a rule that allowed only a vote on a comprehensive Republican substitute; amendments to delete various unpopular elements of the package—the Btu tax and the tax on Social Security payments to high-income recipients—were barred. The rule also prohibited the minority from offering a motion to recommit with instructions, which is another way of amending the bill. The rule thus gave Republicans an opportunity to offer a comprehensive alternative to the Democratic plan, and it gave the whole House a choice between two distinct approaches. The rule, however, made it impossible for Republicans to use the amendment process to unravel the Democratic package by narrowly targeting the least palatable provisions, and it also protected Democrats from having to cast some excruciatingly difficult votes. A vote for a deficit reduction package would be easier for Democrats to explain to their constituents than a stand-alone vote for higher taxes.

In addition to these provisions, the rule contained what is called a "self-executing" provision by which adoption of the rule simultaneously results in adoption of certain legislative language. In this case the deal on the entitlement cap, as well as some other language about enforcement of the budget agreement that was worked out after the bill was reported from committee, was thereby incorporated into the bill without requiring a separate vote.

Democratic Whip Bonior personally headed the whip task force set up to pass the bill. Starting work several weeks before the bill got to the floor, members of the task force, and later the top leaders, unrelentingly pursued every House Democrat. Anyone who might have influence with an undecided or recalcitrant member—state party chairmen, governors, union officials, personal friends—was enlisted to help in the persuasion effort. The administration was very much engaged in the drive to build support for the bill. Cabinet secretaries called and visited Democrats; Secretary of the Treasury Lloyd Bentsen, for example, attended the Texas delegation's regular lunch meeting to sell the bill. Two days before the vote, President Clinton invited about seventy-five House members to the White House; he personally called close to sixty members—some of them repeatedly.

Given the level of effort, no Democrat could fail to understand that how he voted on the bill would affect his future in the House. As Rep. Barney Frank, D-Mass., said, "Nobody got a pass on this" (Hager and Cloud 1993b, 1341). At a Democratic caucus meeting the day before the vote, some members made clear that this was a litmus-test vote, that future decisions on committee and subcommittee chairmanships would be influenced by how members voted. Just before the vote, freshmen circulated a petition demanding that any committee or subcommittee chair who voted against the party be stripped of his or her position by the caucus. Within hours, more than eighty Democrats, including several influential committee chairmen, had signed (Hager and Cloud 1993b, 1345).

The rule was adopted by a vote of 236 to 194, with all but nineteen Democrats and no Republicans supporting it. Republicans were much less united on their substitute; as with the budget resolution, many Republicans believed attacking the Democratic plan without giving Democrats anything on which to attack them was the politically smarter course. The Kasich substitute received only 138 votes; forty Republicans opposed it.

Because of the character of the rule, the key vote would be on passage. The Speaker himself closed floor debate for his party, acknowledging that this was indeed a tough vote: "We seldom do important, valuable and lasting things by taking easy votes, comfortable votes, politically popular votes." He challenged members, saying, "This is a time to stand and deliver; this is a time to justify your election" (Hager and Cloud 1993b, 1341). On May 27 the House passed the legislation, 219–213; again, not a single Republican voted in support; thirty-eight Democrats opposed their party's position.

Reconciliation in the Senate

Although twelve Senate committees were under instructions to report reconciliation provisions, the Finance Committee had by far the most formidable task; the fate of Clinton's economic program depended largely on Finance Committee action. Boren's opposition to the Btu tax and the committee's narrow partisan margin meant that significant changes would have to be made. Some strategists suggested that the Democratic leadership bypass the Finance Committee altogether and bring the tax and other provisions within its jurisdiction to the floor directly. Majority Leader Mitchell decided not to do so, evidently convinced that such a course would only make a hard job harder.

Committee chair Moynihan and Mitchell, who was a member of Finance, took on the task of putting together a package that could pass the committee and the chamber. Given the hardening of the Republicans' antitax position, they knew they had to form their majority from Democrats only. It took "two weeks of grinding negotiations" to craft a compromise package (Cloud, Hager, and Rubin 1993, 1542). As had been expected from the beginning of the negotiations, the Btu tax was jettisoned; that, however, produced a huge revenue shortfall. Eventually, a gas tax, sharper cuts in Medicare, and a host of minor changes were agreed to. Republicans offered a multitude of amendments during markup, but once the deal was struck, Democrats held together and defeated them all.

On June 18 the Finance Committee reported its crucial part of the reconciliation bill on a straight party-line vote of 11 to 9. The other committees had already complied with their instructions and reported their provisions. On June 22 the Budget Committee ordered the reconciliation bill reported.

On June 23 Tennessee Democrat James Sasser, chairman of the Senate Budget Committee, began floor debate on the reconciliation bill by reminding his colleagues what was at stake and thanking the committees for doing their job:

> Mr. President, the Senate today begins consideration of the budget reconciliation bill. The reconciliation bill is really the centerpiece of the President's economic proposal and economic plan. What this reconciliation bill includes is all of the spending cuts that have come from all of the committees stretched across the Senate . . . along with enhanced revenues also coming from the Committee on Finance. All across the Senate the committees and the committee chairmen have done their duties.
>
> I want to express my appreciation to 12 of the Senate committee chairmen for their stalwart work in producing this record reconciliation bill. . . . This was not an easy task. Deficit reduction never is. . . . Everyone is for reducing the deficit in the general sense. But when you get down to the specifics, no one seems to want to do the specifics that are required to actually reduce the deficit. . . . So, deficit reduction is something everybody likes to talk about but no one really wants to do much about it. I think literally hundreds of Academy Awards would be in order for some of the posturing and play acting that I have witnessed over the past few years. . . .
>
> So, the President of the United States and the committees of the U.S. Senate looked the deficit squarely in the eye and they made some very difficult, some very tough, and some very painful choices in developing this reconciliation bill. The fruits of their labor are before us today. We have produced $347 billion in savings over the next 5 years. And a landmark $516 billion . . . in deficit reduction in this total bill when we are through with it. (*Congressional Record,* June 23, 1993, S7662)

Republicans responded by calling the bill "the largest tax increase in history" and charging that it was a "job killer." As Senator Gramm expressed it:

> I oppose this bill because you cannot create more investment by taxing investors. You cannot create more savings by taxing savers. You cannot create more jobs by taxing job creators. Hundreds of thousands of Americans will lose their job because of this bill. Bill Clinton will be one of those Americans, but he will deserve to lose his job. (S7672)

Democrats argued that, while the bill did raise taxes, most of the new taxes would be paid by the very well off. Yes, it was a tough bill, but a fair and responsible one; it really cut the deficit and did so in a way that spread the pain according to citizens' capacity to pay.

Many acknowledged that they did not like numerous provisions in the bill: "Supporting this bill is a hard choice," admitted Sen. John Glenn, D-Ohio, explaining his vote in favor of the legislation. "I do not like every page, every provision, every punctuation point" (S7940). As Sen. Howell Heflin, D-Ala., noted:

> There is one thing that is far worse than even the most distasteful provision in this bill. And that is inaction. . . . It is time to act. And it is high time for honesty here in this town. It is time to come clean about what needs to be done. It is no fun voting for taxes. It is much easier to oppose them.
>
> And it is not easy to vote for spending cuts that will hit the elderly, that will hit retirees, that will hit farmers, that will hit Federal workers. It is much easier to oppose these cuts. But I am not here to take the easy way out.
>
> I am here to make the hard choices. To do what is right for my State and for the Nation. And, Mr. President, that is why I am going to vote for this bill. (*Congressional Record,* June 23, 1993, S7944)

The debate was heated and sometimes nasty. The moderate and not usually highly partisan Sen. David Durenberger, R-Minn., said:

> I rise today in opposition to this reconciliation package. I do so because it represents a breach of faith with the American people—the voters who last November took a chance for change. . . . [I]t is a budget buster and a job killer. (S7679)

To get the bill out of Finance, Mitchell and Moynihan had deleted provisions intended to provide incentives for investment that small business highly prized. This made a number of moderate Democrats unhappy. As Joseph I. Lieberman of Connecticut, one of these senators, explained, "[Some of] us . . . felt that the bill, as reported out of the Finance Committee, was a good deficit-reduction package, but if it was only that and if it is only that, we have not done our job. We must also do something to stimulate the economy" (*Congressional Record,* June 23, 1993, S7697). When scoring of the Finance Committee bill by the Congressional Budget Office indicated the bill actually exceeded the deficit reduction target by a few billion dollars, Majority Leader Mitchell decided to use that money to ensure those senators' votes. Along with Dale Bumpers, D-Ark., chair of the Senate Small Business Committee, he crafted an amendment that provided a capital gains tax cut targeted at small business, and he increased the amount small business could write off for new equipment.

The Mitchell amendment was the first amendment offered. Support fell primarily along party lines. A few Democrats opposed it as ineffective; most Republicans simply did not want to make the reconciliation bill easier to pass. Budget Act rules impose a strict germaneness requirement on amendments, a test the amendment did not meet. If any senator made a point of order, budget rules would have to be waived to allow consideration of the amendment, and that requires sixty votes. After debate on the amendment, Republicans did raise the point of order; the motion to waive budget rules failed on a 54-44 vote, so despite a majority in support, the amendment was ruled out of order.

Mitchell made another attempt the next day with a revised amendment. This one raised to $20,500 the amount small businesses could deduct for equipment and machinery. This amendment was germane. Since it was clear it would pass, few senators saw any benefit in voting against it; the vote was 93-5.

Budget Act rules protected the bill against a filibuster and made successfully amending it more difficult than with other legislation. Republicans, however, were free to offer all sorts of amendments that would put Democrats in a difficult political position. And that they did. Republicans forced Democrats to vote on all the tough provisions by offering amendments to strike them. Some of the votes were agonizingly close—the amendment to strike the gas tax increase failed by only two votes—but Democrats held together and defeated every significant change.

In the wee hours of June 25, after two long and intense days of floor consideration, the time for the vote came. The majority and minority leaders closed debate. "Mr. President," Senator Mitchell began,

> in every human endeavor, there comes a time for action, a time when the words must end and the deeds begin. For those who have so loudly endorsed making real spending cuts and making real deficit reductions, that time is now. (*Congressional Record,* June 25, 1993, S7986)

Senator Dole responded:

> The choice tonight could not be more clear. Senators can vote for President Clinton's record-breaking tax increase or they can cast a vote for America's taxpayers and send a wake-up call to the White House and to the Congress. The President has tried to make this a defining moment of his Presidency. He is right. It is and will be for years to come. He has already earned his place on Mount Taxmore. (S7986)

Senator Mitchell closed:

> For 12 years we have laughed as the national debt has gone up. We have had jokes, not deeds. We have had talk, not action. It is now time for action.

> This Chamber has been filled to overflowing with speeches about the need
> to reduce the deficit and there is only one way to reduce the deficit and that
> is to vote for this package. There is no other alternative. No other serious or
> credible alternative has been presented in either Chamber. If you mean to
> reduce the deficit you must vote for this package.
>
> Mr. President, I ask for the yeas and nays. (S7986)

At about 3 a.m., the Senate passed the bill on a 50-49 vote, with Vice
President Al Gore, as president of the Senate, casting the deciding vote.
Every Republican and six Democrats opposed passage.

Resolving House-Senate Differences

Changes made to pass the bill in the Senate and the narrowness of the
vote to pass the bill in the Senate and House guaranteed that reaching a
conference agreement on a version passable in both houses would be a delicate and difficult task. House liberals—especially members of the Black
Caucus—were dismayed with the cuts in benefits for the poor and for cities
made to compensate for the revenue lost when the Btu tax was replaced by
a gas tax. Many deficit hawk Democrats in the Senate had voted for the
package without enthusiasm, believing it did not do enough; they might
well defect if significant changes were made. A number of western Democrats refused to support a gas tax higher than the 4.3 cents in the Senate
bill.

Because so many committees had played a role in drafting the bill,
the conference committee was huge: 164 House members from sixteen
committees and 53 senators from thirteen committees. The House delegation was formally composed of twenty-seven subgroups, each with specifically delineated jurisdiction; although the Senate designated no formal
subgroups, it was understood that Senate conferees would also work on
the provisions from their own committees. Most of the work of crafting a
compromise proceeded in subconferences made up of members from the
committee that had drafted the legislation and of Budget Committee
members; Budget Committee leaders, including House Majority Leader
Gephardt, the majority party representative on Budget, took part in all of
the subconferences.

The most crucial decisions fell within the jurisdiction of the taxing
committees. As other subconferences worked out their differences outside
the media's glare, Chairmen Rostenkowski and Moynihan, under intense
pressure and scrutiny, began their negotiations. Democratic party leaders
and representatives of the Clinton administration also participated.
Although the conflicting priorities of the various groups of Democrats
who had voted for the bill often made it seem impossible, a compromise
package was worked out.

Out of the media's spotlight, Democratic staff worked to protect the bill from Byrd rule attacks. Before the bill had passed the Senate, Pete Domenici, ranking minority member on the Budget Committee, had put Democrats on notice. If and when the bill returned from conference, he would invoke the Byrd rule to try to knock many provisions out of the bill as "extraneous matter." Any senator can make a point of order that a provision violates the Byrd rule; if the parliamentarian agrees, sixty votes are required to waive the rule and save the provision. With solid Republican opposition, Democrats knew they could not muster the sixty votes. Therefore, as the conference proceeded, they tried to persuade the parliamentarian that their provisions did not violate the rule, or they tried to work out language that would pass the test. In many cases Democrats were forced to remove provisions; the review mechanism for entitlement spending that had been instrumental in getting deficit hawk Democrats to support the bill in the House fell victim to the Byrd rule.

Already tense relations between House and Senate Democrats were made even worse by the dictates of the Byrd rule. Senate Democrats' individualism, the willingness of many to pursue their own interests and agendas at the expense of those of their party, and Senate rules that encouraged such behavior had infuriated House Democrats all year; they did the responsible thing and took the hard votes and then someone like Senator Boren negated their efforts for narrow selfish gain, they believed. Now, with the Byrd rule, Senate rules were forcing decisions on the House and making House Democrats jettison policy changes dear to their hearts. The animosity of House Democrats toward the other body would make the difficult task of passing the conference report even harder, as a House Democrat's complaints about "the insidious influence of the so-called Byrd rule on the conference agreement" made clear:

> In our small section of the conference agreement the Byrd rule was invoked twice and several important provisions were arbitrarily removed from the agreement text of the bill. This occurred after agreements were reached on the basis of many hours of long and intricate negotiations. The House should never enter into negotiations with the other body with our hands tied behind our backs as has happened in this process. We can't let the nameless, the faceless Members of the Senate, treated as a star chamber, dictate at their whim what is extraneous and what is not in the reconciliation process. Mr. Speaker, if this Parliamentary procedure persists it will debilitate the ability of the Congress to do its job. I would suggest our problem is that we are too often barred by archaic rules and procedures of the Senate already, without new impediments being put in place in 1993. (*Congressional Record*, Aug. 5, 1993, H6251)

The End Game: Passing the Conference Report

With a conference agreement in hand, the task of selling it, already under way, intensified. Methodically and relentlessly, the House leadership pursued every Democrat. "There was whip meeting after whip meeting," a participant explained. "Members were getting really sick of being beat on, they would run when we came. But we kept after them." Clinton met personally with almost every organized group of Democrats. His meetings with House groups ranged from the Black Caucus to the Conservative Democratic Forum. He also met with women, freshmen, and even gym users. Many senators and some House members were courted individually as well (Cloud and Hager 1993, 2023–2028; Hook 1993, 2025–2026).

The president and the Democratic leadership argued that the reconciliation bill should be approved because it was good public policy and because Democrats needed to show they could govern. When essential to pick up needed votes, they made deals. Liberals had been mollified by the conference restoring a significant part of the social spending the Senate had cut. On August 4 Clinton by executive order set up an entitlement review process similar to that deleted from the bill because of Byrd rule problems. A last-minute agreement to allow a vote on further spending cuts in the fall satisfied some deficit hawks.

When the mercurial Boren announced he would switch and vote against the conference report, a replacement "yes" vote had to be found. "After four days of feverish wooing" by the administration and Senate leaders, Dennis DeConcini, D-Ariz., agreed to switch his vote; in return he received several policy concessions, including a lessening of the tax bite on Social Security recipients (Hager and Cloud 1993c, 2122–2129). With every vote essential in the Senate, some erstwhile supporters took advantage of their bargaining position to extract benefits for their constituents; freshman senator Russell D. Feingold, D-Wis., cut a deal on regulation of bovine growth hormone. A tête-à-tête at the White House and a promise of a commission on entitlements finally induced Sen. Bob Kerrey, D-Neb., to declare his support after he had very publicly criticized the package and indicated he might defect.

On August 5 the House began consideration of the reconciliation bill conference report under a rule that allowed six hours of debate. Through a self-executing provision, the rule made the entitlement review process a part of standing House rules; this was done to mollify deficit hawk Democrats.

The debate was highly charged, even for the partisan House. "We oppose this plan because it's a giant tax on the American dream and on America's future," staunch Republican Dick Armey said. "This plan is . . .

a recipe for disaster. Democrats may give your President a political victory today, but it's a defeat for our economy and the well-being of the American people." A California Republican charged that "the Clinton tax bill will drive a stake into the heart of California's economy," and another Republican called it "a ship of fools" and urged the House to "sink it." Georgia Republican Newt Gingrich, then the minority whip, predicted the plan would cause "a job-killing recession" (*Congressional Record,* Aug. 5, 1993, H6267–H6269).

Democrats defended the plan and accused Republicans of being unwilling to make the hard choices. "Let me tell you what a 'no' vote on this budget means," said a freshman Democrat bluntly: "no action; no growth; no hope; no guts" (*Congressional Record,* Aug. 5, 1993, H6229). Some also charged that their opponents had waged a war of misrepresentation about the bill. Majority Whip Bonior summed up the arguments Democrats were using:

> [W]e are approaching the closing moments of a long and wrenching national debate. This vote is about just one thing—do we have the courage to stand up and take control of our economic future and to get our Nation's house in order? . . . I know this isn't an easy decision. We in public life are often asked to do difficult things. And this is one of those difficult times. There's no easy way to make record reductions. . . . The last two Presidents have just passed the buck, passed the buck to the next generation. . . .
>
> This is the first plan in 12 years that uses real numbers to achieve real results. It's a fair plan, it's responsible, and it deserves a chance to work. We know the bold details of this plan: A record $496 billion deficit cut that will create jobs; over 200 specific spending cuts; 80 percent of the new taxes paid by the wealthiest 1 percent; and 90 percent of small businesses eligible for tax reduction, to name a few.
>
> But we have to remember that there are faces behind these numbers and stories behind these statistics. Real lives of real people.
>
> Deficit reduction will create jobs that will move autoworkers from the unemployment lines to the assembly lines. Low interest rates will put an extra $175 a month in the pockets of working families able to refinance their homes. The earned income tax credit will give millions of working parents dignity and respect. And small businesses will use tax credits to buy new plants and equipment that will make them more competitive.
>
> That's what this plan will do. That's what it will do for America. That's what it will do for working people. . . .
>
> Let's tell it like it is: [The Republicans] don't have an alternative. . . . And now the choice has come down to our plan or no plan. The American people want change, they voted for change, and it's time we get on with that change. That is what we were sent here to do. . . .
>
> When America's economy is standing tall again, historians will look back to this day and this vote, and say, "That is where it started. That is where it turned around. That is where America's renewal began."

So say "no" to gridlock. Say "no" to the status quo. Don't pass the buck—pass the plan. (*Congressional Record*, Aug. 5, 1993, H6254)

The Republicans' responses to Bonior's passionate remarks showed just how far apart the parties were in their beliefs about what constituted good economic policy. Closing debate for the Republicans, Minority Leader Bob Michel said:

The differences here are philosophical, they are real, profound, differences over fundamentals that transcend partisanship.

We will concede, with all the pressure brought to bear by the present leadership on the Democratic side, that you will probably have your way for this day, but we will be back another day to remind you of your folly. . . . [T]his package will not create any new jobs . . . because you are taxing away the incentives of the small entrepreneurs who create three-fourths of all the new jobs that are created in this country. You have been so obsessed with this $500 billion figure that you have lost your marbles attempting to achieve it.

Mr. Speaker, I strongly urge a vote against this harmful, ill-conceived conference report that taxes today or taxes yesterday, taxes today and, yes, taxes tomorrow. (*Congressional Record*, Aug. 5, 1993, H6270)

Majority Leader Dick Gephardt, speaking shortly before the vote, talked about the hard work and hard choices putting the package together had entailed:

I have been heartened by seeing all of the parts, all of the beliefs in our Democratic Party come together to work on this plan. I have seen liberal members of our party and moderate members and conservative members give and take, compromise, sacrifice, be willing to take positions that they did not know or think they could take, but took them because they knew the common good of the country was at stake.

And each who has voted for this plan in committee or on the floor has done it knowing that there is no way in the world that we can attack this great deficit without making tough, hard choices that no one really wants to take.

And I am proud of the members of my party who have come together, taken the choices, made the decisions, and risen to the occasion.

He implicitly acknowledged that the leadership was still uncertain it had the votes to pass the bill when he alluded to the undecided:

To Members here tonight who are still undecided, let me say this is a challenge, this deficit; this plan is a challenge to our generation that we must meet. . . .

Ladies and gentlemen of the House, . . . surely tonight we can take the responsibility ourselves to see that the country we hand to the next generation is not as good but is better than the country that was handed to us. (*Congressional Record*, Aug. 5, 1993, H6270)

Speaker Tom Foley closed debate:

> This is not an easy bill. We have all noted that. . . . The Republican Party will march in lockstep, so we on this side of the aisle must bear the burden of responsibility. We are ready to do it. We are anxious to do it, and we will do it.
>
> The Bible says that there is a time for everything. Tonight is the time to decide. Tonight is the time for courage. Tonight is the time to put away the old easy ways. Tonight is the time for responsibility. Tonight is the night to vote.
>
> Let us not break faith with our people. Let us pass this plan. Let us move forward to a better day for our country. (*Congressional Record,* Aug. 5, 1993, H6271)

At the end of an exhausting day of feverish, one-on-one lobbying and combative floor rhetoric, the House passed the conference report by a vote of 218 to 216; only a vote switch by Rep. Marjorie Margolies-Mezvinsky, D-Pa., saved the package. When working to put together a majority on a high-profile, contentious bill, congressional party leaders often accumulate "pocket" or "if you need me" votes; these are promises of votes from members who would rather not support the legislation, usually for reelection-related reasons, but who do not want to be responsible for its demise. Margolies-Mezvinsky, a freshman from a Republican district, had promised her constituents she would vote against any tax increase and had opposed the reconciliation bill initially; she was not willing, however, to grievously wound the Clinton presidency, so she switched her vote.[2]

The next day, August 6, the Senate passed the conference report—also by a hair. The vote was 51 to 50, with Vice President Gore casting the deciding ballot, as he had on passage of the reconciliation bill. No Republican in either chamber voted for the legislation. Speaker Foley had been right. The Republicans had marched in lockstep, but the Democrats had held together enough to prevail.

Unified Government, Procedural Control, and Policy Success

Passing the economic program represented a major legislative victory for President Clinton and congressional Democrats. Although many alterations and compromises were made during the long, complex process,

---

2. Representative Margolies-Mezvinsky was defeated in 1994. Given how badly Democrats did in that election, it is unlikely that voting differently on the conference report would have saved her.

the final product followed the outlines of the plan Clinton had laid out in February 1993 and, within the severe constraints imposed by the deficit, reoriented economic policy in a direction Democrats favored. The most significant deviation from the initial proposal and the biggest compromise necessary for passage was substituting a modest gas tax hike for the more ambitious Btu tax.

Democrats accomplished this legislative success by working together across the institutional divide. Throughout the process, Clinton maintained an enormous amount of personal contact with congressional Democrats. The president gave congressional Democrats opportunities to influence the substance of his package and immersed himself in the process of getting it enacted. In early February he invited every member of the House to the White House to consult with him in small groups on the components of the economic plan; he made numerous appearances at Democratic Caucus meetings on the Hill to buck up Democrats; he conducted innumerable one-on-one conversations. A willing participant in the whipping effort, the president learned over time how to nail down a commitment. Early on, congressional participants report, Clinton was too willing to accept excuses from members. The administration also quickly learned to deploy the cabinet and other high-ranking officials to good effect; the ties many of them had to members of Congress served them well in persuasion efforts. "White House budget director Leon E. Panetta, a former House member, and Treasury Secretary Lloyd Bentsen, a former senator, spent so much time on Capitol Hill the week of July 26 that it was easy to forget they ever left the Congress," Congressional Quarterly reported (Hook 1993, 2024). Throughout the process, the Democratic congressional leadership worked closely and loyally with the administration.

As important as cooperation between the president and the congressional majority was to success, the president's program would never have passed were it not for the special procedures the leadership had available and used to maximum effect. In both chambers the leaders worked out postcommittee adjustments to the legislation in order to build majority coalitions. In the House restrictive special rules were crucial to keeping the supportive coalition together. Most important, of course, was the budget process and the packaging it makes possible. Despite voters' professed desire for deficit reduction in the abstract, a real deficit-cutting package will unavoidably contain some unpalatable provisions, and it is unlikely to be popular. Had it been procedurally necessary to bring up those elements as separate bills, few of the provisions would have survived. Packaging allows popular and less popular elements to be combined and reduces the number of fights that need to be won. It also raises the stakes so high that members are faced with repudiating and severely weakening their leaders if they desert them; that makes it high risk for leaders but also gives them leverage. Budget rules give the budget resolution and the reconciliation bill protection against a filibuster and amendments in the Senate that is enormously advantageous.

The budget process makes comprehensive policy change possible; it makes it a bit less difficult for the Congress to make hard choices and unpopular decisions. However, as shown by the saga of Clinton's economic program in 1993 and even more by the Republicans' attempt in 1995 to enact nonincremental policy change, it certainly does not make either comprehensive policy change or hard choices easy.

Success also requires favorable political circumstances. Without a Democratic Congress, President Clinton's economic program would have had no chance at all. With stronger public support, the compromises necessary to pass it would have been less extensive.

c h a p t e r   e l e v e n

Republican Majorities, Divided Government, and Budget Politics

DURING THE 1994 ELECTIONS Republicans promised that, were the voters to make them the congressional majority, they would balance the budget in seven years and enact a host of specific major policy changes. Using all their considerable political resources and all the procedural tools at their command, they tried but failed. Two years later, in different circumstances, congressional Republicans and President Clinton came to an agreement to balance the budget. Yet, despite a strong economy, budget surpluses, and the budget agreement, the last years of the Clinton administration saw continuing intense conflict over budgetary issues. Congress had to resort to extraordinary procedures just to get done the essential legislative work of passing the spending bills.

An examination of budget policy making and politics during the second half of the 1990s, when Republicans controlled Congress and Democrats held the White House, illustrates how political conditions and structural features of the American system of government interact to affect the opportunities for and the barriers to lawmaking. The course of the legislation surveyed in this chapter further shows how many of the procedures and practices of unorthodox lawmaking can contribute to legislative success, but it also makes clear that they are only tools and cannot be expected to engineer legislative success when critical political conditions are adverse.

The Republican Revolution and the Budget Process, 1995–1996

In early January 1995, the new Republican majorities in the House and Senate confronted a monumental task in delivering on their promises. House Republicans had formalized a number of their promises in their Contract with America, which they had pledged to bring to a vote within the first 100 days of the Congress. Balancing the budget (without touching Social Security or reducing defense spending, as they had also promised) would require restructuring and making big reductions in large, complex federal programs such as Medicare, Medicaid, and farm programs. House Republicans had included a big tax cut in the Contract; fulfilling that promise would, of course, make balancing the budget that much harder. The Contract committed House Republicans to revamping federal welfare programs, especially Aid to Families with Dependent Children (AFDC), and Senate Republicans too were dedicated to that task. Thus Republicans faced making a host of highly significant and extraordinarily complex policy decisions—many of which would inflict pain on constituents and thus be extremely controversial—in a limited period of time. House Republicans believed they had to bring all the Contract items to the floor within the promised 100 days, but even the full two years of a Congress is not much time to thoroughly overhaul large numbers of programs developed over decades.

Furthermore, Republicans faced enacting such far-reaching policy change with narrow margins of control in both chambers and a hostile president in the White House. The radical character of the Republicans' agenda assured that the battle over its enactment would be hard fought and that opponents would attempt to stop passage using all available tools. Certainly opponents would appeal to the court of public opinion and attempt to make voting for the components of the program prohibitively expensive in reelection terms for many Republicans. Given the ideological gulf between President Clinton and congressional Republicans, the president, with his veto and his bully pulpit, would be a chief opponent.

The budget process provided the primary procedural tool through which Republicans would attempt to enact their agenda. Without it, the "Republican revolution" of a balanced budget in seven years would have had no chance whatsoever; the Republican congressional leaders knew that getting a large number of major and often painful changes through both chambers and past the president as separate bills was a hopeless task. The budget process allowed the packaging of many policy changes into one piece of legislation; it provided protection against the Senate filibuster; and, combined with an adept strategy, it might make it possible to force Clinton to sign the legislation. (See Table 11.1 for a chronology of the budget process.)

TABLE 11.1 1995 Budget Process: A Chronology

House Action	Senate Action	Appropriations and Debt Limit Legislation
	Budget Resolution and Reconciliation	
	1/26, 2/1 Budget Committee holds hearings.	
3/21, 3/22, 3/30, 4/4 Budget Committee holds hearings.		
5/10, 5/11 Budget Committee considers, marks up, and approves budget resolution.	5/8, 5/9, 5/10 Budget Committee considers and marks up budget resolution.	
5/16 Rules Committee grants modified closed rule allowing votes on four substitutes and suspending the automatic adoption of an increase in the debt limit.	5/11 Budget Committee completes markup and approves budget resolution.	
5/17 House adopts rule.		
5/18 House considers and adopts budget resolution, H.Con.Res. 67, by a 238–193 vote.	5/18, 5/19, 5/22, 5/23, 5/24 Senate considers budget resolution.	
6/8 House conferees named.	5/25 Senate completes consideration and approves budget resolution, S.Con.Res. 13, by a 57–42 vote.	
	6/7 Senate conferees named.	
6/8 Conference begins.		
Gingrich and Dole negotiate an agreement on taxes.		
6/22 Conferees reach agreement.		
6/29 House and Senate approve conference report by votes of 239 to 194 and 54 to 46.		
Budget resolution, having been approved by both chambers, is now in effect.		

7/19–10/11 House committees, under instructions by the budget resolution, hold hearings. They then consider and mark up their recommendations.

8/1 Budget reconciliation recommendations are ordered reported by the National Security Committee.

9/12 Budget reconciliation recommendations are ordered reported by the Judiciary Committee.

9/19 Budget reconciliation recommendations are ordered reported by the Banking and Financial Services Committee and the Resources Committee.

9/21 Budget reconciliation recommendations are ordered reported by the Ways and Means Committee.

9/22 Budget reconciliation recommendations are ordered reported by the Commerce Committee.

9/27 Budget reconciliation recommendations are ordered reported by the International Relations Committee.

9/28 Budget reconciliation recommendations are ordered reported by the Economic and Educational Opportunities, Transportation and Infrastructure, and Veterans' Affairs committees.

7/11–10/19 Senate committees, under instructions by the budget resolution, hold hearings. They then consider and mark up their recommendations.

9/18 Budget reconciliation recommendations are ordered reported by the Armed Services Committee.

9/19 Budget reconciliation recommendations are ordered reported by the Environment and Public Works Committee.

9/20 Budget reconciliation recommendations are ordered reported by the Banking, Housing and Urban Affairs Committee and Veterans' Affairs Committee.

9/21 Budget reconciliation recommendations are ordered reported by the Energy and Natural Resources Committee and the Judiciary Committee.

9/22 Budget reconciliation recommendations are ordered reported by the Labor and Human Resources Committee.

TABLE 11.1 (*Continued*)

House Action	Senate Action	Appropriations and Debt Limit Legislation
	Budget Resolution and Reconciliation	
	9/28 Budget reconciliation recommendations are ordered reported by the Agriculture Committee and the Commerce, Science and Transportation Committee.	10/1 1997 fiscal year begins; FY 1996 appropriations run out; continuing resolution (CR) extending funding through November 13 in effect.
10/12 Budget Committee marks up and orders reported the reconciliation bill, HR2491.	10/19 Budget reconciliation recommendations are ordered reported by the Finance Committee.	
Republican party leaders engage in intense bargaining and agree on postcommittee adjustments.	*Dole negotiates with moderates.*	
10/20 Budget chair Kasich unveils the omnibus reconciliation bill, HR2517. (It includes Medicare, welfare, and tax cut bills passed separately earlier and cuts in agricultural subsidies and in federal pensions that the committees of jurisdiction refused to report.)	10/20 Budget Committee marks up reconciliation bill.	
	Dole and moderates and other holdouts agree on postcommittee adjustments to be offered as amendments on the floor.	
Republican party leaders continue their negotiations and agree on more postcommittee adjustments.	10/23 Budget Committee completes markup and orders reconciliation bill reported.	
10/25 Rules Committee grants rule allowing a vote on one substitute and including a self-executing provision incorporating last-minute deals into the bill.	10/25, 10/26, 10/27 Senate considers reconciliation bill.	

10/26 House approves rule and debates and approves the reconciliation bill, HR2491, which incorporated HR2517. The vote was 227–203.

10/30 House conferees named.

10/27 Senate passes reconciliation bill, S1357, by a 52–47 vote.

11/1 Clinton and Republican congressional leaders meet to discuss budget issues.

11/9, 11/10 House and Senate pass and clear for president a short-term debt limit increase with "strings."

11/8, 11/13 House and Senate pass and clear for president a CR with extraneous matter that Clinton opposes.

11/13 Clinton vetoes CR and debt limit increase; old CR runs out.

11/14 Federal government shuts down.

11/13 Senate conferees named.

11/15 Conferees agree to file conference report.

11/17 House agrees to conference report, 237–189. Portions of bill stricken in Senate as violations of the Byrd rule. Senate agrees, 52–47, to conference report without stricken provision. (Amendments between the chambers used.)

11/18 House agrees to conference report as altered in the Senate, 235–192.

11/19 Clinton and Republican congressional leaders reach agreement to open the government and to hold high-level talks; group of sixteen chosen to negotiate deal.

11/19, 11/20 Senate and House pass and clear for president a CR funding government until December 15.

11/28 Negotiations begin.

Negotiations continue in fits and starts.

12/6 Clinton vetoes reconciliation bill.

11/30 Bill presented to the president.

12/6 President Clinton vetoes reconciliation bill, HR2491.

TABLE 11.1 (*Continued*)

Budget Resolution and Reconciliation	Appropriations and Debt Limit Legislation
	12/15 CR runs out and federal government shuts down again.
	12/19 Clinton and Republican congressional leaders agree to peak-level summit with Clinton participating.
	12/22 Clinton, Dole, and Gingrich meet at White House.
	Talks continue intermittently.
	1/2/96 Senate passes "clean" CR.
	1/5/96 House passes CR, ending the longest government shutdown ever.
	More talks, maneuvering, and negotiations; short-term CRs keep government open. Republican leaders and Clinton administration negotiate deal on debt limit increase.
	3/28/96 Long-term debt limit extension passes.
	Congressional party leaders and appropriators and administration negotiate deal on remaining appropriations.
	4/24/96, 4/25/96 House and Senate pass and clear for president omnibus appropriations bill funding government for the rest of FY 97.
	4/26/96 Clinton signs omnibus appropriations bill, HR3019.

Note: Official actions are in roman type; behind-the-scenes, unofficial actions are in italics.

Committing to a Balanced Budget: The Budget Resolution

On May 18, 1995, the House approved the budget resolution its Budget Committee had reported by a vote of 238 to 193; only one Republican opposed it and only eight Democrats supported it. The resolution proposed balancing the budget in seven years and called for a $353 billion tax cut and deep spending cuts; entitlements such as Medicare and Medicaid and domestic discretionary programs were slated to be severely slashed, with spending for programs to aid the poor being especially hard hit (Hager 1995c, 1302).

The Republican party leadership brought the budget resolution to the House floor under a highly restrictive rule to prevent Democrats from forcing votes on narrow amendments targeting unpopular features of the measure. Anticipating difficulty in getting Clinton to accept legislation enacting the major policy changes required by the budget resolution, the Republican leadership also inserted a special provision in the rule: it suspended a House budget process rule that automatically raised the debt limit by providing for the automatic adoption of a debt limit identical to the level contained in the conference report on the budget resolution. Republican House leaders wanted to keep in reserve the need to increase the debt limit as a weapon in the confrontation with the president that they knew would eventually come.

On May 25, the Senate passed its budget resolution by a vote of 57 to 42, with every Republican and three Democrats supporting it. The Senate resolution called for a smaller tax cut and made it contingent on the passage of a balanced budget plan certified as valid by the Congressional Budget Office (CBO). A number of Senate Republicans were less enthusiastic about a huge tax cut than their House colleagues were. However, others such as Phil Gramm, who was challenging Senate Majority Leader Dole for the Republican presidential nomination, wanted at least as big a cut as the House had approved.

Senate Republican leaders, lacking an instrument like restrictive rules, had to beat back a barrage of amendments, not all of them offered by opposition party members. Nevertheless, budget process rules aided them in passing their resolution. Those rules restrict total debate time and so prohibit a filibuster by opponents. They also require that an amendment increasing spending in one area must be paid for with cuts in another, which tends to work against major changes.

The budget resolution then went to a conference committee. After two weeks of tough bargaining among congressional Republicans (Democrats having been relegated to the sidelines), Gingrich and Dole reached an agreement on taxes, the remaining and most contentious issue separating the chambers. To a very considerable extent, the House won. The House Republicans' iron commitment to a big tax cut, the Senate's eagerness to get a budget resolution because chamber rules prevented movement on appropriations bills until then, and Bob Dole's presidential ambitions worked to the advantage of the House position.[1]

On June 29, both chambers approved the conference report on largely party-line votes. Republicans were ecstatic about what they had accomplished. "We are changing directions," said an elated Senate Budget Committee Chairman Pete Domenici. "It is the framework to change the fiscal policy of America and to change the way the federal government operates" (Hook 1995a, 28A). They were determined to finish the job, Republicans said, no matter how recalcitrant Clinton was. "This is a revolution," declared moderate Chris Shays, vowing to refuse to raise the debt ceiling if Clinton did not agree to a balanced budget. "We are prepared to shut the government down in order to solve this problem," proclaimed Budget Committee Chairman John Kasich (Hager and Rubin 1995b, 1905).

Shooting with Real Bullets: Reconciliation

As difficult as passing the budget resolution had been, a bigger and more politically difficult task lay ahead—passing the reconciliation bill that actually enacts the policy changes into law. The budget resolution is a blueprint; by its passage Congress had promised to make the changes in law necessary to reach balance in the federal budget by fiscal 2002. Now Republicans had to deliver; as Bob Dole had said at the same stage in 1993, "From now on we're shooting with real bullets."

The budget resolution committed Congress to making savings of $894 billion over seven years. It instructed twelve House and eleven Senate committees to change law under their jurisdictions so as to meet spending targets. Much of the savings was slated to come from entitlement programs: $270 billion from Medicare, $182 billion from Medicaid, and $175 billion from a number of other mandatory spending programs such as food stamps, farm subsidies, welfare, and federal pensions. The committees of jurisdiction were free to decide just how to reach these tar-

---

1. The rule against the Senate's considering appropriations bills before final agreement on a budget resolution mattered because of another departure from orthodox lawmaking. The Senate had started moving appropriation bills before the House passed them. In the past, the Senate had always waited for the House to pass an appropriations bill before it did so.

gets, but the magnitude of the required savings dictated a major restructuring of the programs.

The budget resolution also prescribed $190 billion in savings in nondefense discretionary spending, which funds all those government activities—from the federal courts to Head Start to national park maintenance—that are not entitlements. The Budget Committees' reports accompanying the budget resolution contained numerous suggestions for how these cuts could be made; the Budget Committees had proposed closing down whole departments, agencies, and programs. Such specifics just provide guidance; they are not binding. The Appropriations Committees would be responsible for deciding how to make the cuts; but again, given the magnitude of the cuts—about 10 percent in the first year—drastic changes would be required.[2]

About the only pleasant task mandated by the reconciliation instructions was for the tax writing committees to cut taxes by $245 billion; however, given the disagreements within the Republican Party about whether a sizable tax cut made political and policy sense, even that task promised to be difficult. And finally, all this had to be done in a very short period of time. The thirteen appropriations bills are supposed to be enacted by October 1, the beginning of the federal government's fiscal year. There is no such statutory deadline for the passage of the reconciliation bill, but the budget resolution instructed the committees to report their provisions for the bill by September 22.

Congress returned to work in early September after an August recess that had been filled with heated rhetoric in members' districts and on the airwaves. Democrats accused Republicans of sacrificing the elderly's health care in order to pay for huge tax cuts for the wealthy; Republicans claimed they were restructuring Medicare in order to save it from bankruptcy and that Democrats were acting irresponsibly. Returning members from both parties reported that their constituents supported their positions; Republicans, thus, were fortified to proceed with the difficult task ahead.

By the end of September the pieces were coming together. Ten House committees had reported their provisions. In the Senate, all except Finance had reported. The tough political decisions to be made assured that the process would not be smooth; lawmakers were often forced to use unorthodox processes. The politically delicate Medicare provisions were put together by a Gingrich-led "design team." Responding to their con-

---

2. The authorizing committees with jurisdiction would be in charge of making major changes in or abolishing programs; however, by cutting funding drastically, Appropriations can achieve the same effect.

stituents' interests, enough Republicans on the Agriculture Committee resisted their chair's plan to drastically change and reduce the cost of farm policy to prevent the bill from being approved in the committee, despite threats from the party leaders. In Senate Finance, moderate Republican John Chafee forced his fellow Republicans to temper their Medicaid overhaul legislation to get his vote; but then, responding to complaints from Republican governors, Senate Republicans changed the language after the committee had reported.

The House Budget Committee on October 12 approved on a single 24–16 vote the approximately $562 billion in spending cuts made by the authorizing committees. The bill that went to the floor would, however, include in addition the Medicare cuts, the welfare bill, tax cuts, and cuts in agriculture subsidies and federal pensions. The Agriculture Committee and the Government Reform Committee, which have jurisdiction over farm subsidies and federal pension legislation, respectively, had not been able to report those provisions; too many committee members believed they hurt their constituents. Nevertheless, at the instructions of the party leadership and under authority provided by the budget resolution, the agriculture and pension provisions were to be included in the bill. The leadership's plan to dismantle the Commerce Department would also be incorporated in the package (Hager 1995e, 3119).

The House Republican leadership devoted the week preceding floor consideration to last-minute bargaining and intense persuasion. The bill's enormous scope and its importance to the Republican Party made it hard for Republicans to oppose, but the same characteristics also ensured that many members would strongly dislike some provisions and would be tempted to extract a price for their vote. The party leaders had been centrally involved in the budget process from its beginning; now they became the preeminent players. Gingrich agreed to restore $12 billion in Medicaid spending and to distribute the money to states particularly hard hit by the committee's plan; he thereby assuaged the concerns of some moderates and members from fast-growing states. Although the agricultural provisions were not altered, disgruntled farm-state members were brought back on board with implied promises that, since the Senate provisions were less radical, changes to their liking would be made in conference. Moderates upset by environmental provisions were not given any concessions on that issue, but the leadership did agree to drop the repeal of the Davis-Bacon Act, which requires federal contractors to pay the prevailing wage, a move aimed at moderates (Hook 1995b, A20).

These and other changes to which the leadership agreed either were included in the revised bill, HR2517, that Kasich put together and unveiled on October 20 or, in the case of the many last-minute deals, were incorporated into the bill taken to the floor by the rule. The rule granted by the Rules Committee on October 25 contained a self-executing provision specifying that when the House approved the rule it thereby approved HR2517 as modified by the last-minute leadership amendments as a substitute for the bill the Budget Committee had reported. This procedure allowed the leadership to avoid having to offer their changes and additions to the bill reported by the Budget Committee as amendments on the floor. The rule allowed only one amendment, a minority party substitute.

The Democratic leadership did not draft its own alternative; the leaders knew a Democratic substitute would have no chance and feared it would only distract media attention from the Republican plan just when public opinion seemed to be turning against it. The Republican leaders' combination of fervent, high-minded exhortation and nitty-gritty deal making paid off. The biggest and most ambitious reconciliation bill ever passed the House on a 227–203 vote, with only ten Republicans defecting.

To engineer passage in the Senate, Majority Leader Dole had to placate Republican moderates who had serious concerns about a number of the bill's provisions. The bill passed on a 52–47 vote; no Democrat voted for it but all but one Republican did. Dole's concessions as well as a few additional victories on the floor brought all the other Republican moderates on board. Ironically, Clinton's vow to veto the bill made it easier for moderate Republicans to vote for passage. "We know this isn't the last station," Chafee said (Rubin 1995e, 3290).

Summitry: Struggling to Reconcile Irreconcilable Differences

Politics and procedure had relegated President Clinton to the sidelines during much of the budget process. Clinton had, of course, submitted a budget in January as law requires the president to do. In June he had unveiled a new budget that reached balance in ten years. Republicans, however, insisted that any plan balance the budget in seven years according to conservative CBO figures. Convinced that the 1994 elections had given them a mandate that superseded any Clinton may have had and finding nothing of value in either of Clinton's budget plans, Republicans had proceeded on their own. Since the budget resolution does not require the president's signature, Republicans were not forced to take Clinton's preferences into account. However, the president can veto the reconciliation bill, and Republicans knew they could not muster the votes to override.

As Republicans were crafting their bill, President Clinton made clear that he strongly opposed many of its provisions. The bill, Clinton argued, cut much too deeply in Medicaid, Medicare, welfare, education, and the environment; ending poor people's entitlement to health care under Medicaid and slashing the earned income tax credit for the working poor while providing huge tax cuts to the well-off were unacceptable.

If, as he had repeatedly threatened, Clinton vetoed the reconciliation bill, Republicans would have to bargain with him; otherwise the legislation on which they had spent so much of their first year in power would die. They hoped that public opinion—which, they were convinced, strongly supported a balanced budget—would force Clinton to sign the bill or at least to agree to a deal to their liking. However, they had from early in the year contemplated the use of additional weapons. To provide the funds necessary to keep the government functioning, appropriations legislation has to be passed every year; otherwise large chunks of the government must shut down. Perhaps even more of a weapon was legislation raising the debt ceiling. Congress must periodically pass such legislation so that the federal government can borrow the funds necessary to pay its debts; if borrowing authority were to run out, the federal government would have to default on its obligations, a course potentially disastrous for the economy and the credibility of the United States. Republicans believed they could use the threat of shutting down the federal government or of bringing it to the brink of default as bargaining tools.

All thirteen appropriations bills are supposed to be enacted by the October 1 beginning of the new fiscal year. In 1995, the process was far behind schedule, slowed by the time the House had spent on the Contract, the big cuts that the Appropriations Committees were required to make, and legislative riders. With the party leadership orchestrating the effort, House Republicans, eager to make changes in law quickly, attached numerous controversial legislative provisions—known as riders—to appropriations bills. Intended to protect the provisions from a presidential veto, the strategy in many cases made House-Senate agreement on the bills excruciatingly difficult to reach. Moderate Senate Republicans were much less enthusiastic about hobbling the Environmental Protection Agency, imposing new restrictions on abortion, or effectively barring liberal interest groups from lobbying than hard-line House Republicans were.

By late September, only two of thirteen appropriations bills had been cleared for the president. Not wanting to call attention to their inability to meet deadlines, congressional Republicans agreed with the president on a continuing (appropriations) resolution to fund government programs for forty-four days. This was a "clean" continuing resolution (CR) in that it contained no extraneous provisions and was not controversial.

The early rounds and the first government shutdown. Both sides knew that they would have to talk. On November 1, President Clinton and the

Republican leadership met for two hours at the White House to discuss budget issues, including the debt limit, but no agreements were reached.

Implementing their strategy of using must-pass legislation to pressure the president into an agreement, congressional Republicans passed a CR and a debt ceiling increase, including in both pieces of legislation provisions the president strongly opposed. On November 13 Clinton vetoed both bills, as he had said he would.

In a final attempt to avert a government shutdown, Clinton sent Leon Panetta, White House chief of staff, to the Hill to confer with Gingrich and Dole; however, when Panetta insisted that congressional Democrats be included in the talks, the Republican leaders refused and no negotiations took place. On November 14 the federal government shut down. At that point, only two of the regular appropriations bills had been signed into law by the president.

Under law, "essential" government services—law enforcement, for example—continue even if appropriations bills are not passed; but all other services and programs not yet funded have to close down. About 800,000 federal employees were sent home all across the country; national parks were shut; the Small Business Administration stopped processing loan requests; new applicants for Social Security were out of luck, though the checks (an entitlement and therefore not funded by appropriations) continued to go out.

On November 15, with no debt limit bill having passed, Treasury Secretary Robert Rubin made use of an extraordinary procedure to prevent default. Two days later both chambers passed the reconciliation bill conference report. Resolving the differences between the House and Senate bills had been a huge task. The bills, after all, dealt with hundreds of issues and programs. Agriculture, Medicare, Medicaid, welfare, and taxes presented the trickiest problems. In addition to being faced with many tough issues, the negotiators were constrained by the numerous promises that had been made during the effort to pass the bill. In both chambers the leaders had over and over again promised members concerned with some provision that "we'll fix it in conference."

Countering this formidable set of problems was the momentum created by the passage of the legislation in both chambers. Members had made a host of difficult decisions; they had put their careers on the line; if no agreement were reached it would all be for naught. And, given that important deadlines had already been missed, more long delay was likely to hurt the Republican Party's image. The leaders were determined to get a bill to the president before Thanksgiving.

The conference committee consisted of forty-three senators divided into twelve subgroups and seventy-one House members divided into fourteen subgroups. Had Gingrich not assertively exercised the Speaker's discretion in the appointment of conferees, the House delegation could easily have been much larger. Fearing that sheer numbers would delay resolution, Gingrich chose whenever possible members who could do double duty because they served on the Budget Committee and another concerned committee; in this and other ways he kept the number of conferees down.

A subgroup of eight House members had authority over the entire bill and included, in addition to high-ranking Budget Committee members, a number of party leaders—Majority Leader Dick Armey, Whip Tom DeLay, and conference chair John A. Boehner of Ohio on the Republican side and Whip David Bonior on the Democratic side. In the Senate, the group of three that had authority over the entire bill was confined to the Budget Committee leaders. The other subgroups consisted of members from the committees with provisions in the bill and had authority over the relevant provisions only. The Republican members of these subgroups made most of the many decisions that a bill of such broad scope required. On the big, tough issues, however, the party leaders were centrally involved. Gingrich and Dole, working with shifting groups of committee leaders, depending on the issue, hammered out agreements on the most sensitive issues.

On agriculture the agreement provides an example of the power of conferees; much of the fairly radical House language was adopted, even though the House Agriculture Committee had turned it down and the Senate version entailed less drastic change. The chair of the House Agriculture Committee, who was the author of the "freedom to farm" version, headed the House conferees and the top House party leaders supported him; the chair of the Senate Agriculture Committee also liked much of the House version even though his committee had reported a more moderate bill.

The conferees approved the conference report on November 15, and on November 17 both houses approved the report on largely party line votes. Democrats in the Senate used the Byrd rule to force deletion of a number of extraneous provisions as they had during initial floor consideration. Again Republicans could not muster the sixty votes needed to waive the rule. Since the House had already approved the conference report with the offending provisions, the legislation had to go back to the House for approval in altered form. When on November 20 the House concurred in the Senate amendment, both chambers had passed the bill in identical form.

Agreements, disagreements, and the second government shutdown. On November 19 President Clinton and Republican leaders announced an agreement to end the six-day shutdown. To their surprise, Republicans found the public blaming them rather than the president by a 2-to-1 margin. Threats of defection by significant numbers of congressional Democrats put Clinton under pressure as well. The deal, which was incorporated in a CR passed the next day, funded the government until December 15 and bound the president and Congress to enacting a budget that the CBO certified as balanced by 2002 and that, at the same time, protected future generations; ensured Medicare solvency; reformed welfare; and provided adequate funding for Medicaid, education, agriculture, national defense, veterans, and the environment (Rubin 1995g, 3598).

To carry out the face-to-face negotiations, a group of sixteen was chosen, eight from each side. The Republican group consisted of a combination of party and Budget Committee leaders from each chamber: House Republicans were represented by Majority Leader Dick Armey, Whip Tom DeLay, Budget Committee Chairman John Kasich, and Robert Walker of Pennsylvania, a high-ranking member of the Budget Committee and a confidant of the Speaker; Whip Trent Lott, Budget Committee Chairman Pete Domenici, and the two next most senior members of the Budget Committee, Charles Grassley of Iowa and Don Nickles, made up the Senate Republican contingent. The administration was represented by White House Chief of Staff Leon Panetta, Treasury Secretary Robert Rubin, and Office of Management and Budget (OMB) Director Alice Rivlin. Republicans had wanted to limit participants to representatives of the administration and congressional Republicans; the White House had, however, insisted that congressional Democrats be included. The difficult political environment for Democrats since the 1994 elections had strained relations between the White House and congressional Democrats; excluding them from the talks was a prescription for disaster. Thus Rep. Martin Sabo of Minnesota and Sen. Jim Exon of Nebraska, ranking members of the House and Senate Budget Committees, respectively, House Democratic Whip David Bonior, Charles Stenholm (a senior member of the House Budget Committee and a leader of the Coalition, a group of conservative Democrats), and Byron Dorgan of North Dakota, representing the Senate Democratic leadership, were included (*Congressional Quarterly Weekly Report*, Dec. 2, 1995, 3640). In the background would be Speaker Gingrich, Senate Majority Leader Bob Dole and the president, all of whom would have to sign off on any deal.

The negotiators met for the first time on November 28 in the Capitol. On November 30, after three bargaining sessions of a few hours each, the talks stalled. Each side accused the other of bad faith. Republicans charged that Clinton had still not proposed a detailed alternative plan; the White House responded that Republicans refused to follow a previously agreed upon agenda for the meetings.

On December 6 the president vetoed the reconciliation bill, using the pen with which President Lyndon B. Johnson had signed the Medicaid/Medicare bill into law in 1965. At the same time he announced that he would unveil a seven-year alternative budget. Clinton's new budget did not rely on the more pessimistic CBO numbers (which required deeper cuts), as the Republicans had demanded, and they dismissed it out of hand. Still another White House proposal met with the same reception on December 14 (Hager and Rubin 1995c, 3789).

With the talks again stalled, Republicans refused to approve another short-term CR and the government shut down again. Many were convinced that the president did not really want a balanced budget deal and that they would have to play hardball to force him to agree. Treasury Secretary Rubin's extraordinary but legal financial maneuvering had, at least temporarily, removed the debt limit as a lever. Thus appropriations remained their best weapon. Vowing that the House would not pass another CR, Gingrich confidant Bob Walker said, "We will politically endure as much pain as it takes to get a [balanced-budget] deal" (Hager 1995g, 3876).

Peak-level summitry and the longest shutdown. On December 19 President Clinton called Gingrich and Dole; that afternoon, after a two-hour meeting at the White House, the Republican leaders announced a breakthrough—Clinton had agreed to negotiate by the end of the year a seven-year budget deal starting from CBO numbers. Furthermore, Clinton had promised to participate personally in the negotiations.

Republican leaders had promised that once good faith talks were under way Congress would pass a CR. However, House Republicans absolutely refused. A statement by Vice President Gore, seeming to dispute that Clinton had agreed to CBO numbers, though quickly contradicted by the White House, fed already suspicious Republicans' distrust and hardened their inclination to hold fast. By a near-unanimous vote, the House Republican Conference voted to hold out until Clinton agreed to a balanced budget deal. The freshmen, many of whom lacked political experience and disdained compromise, were especially adamant. "This government is going to remain shut down until he [President Clinton] realizes that we are not going to compromise on a balanced budget," said Mark W. Neumann, R-Wis. (Fiore 1995, A1).

When Congress returned in early January, the government shutdown had lasted far longer than any before. Although several more appropriations bills had become law before the second shutdown started, six were still outstanding. The press was full of articles about the harm the shutdown might cause—the preparation of the next year's flu vaccine was being hindered, for example—and about the suffering of federal employees. The public was blaming Republicans far more than the president for the impasse. Never enthusiastic about the strategy of closing the government down and concerned that the focus had shifted from budget balancing to the shutdown, Majority Leader Dole on January 2 pushed through the Senate a condition-free CR to fund the government until January 12 while budget talks proceeded. To move the legislation so quickly, Dole took up a most-favored-nation bill for Bulgaria and offered the CR as a substitute amendment to it, a maneuver which the Senate's loose rules on germaneness made possible. When the Senate adopted the "amendment," the CR was substituted for the original bill.

The House Republican leadership decided that House Republicans were in a politically untenable position; a change in strategy was needed. The leaders proposed a CR that would run through March 15, but at a contentious party conference the membership refused to go along. "I am vehemently and steadfastly opposed to this . . . defeatist strategy, which is going to blur the differences between the parties," said Frank Riggs of California, reflecting the views of many of his fellow freshmen (Hook and Richter 1996, A16). Republican leaders regrouped, came up with another plan, and, at a conference the next morning, pressed their members to support it. House Republicans had been so successful in 1995 because they had acted as a team, Gingrich told his members. If they wanted to stay a part of the team, they would vote for the CR, he added pointedly. Later in the day, the leadership-supported measures were approved by the House; fifteen Republicans refused to vote in favor of reopening the government.

Clinton responded by putting forth his own plan to balance the budget in seven years according to CBO numbers; since Clinton had thereby finally met what Republicans said was their one "nonnegotiable" demand, this initially seemed like a breakthrough. But the talks soon stalled again. Increasingly, it was becoming clear that the policy differences between the president and congressional Republicans were too great to bridge. Even as negotiations narrowed the dollar amount differences between the sides, Republicans found the ways in which the administration proposed balancing the budget unacceptable because they did not include the sort of basic restructuring of entitlement programs to which Republicans were committed. The president and congressional Democrats, although they had conceded on balancing the budget, deemed the Republicans' means of doing so unacceptable because they weakened or destroyed government programs Democrats considered essential. "It's not a debate about numbers, it's a debate about policies," Majority Leader Dole said succinctly (Rubin and Hager 1996, 89).

With the prospects of an agreement dimming but with neither side wanting to throw in the towel and reap the blame for failure, negotiations spluttered along, more frequently in suspension than in full throttle. In late January, congressional Republicans and the White House worked out a mutually agreeable CR that extended funding until mid-March.

Raising the debt limit. Not long into the new year the debt limit reemerged as a front-burner issue; Treasury Secretary Rubin was running out of stopgap measures to ward off default. The Republican House leadership no longer talked blithely about preferring default to compromise; the government shutdown had cost the Republican Party dearly with the public; Republicans could not afford another such debacle. Yet the leaders desperately wanted to be able to claim if not a victory at least not a total defeat, and they, of course, had to amass a majority vote for the debt limit increase. Both considerations dictated adding provisions favored by Republicans to the debt limit bill.

The Republican leaders negotiated a deal with the Clinton administration to include language in the bill providing for a long-term increase in the debt ceiling, some regulatory relief for small business, an increase in the earnings limit for Social Security recipients, and the line-item veto. These "sweeteners," especially the line-item veto, were sufficient to enable most Republicans, even the hard-line House freshmen, to vote for the debt limit increase and to give the Republican Party something to brag about. Essentially, Republican leaders made the best of a weak hand.

Both chambers passed HR3136 on March 28, and Clinton signed it the next day, thereby ending the threat of default but also depriving Republicans of the lever they had hoped to use to force the president to accept their policy proposals.

With a whimper. The curtain finally came down on the 1995 budget battle in late April, when Congress passed and Clinton signed an omnibus appropriations bill to fund the nine departments and dozens of agencies covered by the five regular appropriations bills that had not been enacted. Six months late, after fourteen continuing resolutions and two government shutdowns, the government was finally funded for the fiscal year that ended October 1, 1996.

Both chambers passed their own versions of the omnibus appropriations bill in March, but reaching a final agreement required weeks of negotiations between House and Senate Republicans and with the White House. Both funding levels and policy riders were at issue. Hard-line House Republicans were resistant to increasing funding, especially for the programs such as AmeriCorps (the national service program) and Goals 2000 dearest to Clinton's heart, and to dropping policy riders on hot-button topics such as abortion and the environment; Clinton, buoyed by his increasing popularity, also hung tough; Senate Republicans often found themselves in between. There was much less support for the policy riders in the Senate than in the House, and the Senate bill included more money than the House bill—though not as much as Clinton wanted.

Extensive negotiations between House and Senate appropriators in small groups, in which a multitude of compromises were reached, were followed by a series of high-level talks. Finally, on Wednesday, April 24, the core negotiating group of White House Chief of Staff Leon Panetta and the chairs and ranking minority members of the House and Senate Appropriations Committees reached agreement. House Republicans were forced to make major concessions on both funding levels and policy riders; considerable money for Clinton's priorities in the areas of education and the environment was restored, and most of the riders were dropped or the president was given the authority to waive them. "We got rolled," House freshman Mark Souder complained (Hook 1996, A15). Despite much grumbling by House Republicans, the House as well as the Senate overwhelmingly approved the conference report that contained the agreement. As senior House Republican and appropriator Bill Young of Florida said succinctly, "At this stage, we've got to get it settled" (Hook 1996, A15).

The Budget Process and "Revolutionary" Policy Change: Possibilities and Limits

Using the budget process, the new Republican majorities managed to cut domestic appropriations by 9 percent over the previous year, a very considerable achievement from their perspective (Hager 1996, 1156). They failed in their much more ambitious attempt to cut spending in and to fundamentally restructure the big entitlement programs, especially Medicare and Medicaid.

The procedures and practices of unorthodox lawmaking were essential tools in the Republicans' strategy to accomplish their ambitious goal; without the packaging the budget process allowed and the protection from filibusters it afforded the legislation in the Senate, passing such nonincremental policy change would not have been possible. Had the minority Democrats in the Senate been able to filibuster the reconciliation bill, they certainly would have done so, just as the minority Republicans would have filibustered the Clinton economic program in the 103rd Congress. Other tools of unorthodox lawmaking were instrumental at a number of stages in the process as well. To ensure that the bill would pass the chamber and satisfy most Republicans, the Republican leadership used task forces, negotiated postcommittee adjustments, and, in some instances, bypassed committees altogether. As employed by an activist party leadership, special rules were critically important to Republican strategy; such rules were used to hold the package together at a number of crucial stages.

The procedures and practices of unorthodox lawmaking are, however, just tools and are by no means sufficient to produce nonincremental policy change. Summits are, in fact, a procedure of last resort; the president and Congress agree to try to settle their differences through a summit when more orthodox procedures have failed. The American governmental system of separate institutions sharing power has a status quo bias; making major policy changes is difficult and usually requires compromise. When the philosophical differences between the president and the congressional majority are so great that what one considers a reasonable compromise the other regards as selling out, significant policy change is unlikely unless the actor advocating such change can marshal strong public support and thereby make holding out too costly in electoral terms for the other actor. In fact, in the summer of 1996, Republicans scored a major victory when President Clinton signed a welfare overhaul bill. Although Clinton had extracted a number of significant compromises, the legislation ended welfare as an entitlement and, in other provisions as well, bore a clear Republican stamp. This was a case in which the Republicans were backed by a strong public desire for policy change; Clinton and many other Democrats feared the electoral consequences of killing the legislation. On the budget, Republicans had hoped that public support for a balanced budget in the abstract would translate into strong public pressure on Clinton to make a deal on their terms. Instead, the Democrats' warnings that the Republicans' plan would cut Medicare, education, and environmental protection proved more persuasive. When Clinton won the battle for public opinion, Republicans lost their chance of winning the policy war.

Balancing the Budget, 1997

By 1997 the political context offered new opportunities for a balanced budget deal. Having been reelected, President Clinton clearly wanted a budget deal to burnish his legacy. The hard experiences of 1995 and 1996—the government shutdown for which they were blamed, the "near death" experience of the 1996 elections, in which they only narrowly maintained control of the House—had made Republicans more realistic about what they could accomplish under conditions of divided government and so more willing to deal. Furthermore, Republicans knew they would have real difficulty proceeding on their own. After the public pounding they had taken from Democrats, many Republicans were unwilling to take the lead on making the unpopular decisions on programs like

Medicare; the only way of making those choices less draconian was to scale back substantially their tax cut proposals, a course of action anathema to many Republicans. Since House Republicans could count on no Democratic votes for a partisan budget resolution and thus had to hold all but a handful of their own members, they probably could not pass such a budget resolution.

Getting a Deal

On February 6, President Clinton unveiled a budget that balanced by fiscal 2002, contained significant tax cuts, including the $500 per child tax credit, and cut projected Medicare spending. Clinton's meetings with Republican party and committee leaders immediately following the elections and then this proposal signaled his desire for a budget deal. Yet, although the president had accepted a number of the Republicans' proposals, his priorities and theirs were still far apart. Clinton's budget was based on the more optimistic OMB numbers, not on the CBO numbers Republicans insisted on; his net tax increase was much more modest than theirs and differently distributed, much of it targeted at education; and he proposed spending more money on selected domestic programs, including education and a restoration of some welfare benefits for legal aliens.

Low-key talks between White House officials and congressional budget leaders began in early February. In public, both sides jockeyed for advantage. The budget committees held hearings on the president's budget, with Republicans criticizing it as not credible. In March House Republicans passed a nonbinding resolution calling on the president to submit a new budget that was balanced using CBO numbers. As negotiations proceeded, members not involved in the talks pressured their fellow partisans to hang tough on matters of special interest to them. House Democrats had been unenthusiastic about negotiations, believing that Republicans should have been forced to come up with their own proposal before talks. When liberal Democrats heard that the negotiators were seriously considering a downward adjustment in the Consumer Price Index to save money, they pressured their leaders and the White House to drop the idea. When Speaker Gingrich raised the possibility of postponing the tax cuts until deficit reduction had taken place, conservative Republicans reacted with horror and disbelief, and the Republican leadership quickly disavowed the idea.

With the mid-April deadline for the budget resolution quickly approaching, negotiations became intense during the week of April 7. Representing the While House were OMB Director Fredrick Raines, legislative liaison John Hilley, and director of the President's National Eco-

nomic Council Gene Sperling; House Budget Committee Chairman John
Kasich and Senate Budget Committee Chairman Pete Domenici spoke for
the Republicans. The ranking minority members of the Budget Committees, Rep. John Spratt of South Carolina and Sen. Frank R. Lautenberg of
New Jersey, represented congressional Democrats. Each of the negotiators
consulted regularly with his congressional party leadership or, in the case
of the White House representatives, with the president. No deal could be
final until the congressional majority party leaders and the president
signed off on it.

Pressure from liberal Democrats and conservative Republicans intensified, and negotiators realized that an agreement had to be reached soon
if it were to receive the majority approval that it needed. As secret talks
proceeded, members not in the room were becoming increasingly suspicious and were beginning to lock themselves into hard positions. White
House representatives met with Republican budget leaders; congressional
Democrats were outraged about their exclusion, but a deal was coming
together. The hostile reception the tentative deal received from congressional Democrats when White House officials presented it suggested serious problems ahead. However, a last-minute change in CBO projections
saved the day. The unexpectedly strong economy had made the original
deal possible by limiting how much had to be cut; now the CBO estimated
that, with the economy even stronger than it had projected earlier in the
year, the cuts could be scaled back further. Negotiators agreed to drop
some of the politically more problematical cuts, making the deal more
acceptable to congressional Democrats.

President Clinton and congressional Republicans announced the
deal at separate news conferences on May 2. Yet, at this point, the deal was
primarily an oral one, and it quickly became apparent that Republicans
and Democrats understood what had been agreed upon differently in
many important respects. Congressional Democrats and the White House
wanted a written agreement in as much detail as possible so as to con-
strain the Republicans when they actually drafted the legislation that
would turn the deal into law. Republicans, of course, wanted as much discretion as possible, and Republican committee leaders not directly
involved in the negotiations bridled at being instructed in detail about
matters under their jurisdiction. Nevertheless, after two more weeks of
negotiations in which Speaker Gingrich and Senate Majority Leader Lott
took a lead role, a final, written agreement was worked out.

Passing the Budget Resolution

The House Budget Committee quickly approved by a 31–7 vote a
budget resolution incorporating the deal. Even though Democratic

attempts to write still more specifics into the resolution failed on a series of votes in committee, a majority of Democrats as well as all Republicans supported the resolution. A few days later, the Senate Budget Committee approved an almost identical resolution on a 14–4 vote, with two conservative Republicans and two Democrats dissenting.

In the House, the leadership brought the resolution to the floor under a rule that allowed votes on five substitutes. As the leadership had feared, the Shuster-Oberstar substitute proved to be the greatest threat to the bipartisan deal. (The leaders allowed a vote on this substitute only because they realized they could not pass a rule that barred such a vote.) Bud Shuster, R-Pa., chairman of the House Transportation and Infrastructure Committee, had made clear throughout the process his dissatisfaction with the transportation funding in the deal. With support from his ranking minority member James L. Oberstar, D-Minn., he proposed a budget substitute that increased transportation funding and paid for it by an across-the-board cut in spending and smaller tax cuts. The Shuster proposal offered members much-prized projects for their districts, and Shuster and his allies in the House and in the lobbying community made sure members were aware of what they stood to gain if they voted with Shuster. Yet, for the Republican party leadership and the White House, the Shuster substitute was a deal breaker; it made cuts both groups opposed and, perhaps worse, it reopened negotiations on the fragile agreement and might well lead to its unraveling.

Although White House officials made their opposition to Shuster clear to House Democrats, the Republican leadership had to do the heavy lifting in defeating it. Minority Leader Dick Gephardt opposed the budget deal and, although he carefully refrained from working against it, he was not willing to use the party whip system to defeat Shuster. The Republican leaders worked their members hard, pleading with them at a special 10 p.m. Republican Conference meeting to vote against Shuster. Members of the whip system and the leaders themselves talked to waiverers one on one, warning that the deal would probably unravel if the Shuster substitute won. The leaders promised they would prevent Shuster from retaliating against members who opposed him. The Shuster-Oberstar substitute was defeated on a 214–216 vote; Republicans voted 58–168 against, Democrats 155–48 for.

The passage vote was anticlimactic; the budget resolution passed 333–99. Even many hard-core conservatives and liberals—the majority of the firebrand 1994 Republican class and Democratic Whip David Bonior among them—voted for the resolution. During the eleven hours of debate, many supporters had made clear that there was much about the deal they did not like but that, given divided government, this was the best that was attainable. Opposing the resolution were twenty-six

Republicans, mostly rigid conservatives, and seventy-two Democrats, mostly liberals.

After four days of debate and more than fifty amendments, the Senate approved a budget resolution little changed from that reported by its Budget Committee. Lacking the procedural tools for limiting amendments, leaders had to beat them back by other means. Most problematic was an amendment jointly sponsored by Orrin Hatch and Ted Kennedy to raise the tax on cigarettes by 43 cents a pack and use the money to provide additional health insurance for uninsured children and to reduce the deficit. Portrayed in posters and newspaper ads as a choice between Joe Camel (the tobacco companies) and a cute little boy named Joey, this was a hard amendment for many senators to oppose. Yet, like the Shuster substitute, it was a deal breaker; if the amendment passed, Republican support for the deal would bleed away. Majority Leader Trent Lott insisted that the president give Republicans cover for voting against the amendment by coming out against it. Clinton had White House spokesman Mike McCurry explain that, if this were a freestanding amendment, Clinton would support it; but that was not the case here, and Clinton did not want to see the deal unravel. The amendment was tabled, that is, killed, on a 55–45 vote, with eight Democrats opposing it and eight Republicans voting in favor. As in the House, the final vote was anticlimactic; on May 23, the resolution passed 78–22, with only fourteen Republicans and eight Democrats voting against it.

After the Memorial Day recess, conferees quickly worked out the minor differences between the House and Senate versions and the two chambers approved the final resolution by big votes. Since this agreement was a concurrent resolution and would not become law, it did not need to go to the president for his signature.

The Tough Road to Reconciliation

By approving the resolution the House and Senate had bound themselves to pass legislation that would reduce the deficit by $204.3 billion over five years, including a $115 billion savings from Medicare; make $85 billion net in tax cuts; institute a child health initiative costing $16 billion; and restore various benefits to legal aliens (*Congressional Quarterly Almanac* 1997, 2–23). The resolution specified that two separate reconciliation bills would be enacted, one with the spending cuts and the other with the tax cuts. Packaging the changes into two bills rather than one would allow for the building of somewhat different coalitions on the two bills, a possibility given that this was a bipartisan deal, and would let members vote for one of the bills if, for policy or reelection reasons, they could not vote for both.

By June 5, when the budget resolution conference report received final approval, the committees that would make the changes in law had already started their work. On June 9, House Ways and Means Committee Chairman Bill Archer, R-Texas, released his draft proposal (called the chairman's mark) of the tax bill. Congressional Democrats and the White House immediately cried foul; Archer had skewed the tax cuts so as to benefit the well-off at the expense of low-income people. Even many Republicans were worried about the message sent by the large corporate tax breaks Archer's proposal contained. Especially problematic for Republicans was his proposal to abolish the alternative minimum tax for corporations and pay for that by phasing in the cut in estate (inheritance) taxes more slowly. Small business and farm groups, representing core Republican constituencies, objected strenuously to the estate tax provisions and, under intense pressure from the Republican leadership, Archer revised that part of his bill before he took it to markup.

The markup in Ways and Means began June 12 and was rancorous and highly partisan. Republicans turned down the Democratic substitute, which reflected Clinton administration priorities, on a strict party line vote. The bill was then approved on an almost straight party-line vote of 22–16, with only Jim Nussle, R-Iowa, defecting because Archer's bill ended the tax credit for ethanol, a fuel made from corn.

On June 19 Senate Finance approved its bill on a bipartisan 18–2 vote, with two conservative Republicans opposing it. Members of the committee had closed their markup and, after a freewheeling eight-hour session, had emerged with a deal that garnered broad support. It included a smaller net tax cut than the House bill, an increase in the cigarette tax, a child tax credit that was more generous to lower-income families than that in the House bill, and more money for children's health care.

In staged news events, television interviews, and floor speeches, House Democrats amplified their criticism of the Ways and Means bill, decrying it as unfair to the average American family. Lobbyists for interests unhappy with how they were treated in the Archer bill stepped up their campaign for changes; many of them were GOP allies and conveyed their complaints to the Republican party leadership either directly or through Republican members whose districts were adversely affected.

The Republican leadership used all the tools at its command to pass the bill. Speaker Gringrich insisted on a number of postcommittee adjustments to the bill; thus the ethanol provision was dropped and the child tax credit made a bit more generous to lower-income families. Interest group allies were mobilized to lobby members for support; the leaders mounted a media campaign and the whip system engaged in intensive one-on-one persuasion.

The postcommittee adjustments were incorporated into the Ways and Means bill through a self-executing rule, thereby making separate votes on those provisions unnecessary. After a sharply partisan debate, the Democratic substitute was defeated on a 197–235 vote, with no Republicans and only eight Democrats crossing party lines. No other amendments were allowed under the rule, and the bill passed 253–179; one Republican voted against the bill, and twenty-seven Democrats supported it.

One day later, on June 27, the Senate passed its tax bill by an 80–18 vote; fifty-one Republicans and twenty-nine Democrats supported the bill; four Republicans and fourteen Democrats opposed it. Both Democratic and Republican supporters criticized provisions of the bill; Majority Leader Lott vowed that the tobacco tax would be dropped and the net tax cut increased in conference. Nevertheless, although a multitude of amendments were offered and about thirty pushed to a roll call vote, the bill emerged from the process little changed.

As the tax bill wound its way through the process, so did the companion spending cut bill. The budget resolution called for over $260 billion in gross spending cuts over five years, with $140 billion to come from discretionary spending controlled by the appropriations process and $122 billion to come from entitlement programs, $115 of that from Medicare. The resolution, following the budget deal, also specified increases in spending for specific purposes, most notably for a new child health initiative and the restoration of some welfare benefits for legal aliens. Eight committees in each chamber had jurisdiction over the programs at issue and were instructed to report legislation making the savings. The biggest burden fell on the Ways and Means and Commerce Committees in the House and the Finance Committee in the Senate because those committees have jurisdiction over the Medicare program.

House Ways and Means managed to produce a bipartisan Medicare bill, making most of its savings by reducing payment rates to health care providers and adding a preventative-care benefits package. The Commerce Committee, in contrast, split along partisan lines on both its Medicare and its Medicaid bills and, on the latter, also failed to comply with the budget resolution. On the welfare provisions, both the Ways and Means Committee and the Education and the Workforce Committee, which shared jurisdiction, produced Republican bills that congressional Democrats and the White House strongly opposed.

By mid-June, the House committees had reported their reconciliation recommendations to the Budget Committee. The Budget Committee cannot change those recommendations, yet at this point considerable bargaining frequently takes place. In several cases, committees with joint jurisdiction had reported conflicting provisions; in others, committees' provisions did not comply with the budget resolution; and, in still others, the White House adamantly opposed what committees had done. Clearly the bill needed some adjustment before it was ready for the floor. Budget Committee Chairman John Kasich undertook negotiations with Republican committee chairs, John Spratt (the ranking Democrat on the Budget Committee), and White House officials. Under the supervision of and with guidance from Speaker Gingrich, Kasich worked out a number of deals; although Democrats were far from satisfied, the deals were good enough to move the process along.

Under instructions from the Speaker, the Rules Committee drafted a rule that included a self-executing provision by which approval of the rule would also incorporate these postcommittee adjustments into the bill. The rule allowed no Democratic amendments.

Despite the adjustments, most Democrats were still unhappy with the bill and believed it violated in numerous important ways the budget deal. The White House agreed but urged that the bill be passed so changes could be made in conference. After a heated debate, the House on June 25 passed the spending cut bill 270–162, with fifty-one Democrats joining all but seven Republicans in support.

In the Senate, almost all the major issues fell under the jurisdiction of the Finance Committee. Under the leadership of its chairman, William Roth, the committee drafted its Medicare, Medicaid, and welfare provisions through a bipartisan process. Aided by the composition of its membership, which included a number of proponents of entitlement reform among its Democrats, the committee went well beyond the budget deal and approved means-testing Medicare, increasing the Medicare eligibility age, and instituting a $5 co-payment for home health care visits. An ideological fight did erupt on the child health care initiative; a conservative proposal sponsored by Phil Gramm defeated a more liberal proposal co-sponsored by Jay Rockefeller, D-W.Va., and John Chafee and supported by the White House. Finance approved its bill by a 20–0 vote on June 18 and sent it to Senate Budget, which packaged it with the recommendations of the other committees and approved the resulting bill on June 20.

The Senate debated the spending cut bill for two days. Liberals tried to knock out the home health care co-payment, the increase in the Medicare eligibility age, and the means-testing of Medicare but failed on a series of votes. The Senate did approve amendments liberalizing somewhat the welfare provisions and the child health care initiative. The body then passed the bill by a vote of 73–27; Democrats split 21–24.

Thus by late June, both the House and the Senate had passed two reconciliation bills—a tax bill and a spending cut bill—that turned the recommendations in the budget resolution into law. However, the House and

Senate bills differed substantially; on both taxes and spending cuts, the House had produced its bills through a more partisan process than had the Senate, and the outcomes reflected the process. Furthermore, President Clinton strongly objected to many provisions in all the bills. If congressional Republicans wanted the president to sign the bills, they would have to address his concerns.

Negotiating the Final Deal

The conference committee met and broke down into thirteen subconferences to negotiate on the myriad issues that had to be reconciled. After a week, Republicans concluded that the normal process would not work; to negotiate from a position of strength with Clinton, they needed a united position. From July 18 to July 23, key House and Senate Republicans met in Speaker Gingrich's office to develop a unified Republican position. House party leaders immediately insisted that the structural changes in Medicare the Senate had approved (means-testing, a rise in the eligibility age) be dropped; their members were not willing to take the heat such changes were likely to generate from senior citizens. On most other issues, Republicans agreed to take the more conservative of the House or Senate positions into negotiations with Clinton. They believed this would give them maximum bargaining leverage.

Serious negotiations with the White House began July 24; on July 25, the negotiation group was pared down to Republican leaders Lott and Gringrich and three White House Representatives, Chief of Staff Erskine Bowles, Legislative Liaison John Hilley, and Treasury Secretary Rubin. Over the next several days, in fits and starts, they and a few other key players—Chairman Archer on taxes, for example—worked out a series of compromises. On July 28 an overall agreement was reached, and on July 29 Republicans and Democrats touted the deal at separate rallies.

The final deal represented a compromise between the parties' very different positions and philosophies. Republicans got a balanced budget by fiscal 2002, cuts in projected entitlement spending, mostly from Medicare, and substantial tax cuts. Included was a cut in the capital gains tax and in estate taxes. Clinton and congressional Democrats got the education tax credit provisions Clinton wanted, a child health initiative larger than that specified in the original deal, funded in part by an increase in the cigarette tax, and the restoration of some welfare benefits for legal aliens. They had also cut down the size of the tax cut from what Republicans originally wanted and had made many of the tax provisions more progressive.

Both House and Senate approved the conference reports easily, and on August 5 President Clinton signed the two reconciliation bills into law. (See Table 11.2 for a chronology of the budget process.)

Why a Balanced Budget Deal in 1997?

Why were congressional Republicans and President Clinton able to reach an agreement to balance the budget in 1997 when they could not in 1995 and 1996? Certainly the booming economy was critical because it made the task much easier. Also important was the Republican majority's growing policy and political realism. By 1997 most Republicans had come to terms with the imperatives of the American political system; if they were to accomplish any policy change, compromise would be required. Furthermore, keeping their majority dictated working with Clinton so as to have something to show for their tenure. Many hard-line conservatives outside Congress blasted the deal as timid and minimalist; but, within Congress, even the firebrands of the 1994 class mostly held their fire. They might have grumbled in private, but they realized that the deal was the best that could be gotten so long as the president, with his bully pulpit and his veto, was a Democrat.

The differences in policy preferences and electoral needs between the congressional Republicans and President Clinton were great enough that ordinary processes could not produce legislation. A summit—direct and relatively formal negotiations at a high level—was required to reach the initial budget agreement and then to work out the actual legislation. The budget process by which large numbers of often difficult policy decisions could be packaged and protected from Senate obstructionism was essential to the successful transformation of the initial deal into legislation. Along the way, leaders used other "unorthodox process" tools to aid the legislation, most notably restrictive and self-executing rules in the House. The process tools available to leaders facilitated legislative success.

Budget Politics after the Balanced Budget Deal, 1998–1999

Over half of the spending cuts the budget deal required were to come from discretionary spending, which is under the purview of the Appropriations Committees. The deal imposed caps on such spending, ones that became tighter each year. Some liberal Democrats had argued that the spending caps were highly unrealistic for the later years of the budget deal. The caps certainly made the budget and appropriations processes extremely difficult for Republicans starting in 1998.

In 1998, for the first time, Congress failed to agree on a budget resolution. The Senate passed a resolution that basically rubber-stamped the 1997 budget deal; but the House, after a long and arduous process, passed

TABLE 11.2   1997 Budget Process: A Chronology

House Action	Senate Action	Postpassage Action
	2/6 President Clinton unveils a budget that balances by 2002.	
	Feb. Talks between White House and Congress begin.	
	4/7 Talks intensify.	
	5/2 President Clinton and congressional Republicans announce a deal.	
	5/2–5/15 Two weeks of negotiation transform oral deal into agreed-upon written terms.	

Budget Resolution

House Action	Senate Action	Postpassage Action
5/18 Budget Committee reports budget resolution.	5/19 Budget Committee reports budget resolution.	
5/20 Budget resolution debated on the House floor.	5/20, 21, 22 Budget resolution debated on Senate floor.	
5/21 Budget resolution debated and passed by House 333–99.	5/23 Budget resolution passed by the Senate.	
		6/3 House and Senate appoint conferees and conference begins.
		6/4 Conferees reach agreement and file conference report.
		6/5 House and Senate agree to conference report.

Reconciliation Bills

6/12 Ways and Means Committee approves tax provisions.

June House committees draft and then send their reconciliation provisions to the Budget Committee.

6/24 Budget Committee reports HR2014 (containing tax provisions) and HR2015 (containing spending cuts).

6/25 House debates and passes HR2015.

6/26 House debates and passes HR2014.

6/19 Finance reports tax provisions as S949.

June Senate committees draft and then send their other reconciliation provisions to the Budget Committee.

6/20 Budget Committee reports S947 (spending cuts).

6/23, 6/24 Senate debates S947 (spending cuts).

6/25 Senate passes S947 and begins debate on S949 (tax bill).

6/26 Senate debates S949.

6/27 Senate debates and passes S949 (tax bill)

6/27 Senate appoints conferees for both bills.

7/10 House appoints conferees for both bills and spending bill conference begins.

7/11 Tax bill conference begins.

7/18–7/23 Key House and Senate Republicans meet to develop a unified Republican position.

7/24 Serious negotiations between White House and congressional Republicans begin.

7/28 An overall agreement is reached.

7/30 Conference reports filed on spending cut bill and on tax bill.

7/30 House approves spending cut bill conference report.

7/31 House approves tax bill conference report and Senate approves both spending cut bill and tax bill conference reports.

8/5 President Clinton signs both bills.

Note: Official actions are in roman type; behind-the-scenes, unofficial actions are in italics.

a more ambitious resolution calling for big tax cuts and even bigger spending cuts. Senate Budget Committee Chair Pete Domenici considered the House budget resolution totally unrealistic and refused to negotiate a compromise.

Failing to pass a budget resolution makes Congress look bad; failing to pass appropriations is not an option—as Republicans had learned so painfully in 1995. Because of the policy differences between Democrats and Republicans accentuated by the need to make painful spending decisions, the majority Republicans attempted to pass their appropriations bills on a partisan basis; with their narrow seat margin in the House, that too proved to be difficult, and the Republicans found themselves far behind schedule in the fall of 1998. An election was looming, and Republicans knew that shutting down the government was a prescription for electoral disaster. They were, thus, forced into negotiations with the administration. In mid-October, White House officials, led by Chief of Staff Erskine Bowles and OMB Director Jack Lew, met with Republican leaders, often in the office of Speaker Gingrich, to hammer out an agreement on the hundreds of items in dispute on the eight appropriations bills not yet finished. Clinton emerged the clear winner in the negotiations; he obtained funding for his priority programs and succeeded in having many of the legislative riders Democrats opposed dropped from the omnibus appropriations bill in which the deal was incorporated. Deficit hawk Republicans were outraged because the deal busted the spending caps and funded many programs they opposed, but in the end enough voted for it to pass it. The alternative was unthinkable.

Although vowing to avoid a similar scenario in 1999, Republicans were again forced into end-of-the-session negotiations with Clinton on unfinished appropriations bills. Republicans had managed to pass a budget resolution and a big reconciliation bill which consisted mostly of huge tax cuts. They had done so on a strictly partisan basis, however. Before actually sending the tax bill to President Clinton, who had threatened all along to veto it, the Republican party mounted a major PR campaign aimed at mobilizing the public to demand the tax cuts. This failed, Clinton vetoed the bill, and Republicans did not even attempt to override his veto.

The struggle then turned to appropriations bills. New Speaker Dennis Hastert was determined to pass all the bills in the House, despite the problem created by the caps. All but the most committed deficit hawks acknowledged that staying under the caps would be impossible, but "busting the caps" was obviously politically perilous. House Republicans almost achieved their aim; they passed all but one of the appropriations bills as freestanding bills. Lacking the votes to pass it on its own, the leadership wrapped the Labor-HHS-Education bill into the conference report of another appropriations bill.

Many of the bills were unacceptable to Clinton and under veto threat. So in the end, to get a complete agreement, negotiations between the White House and Republican leaders were again required. OMB Director Jack Lew and Senate Budget Chair Pete Domenici took the lead, but several phone conversations between Speaker Hastert and President Clinton, who was in Greece and Turkey, were required to get agreement on the final sticking points.

To speed action, the leaders inserted all the bills into the conference report for the District of Columbia appropriations bill—a most unorthodox procedure! Because conference reports cannot be amended, this procedure also protected the deal from being unraveled on the floor. The deal had been reached Wednesday night, November 17. House leaders called a meeting of the Rules Committee in the middle of the night to get a rule, then took the bill to the floor the next day—Thursday, November 18—and passed it without difficulty. The Senate approved the bill on Friday, but only after placating a number of disgruntled senators (see Chapter 3). The bill was flown to Turkey for President Clinton to sign before the last of several temporary CRs ran out.

Since "only" five appropriations bills were at issue, Republicans believed they had narrowed Clinton's bargaining room, yet again Clinton got much of what he wanted both in terms of money and in terms of the deletion of legislative riders. The caps had been breached again, but neither side had any interest in highlighting that fact.

Clearly, the 1997 balanced budget deal did not end controversy on budgetary matters. A budget deal sets the framework for later spending and taxing decisions, but leaves many particulars to be decided later. Furthermore, because the 1997 agreement was a compromise between bitter antagonists with very different notions of good public policy and diametrically opposed electoral interests, neither side was fully satisfied with the deal. When opportunities later arose, each attempted to achieve policy goals that they had not accomplished in 1997. Thus, in both 1998 and 1999, Republicans pushed hard, if unsuccessfully, for big tax cuts. Even within the context of a budget deal, key actors differed enough in legislative preferences to require a resort to summits and omnibus legislation to get the essential appropriations bills enacted.

chapter twelve

The Consequences
of Unorthodox Lawmaking

UNORTHODOX LAWMAKING has become standard operating procedure in the U.S. Congress. Not only does the textbook model no longer describe how most major legislation becomes—or fails to become—law, no single model has replaced it. Variety, not uniformity, characterizes the contemporary legislative process.

After briefly reviewing the contours of unorthodox lawmaking, this chapter examines its consequences. Do the procedures and practices that constitute unorthodox lawmaking as here defined enhance or hinder a bill's chances of becoming law? Are there other less measurable costs and benefits of unorthodox lawmaking? Overall, how should observers of Congress assess unorthodox lawmaking?

Lawmaking in the Contemporary Congress

Once, most major legislation followed a single, well-defined process; the question at each stage was simply whether the bill would survive (and in what form) to go on to the next. Now bills and other important measures confront a series of decision points where more complex choices are at issue. Will the bill be referred to more than one committee? In the House, rules of committee jurisdiction are the most important determinant of the answer, but the Speaker does have some discretion. Usually the Speaker designates one lead committee, but he may bring in other committees through additional initial referrals, and he likely will impose on those committees time limits for action, which may be generous or tight. When a number of committees work on a bill, many perspectives and interests are represented in the bill-drafting process. If the committees come to an agreement among themselves, the supportive coalition for the bill becomes formidable. But the more committees involved, the longer the process is likely to take and the more difficult working out disagreements among the committees is likely to be.

In the Senate, committee leaders usually work out problems of conflicting jurisdiction among themselves, sometimes by agreeing to multiple referral, more often informally; the majority leader lacks the procedural powers the Speaker has and is less likely to take a hand. Fairly frequently, several Senate committees work on different bills that deal with the same subject; such instances can raise many of the same questions and problems as multiple referral does in the House.

Although in both chambers most legislation is referred to committee, the option of bypassing the committee stage altogether does exist; it is one that, most of the time, only the party leaders can exercise. Bypassing committee can speed up the process significantly. For that reason, committee leaders sometimes agree wholeheartedly to the strategy, particularly if the committee reported the bill or a very similar one in the previous Congress. Party leaders occasionally bypass committee and draft the legislation themselves or delegate the drafting to a special task force because they believe the committee will not do a satisfactory job. They fear that, because of its membership or the political delicacy of the issue, the committee will not be able to come to an agreement in a reasonable period of time or that it will produce a bill that cannot pass the chamber or that is unsatisfactory to significant numbers of majority party members. When legislation is drafted in a task force, the party leadership controls the composition of the drafting group and, in the House, can and often does exclude all minority party members. Speaker Newt Gingrich, for example, headed a task force that drafted the Medicare overhaul plan in 1995; the Republican leaders of the committees of jurisdiction were included on the task force, but no Democratic members of the committee were. Frequent bypassing of committees is, however, likely to engender considerable hostility from the membership, majority as well as minority, and leaders who need their party members' votes for reelection to their positions are unlikely to do so except under extraordinary circumstances.

Once a bill has been reported from committee, the majority party leadership must decide if the bill as reported is ready for floor consideration. That decision depends on the answers to a series of questions. If the bill has been reported from several committees, are there major outstanding differences between the committees' versions? Does the bill as reported command enough support to pass the chamber? Is it satisfactory to most majority party members? If the answer to any of these questions is no, postcommittee changes to the legislation will have to be negotiated. Once leaders decide postcommittee adjustments are necessary, they are faced with a host of choices about the form such changes should take.

In the House the next decision centers on the type of special rule under which to bring the legislation to the floor. Are there special problems that confront the legislation as a result of multiple referral? Do special provisions have to be made for incorporating a postcommittee compromise into the bill? Are there amendments that members very much do or do not want to vote on? The majority party leadership in consultation with the Rules Committee majority designs a rule intended to give the legislation its best chance on the floor. Whereas in the past most rules were simple open rules, and the rest were simple closed rules, now only leaders' creativity and the need for House approval limit the form of rules. A majority of the House membership can defeat a rule, but because leaders are sensitive to their party members' preferences, this seldom happens.

In the Senate the majority leader has no such powerful tool at his command. He will often try to work out a unanimous consent agreement for expeditious and orderly consideration of the legislation on the floor; but, for success, he is dependent on the acquiescence of all senators.

The prerogatives individual senators and the minority party possess give them choices to make at this stage. If they dislike the legislation, should they try to block it from being brought to the floor by putting a hold on it? Should they explicitly threaten to filibuster it? Should they make known to the bill's supporters that they are willing to negotiate? Whatever their sentiments about the bill, if it does come to the floor, what amendments will they offer to the legislation? Should they offer measures that are not related to the bill's subject matter as nongermane amendments—either to load down the legislation and hurt its chances of enactment or to piggyback their own pet ideas on a popular bill? If a bill they strongly dislike passes the chamber, should they try to prevent it from going to conference or filibuster the conference report?

These are the sorts of choices confronting actors in the legislative process on more-or-less ordinary major bills—the kind of legislation discussed in Chapters 7 and 8. Legislative actors can also choose or be faced with new forms of legislation and entirely new processes. For example, leaders can decide to package a broad array of provisions into an omnibus bill—in order to raise the visibility of individually modest measures on a popular issue or to make possible passing unpalatable but necessary provisions by bundling them with more popular ones. The budget process makes omnibus measures a regular part of the legislative process and forces majority party leaders regularly to deal with the problems passing such broad measures creates. Central leaders—the majority party leaders but also the president—can use the budget process as a mechanism for attempting to make comprehensive policy change, something that the legislative process as it functioned before the 1974 Congressional Budget and Impoundment Control Act made extremely difficult.

When the president and the congressional majority cannot come to an agreement on major legislation through normal processes, they may decide to try a summit—formal negotiations between congressional leaders and high-level representatives of the president or even the president himself.

Congressional actors—especially congressional majority party leaders but also individual senators and the Senate minority party—now have more choices, and the alternatives they choose lead to different legislative processes. Majority party leaders make most of their choices with the aim of facilitating the passage of legislation; individual senators and the Senate minority party may have quite different aims in mind. When, as they often do, congressional actors make choices that produce a legislative process that is unorthodox by the standards of the old textbook model, what is the effect on whether the bill becomes a law?

Unorthodox Lawmaking and Legislative Outcomes

I have argued that changes in the legislative process can be seen as the responses of members to the problems and opportunities that the institutional structure and the political environment present as members pursue, as individuals or collectively, their goals of reelection, influence in the chamber, and good public policy. Specifically, I contended that a number of the innovations and modifications were driven by the difficulties in legislating that internal reforms and a hostile political climate created for majority Democrats. If the aim was to facilitate successful lawmaking, does unorthodox lawmaking, in fact, do so?

Most bills do not become law. The House has been passing about 14 percent on average of the bills introduced by its members in recent Congresses (100th through 104th) and the Senate slightly less than 25 percent; of course, passage in one chamber does not ensure enactment (Ornstein, Mann, and Malbin 1998, 160–162). Thousands of bills are introduced in each chamber during each Congress; neither chamber could possibly consider each one, so most are referred to committee and die there without any further action. Members introduce legislation for a variety of reasons, ranging from placating a pesky interest group in their home state or district to publicizing a little recognized problem or an innovative approach to an acknowledged problem. Members may not

TABLE 12.1   The Fate of All Major Legislation, 1989–1990, 1993–1998

	Percentage of major measures	Number of major measures
Total measures	100	210
Reached House floor	92	193
Reached Senate floor	85	179
Passed House	87	182
Passed Senate	74	155
Passed House and Senate	73	153
Became law[a]	58	122

[a] Or otherwise successfully completed the legislative process. This means approval of the conference report in both chambers in the case of budget resolutions and approval by two-thirds vote in each chamber in the case of constitutional amendments.

Source: Computed by the author.

expect certain of their bills to pass and, sometimes, may not even want them to.

Major legislation is different; by definition, it is significant legislation that has made it onto the congressional agenda where it is being seriously considered. As Table 12.1 shows, its prospects are considerably brighter than that of all legislation. Most major measures get to the floor of at least one chamber, and those that do usually pass—though the likelihood is considerably greater in the House than in the Senate. A little less than three out of four major measures pass both chambers, and six out of ten become law or otherwise successfully finish the process.[1] Thus, measures that have attained the status of being considered major legislation on the congressional agenda do tend to become law, but it is no sure thing; about four out of ten do not succeed.

How do the special procedures and practices that often characterize the legislative process on these major measures affect the measures' probability of successful enactment? An examination of the relationship between the number of special procedures and practices used and legislative success provides at least a partial answer. The cumulative indexes introduced in Chapter 5 are used. For each of the major measures in five recent Congresses (the 100th, 101st, 103rd, 104th, and 105th), the House measure counts the number of the following special procedures and prac-

---

1. Legislative success is defined as enactment in the case of bills, as approval of the conference report in both chambers in the case of budget resolutions, and as approval by two-thirds vote in each chamber in the case of constitutional amendments.

TABLE 12.2 The Effect of Unorthodox Lawmaking on Legislative Success, by Chamber, 1987–1990, 1993–1998

	Number of special practices and procedures[a]	All major measures	
		Percentage that passed chamber	Percentage enacted
House	0	77	57
	1	81	56
	2	93	65
	3 or more	96	73
Senate	0	72	60
	1	77	56
	2 or more	90	79

[a] The number of the following special procedures and practices that the legislation encountered as it worked its way through the chamber: for the House, multiple referral, omnibus legislation, legislation was the result of a legislative-executive branch summit, the bypassing of committees, postcommittee adjustments, and consideration under a complex or closed rule; for the Senate, all of the above except consideration under a complex or closed rule.

Source: Computed by the author.

tices that the legislation encountered as it worked its way through that chamber: multiple referral, omnibus, the result of a summit, committee bypassed, postcommittee adjustments, and consideration under a complex or closed rule. The Senate measure is identical except that it does not include consideration under a complex or closed rule.

When the legislative process on a bill in the House includes two or more special procedures or practices, that legislation is considerably more likely to pass the House than if it includes one or none (see Table 12.2). The same relationship holds in the Senate. The likelihood that a bill will become law increases with the number of special procedures and practices employed in the House. Again the relationship is similar for the Senate. Because becoming law requires that both chambers pass the legislation, the combination of special procedures and practices in the two chambers should make a difference. As Table 12.3 shows, it does. Of measures subject to two or more special procedures and practices in both chambers, 80 percent were successful; at the other extreme, if subject to none in either chamber, only 61 percent were successful. In sum, legislation is more likely to complete the legislative process successfully if that process includes these special procedures and practices.

TABLE 12.3   The Cumulative Effect of Unorthodox Lawmaking on Legislative
Success, 1987–1990, 1993–1998

Number of special procedures and practices[a]	Percentage of all major measures enacted
None in either chamber	61
None in one chamber, one in the other chamber, or one in each chamber	51
All other combinations except two or more in both chambers	65
Two or more in both chambers	80

[a] The number of the following special procedures and practices that the legislation encountered as it worked its way through the chamber: for the House, multiple referral, omnibus legislation, legislation was the result of a legislative-executive branch summit, the bypassing of committees, postcommittee adjustments, and consideration under a complex or closed rule; for the Senate, all of the above except consideration under a complex or closed rule.

Source: Computed by the author.

When the circumstances that stimulate the employment of unorthodox lawmaking are considered, these findings are all the more impressive. Leaders are unlikely to employ the special procedures and practices under their control unless they expect passing the bill in satisfactory form to be problematic. Negotiating postcommittee adjustments and crafting and passing restrictive rules, not to mention bypassing committee, take time and resources; if the legislation is going to pass without trouble, why expend either? Therefore, when the legislative process displays several of the special procedures and practices, the chances are that the bill was in some trouble and that, without intervention, its chances of legislative success were lower than those of other legislation. Since the data show a higher frequency of legislative success, these special procedures and practices do appear to accomplish their purpose.

The special practices stemming from the Senate's unique rules can be used by individual senators and by the minority party and may well be employed for different purposes and have different consequences than those that are primarily leadership tools. What impact do amending marathons and filibusters have on legislative outcomes?

Amending marathons are associated with legislative success. Bills subject to ten or more Senate amendments decided by roll call votes are as likely to pass the Senate and more likely to become law than are other measures (see Table 12.4). The adoption of floor amendments may enhance a bill's chances of ultimate legislative success; amendments may make a bill more broadly attractive or at least give the sponsors of successful amendments a greater stake in the legislation's enactment. However,

TABLE 12.4   Amending Marathons, Filibusters, and Legislative Outcomes for
Major Measures, 1987–1990, 1993–1998 (in percentages)

Outcome	Amending marathon[a]		Filibuster problem	
	Yes	No	Yes	No
Passed Senate	91	87	74	87
Enacted	82	68	58	72

[a] An amending marathon is defined as ten or more amendments offered and pushed to a roll call vote. Only measures that reached the Senate floor are included.

Source: Computed by the author.

the substantial differences in success rates between bills subject to high amending activity and those subject to low amending activity (regardless of whether the amendments that were offered passed) strongly suggest that senators engage in amending marathons on bills highly likely to become law; senators use such bills as vehicles for lawmaking. Senators sometimes use the Senate's permissive amending rules to try to kill legislation, but that is not their primary use.

The uses senators make of extended debate are much less benign in purpose and in effect. Legislation subject to a filibuster problem (a hold, a threatened filibuster, or a filibuster) is less likely to pass the Senate and less likely to become law than is other legislation (see Table 12.4). In recent Congresses 87 percent of legislation that did not encounter any extended debate–related problem passed the Senate and 72 percent became law; in contrast, only 74 percent of measures that ran into a filibuster-related problem passed the Senate and 58 percent became law. Over half of the major measures that failed to pass the Senate (56 percent) encountered a filibuster problem. Of all measures that failed to complete the entire process, 48 percent encountered a filibuster problem.

Extended debate–related problems have had quite different effects on legislative success in different Congresses. In the 101st Congress whether a measure ran into a filibuster problem had little impact on its chances of enactment, and the same is true for the 97th Congress, for which data are also available; in the 103rd through 105th Congresses the impact was major. In the 103rd, during which minority party Republicans pursued a strategy heavily based on the filibuster, 85 percent of major measures not subject to an extended debate–related problem passed the Senate, and 82 percent were enacted; 71 percent of those that encountered a filibuster problem passed the Senate, and 58 percent were enacted. In the 104th and 105th Congresses, the minority Democrats pursued a filibuster-based strategy with considerable effect; of those major measures that did not encounter an extended debate–related problem, 85 percent passed the Senate and 65 percent became law; of those that did encounter such a problem, 71 percent passed the Senate and 51 percent became law. Since about half of all major measures in these Congresses were subject to a filibuster problem, the impact on enactment was substantial. Extended debate has its most severe impact on legislative outputs when it is employed as a partisan tool.

Of course, filibusters, actual and threatened, can influence outcomes without killing the legislation at issue. The perpetrators' aim, in fact, may be to extort substantive concessions from the bill's supporters rather than to kill the bill altogether. Those measures that became law despite a filibuster problem show a high incidence of postcommittee adjustments (46 percent for the 101st and 103rd–105th), suggesting that substantive alterations were required to overcome the filibuster problem.

The combination of divided government and the use of the filibuster as a partisan tool seems to have an especially severe impact on legislative outputs. The use of filibusters as partisan tools signals an era of partisan polarization. Under those circumstances, enacting legislation requires the congressional majority party not only to build a supermajority coalition in the Senate but also to either satisfy the president, whose legislative preferences are likely distant from its own, or amass a two-thirds majority in both chambers. Similarly, to enact his programs, a president must put together a majority coalition in the House and a supermajority coalition in the Senate, both of which are controlled by an opposition party with whom he seldom agrees. Thus, in the 104th and 105th Congresses, characterized by both divided government and highly partisan use of Senate rules, on average only 52 percent of major measures were enacted; in contrast, in the 101st and 103rd, on average 63 percent were.[2]

Other Costs and Benefits

What effect does unorthodox lawmaking have beyond its impact on legislative outcomes? Scholars long ago learned that even planned changes in complex organizations and processes are likely to have unintended consequences; many of the changes examined here were not planned but evolved out of ad hoc responses to pressing problems.

---

2. Government was divided during the 101st Congress (Republican George Bush was president and the Congress Democratic), but filibusters had not yet become a routinely used partisan tool; in the 103rd, filibusters were used as a partisan tool but government was unified.

Congress has long done its serious substantive work on legislation in committees. A number of the procedures and practices that constitute unorthodox lawmaking were a response to the decline in the committees' autonomy and power; however, procedures and practices such as multiple referral, postcommittee adjustments, and the bypassing of committees have further eroded the committees' influence, at least to some extent. Has the result been less expertly crafted legislation and less deliberation at the pre-floor stage of the process? If so, this would be a serious negative byproduct of unorthodox lawmaking since this is when real deliberation takes place, if it takes place at all.

At least before the 104th Congress, pre-floor deliberation had not, by and large, been sacrificed. It is when committees are bypassed that the possibility that deliberation will be truncated is greatest. Yet in many cases when a committee is bypassed in a particular Congress, the committee had, in fact, reported the legislation in a previous Congress. In those instances when Democratic House leaders used task forces rather than committees to draft legislation, they chose as task force leaders members who brought great substantive as well as political expertise to bear on the issue (Sinclair 1995, 188–192).

During the 104th Congress, House Republican leaders put extraordinary pressure on committees to report legislation quickly. Hearings, if they were held at all, were perfunctory; markups were often so hurried, and held before most members had had an opportunity to study the legislative language at issue, that they were, in effect, pro forma. Party leaders and task forces on which inexperienced freshmen predominated exercised considerable influence on the substance of legislation in committee or through postcommittee adjustments; and committees were frequently bypassed both to move legislation more quickly and for substantive reasons. Deliberation and the quality of legislation did suffer. Many Republicans, members and staff alike, concede privately that the legislation brought to the floor was sloppy at best; the careful substantive work had not been done.

The power of Congress, especially that of the House, in the political system depends on its specialized, expert committees. The issues and problems with which the federal government deals are too numerous, diverse, and complex for any one person to master. For a relatively small body such as Congress to hold its own vis-à-vis the executive branch and outside interests, it must divide labor and rely on its members' expertise in their area of specialization. Has unorthodox lawmaking decreased the incentives for members to specialize and gain expertise?

If the modes of decision making prevalent in the 104th House had become standard operating procedure, incentives would decline substantially; substantive expertise and hard work on one's committee had relatively little payoff in influence during that Congress, especially during 1995. With the benefit of hindsight, we can now conclude that those modes of decision making arose out of highly unusual circumstances—a new House majority after forty years and the attendant sense of mandate—and were a temporary response to them. To be sure, so long as the parties remain as polarized—and as closely balanced in seats—as they were in the late 1990s, somewhat greater centralization is likely to persist. The difficulties of legislating under these circumstances force the majority party leadership to involve itself in all phases of the legislative process. Even a leader such as Speaker Hastert who committed himself to a return to regular order found himself drawn into what would otherwise be committee business over and over again in 1999. Nevertheless, committees had begun to regain influence as early as 1996, and in the foreseeable future are unlikely to be again relegated to the subordinate role they played in 1995.

The incentives for members of the House to develop committee expertise, although weaker than in the committee government days before the mid-1970s, are still strong. Becoming a committee specialist is not the only route to influence, but it remains a major one. Senators do specialize less than they used to, but notable specialists still exist. The effective senator must develop some expertise; a senator must know what she or he is talking about to be taken seriously. To some extent, senators can substitute staff expertise for personal expertise, and in both chambers the increase in staff has made it possible for members to involve themselves effectively in more issues than once was possible.

In sum, unorthodox lawmaking has not reduced the influence of committees so much that members no longer find it worthwhile to develop committee-related expertise; expertise still pays off in influence. Nevertheless, central leaders do need to be aware that their strategies affect members' incentives and that, for the good of the institution, they should avoid seriously undermining their members' incentives to develop expertise.

As important as expertise to an effective legislative process is ensuring that the broadest possible range of interests is heard and considered. What effect has unorthodox lawmaking had on the likelihood that the full range of views and interests will find a hearing? From that perspective, unorthodox lawmaking as practiced in the 104th House was problematic. When, as was common during the Contract with America period in early 1995, committees do not hold meaningful hearings, an important forum for the expression of a diversity of views is unavailable. To an unprecedented extent, the minority party was excluded from decision making at the pre-floor stage; committee procedures made meaningful participation impossible, and often the real decisions were made elsewhere, within Republican-only task forces or by the Republican leadership itself. Interest groups that the Republican Party considered hostile—environmental groups, for example—were not given access to make their case, while the party's business allies participated in drafting legislation in which they had a direct interest.

Understandably, the first Republican House majority in forty years had a lot it wanted to accomplish; these extraordinary circumstances led to the truncated process. Furthermore, Republicans paid a price for their exclusionary procedures. Because neither the committees nor the leadership did the hard and often ideologically painful work of building a coalition broad enough to survive the entire process, much of the legislation passed by the House did not become law; excluded interests blocked it elsewhere.

The high costs of exclusion have led the House Republicans to temper their ways. Extensive hearings have again become the norm; Republicans are more willing to give groups that do not regularly support them an opportunity to express their views; at the committee level, attempts at bipartisan compromise are more frequently made.

Furthermore, although the minority exclusion practiced by House Republicans in the 104th was extraordinary, Democrats, when they were the majority party, employed some of the practices and procedures of unorthodox lawmaking in a way that excluded the minority from effective decision making in the pre-floor legislative process in the House. In the 1980s and early 1990s, most though not all Democratic task forces consisted of Democrats only. When Democratic leaders negotiated postcommittee adjustments to bills, they were most likely to do so among Democrats. As a more diverse party and one accustomed to governing, Democrats did not exclude major interests from receiving a hearing, nor did they truncate the committee process in the way Republicans did. However, the ideological gulf between the parties that grew ever wider during the 1980s and 1990s made bipartisan decision making increasingly difficult and continues to do so today.

Although unorthodox lawmaking in the House can be employed to cut legitimate actors out of certain stages of the process, it also can have just the opposite effect. Multiple referral involves more members, and thus more and different perspectives and interests, in policy making and gives more members opportunities to participate in the legislative process on issues that interest them. The way postcommittee adjustments are made often does the same, though the members brought into the process are usually only majority party members.

Finally, in evaluating the effects of unorthodox lawmaking on the inclusiveness of the pre-floor legislative process in the House, one must remember that the orthodox process could often be highly exclusionary. One committee had a monopoly on legislative action in a given area and was not necessarily responsive to the wishes of the chamber or of the majority party. Decisions were made behind closed doors. And the membership of many committees was biased in a way that favored some interests and excluded others. Diffuse interests—consumer and environmental interests in particular, which are seldom represented by wealthy and well-connected organizations—had little access.

Have specially tailored and usually restrictive special rules for House floor consideration of legislation degraded floor deliberation, as both Republican and Democratic minorities have claimed? That contention is based on a false premise; it is unrealistic, I would argue, to expect deliberation, as a great many people use the term, to take place on the floor of either chamber and certainly not in the House. If deliberation is defined as the process by which a group of people get together and talk through a complex problem, mapping the problem's contours, defining the alternatives, and figuring out where they stand, it is unrealistic to expect all of that to occur on the chamber floors. Deliberation is a nonlinear, free-form process that depends on strict limits on the size of the group; subcommittees, other small groups, and possibly committees are the forums where it might be fostered. Deliberation so defined certainly did not occur on the House floor before restrictive rules became prevalent.

What we can and should expect on the chamber floors is informed and informative debate and sound decision making. Restrictive rules can, in fact, contribute toward those goals. Rules can provide order and predictability to the floor consideration of complex and controversial legislation; they can be used to ensure that floor time is apportioned in a reasonably sensible way, both within a given bill and across legislation, and that debate focuses on the major alternatives, not on minor or side issues. In addition, through the use of restrictive rules, committee compromises can be protected from being picked apart on the floor.[3]

One's conclusions about the appropriate form of special rules depend on what sorts of decisions one believes can and cannot be made well on the House floor. The membership as a whole can and should

---

3. Formal theorists have shown that, for any bill of more than minimal complexity (technically, any bill involving more than one dimension of choice), there exists an alternative that can defeat it (and, of course, there then exists an alternative that can defeat that one, ad infinitum). This result means that the legislators' preferences are not and cannot be the sole determinant of the legislative outcome because there is no single choice that a majority prefers to all others; the legislative outcome is also a function of the body's rules. For an accessible review of this literature, see Krehbiel (1988).

make the big decisions; it can and should choose among the major alternatives that have been proposed. A body of 435 should not, I believe, get involved in a detailed rewriting of legislation on the floor via multitudes of individual amendments; the chamber is too large and unwieldy, the necessary expertise often is lacking, and the time almost always is too short for full consideration of the impact of proposed changes. Restrictive rules, in and of themselves, have not damaged the quality of House floor consideration. To be sure, both Democrats and Republicans, when in the majority, have sometimes used rules that were unnecessarily restrictive. Nevertheless, despite the rhetoric implying otherwise, the House seldom considers legislation under closed rules barring all amendments. Most rules, by making in order one or more major substitutes, do allow the membership as a whole to make at least the biggest decisions.

Informed floor decision making requires that members not directly involved in the crafting of legislation nevertheless have available sufficient information to make a considered choice. When Congress legislates through large omnibus measures, the likelihood increases that members will not know about or understand all the measures' provisions. When high-level summits make legislative decisions, members are also likely to face information problems. This is not a situation unique to such unorthodox processes of lawmaking; it also occurs with much other complex legislation. In all these cases the problem can be ameliorated by strictly abiding by layover rules that require that language be available for a given period of time before a vote can be taken.

The use of summits as decision-making mechanisms raises another problem. Their frequent use would undermine the committee system. The costs to party leaders of summit decision making are high; because summits are an exclusionary rather than an inclusionary mode of decision making, they leave most members feeling cut out of the action and thus disgruntled. For that reason, party leaders by and large try to avoid summits; yet divided government in an era of partisan polarization tends to force that mode of decision making upon them.

The procedures and practices of unorthodox lawmaking discussed to this point entail limited costs and have the benefit of facilitating lawmaking. Senators' increasingly frequent exploitation of extended debate, however, hinders lawmaking. Does this trend in the Senate have consequences beyond the blocking of specific legislation? Are there benefits not otherwise attainable that outweigh the costs?

The habitual exploitation of extended debate by senators has a pervasive impact on the legislative process that extends far beyond its effect on specific legislation. By requiring a supermajority to pass legislation that is at all controversial, it makes the coalition-building process much more difficult and increases a status quo–oriented system's tendency toward gridlock. The costs of prolonged gridlock can be severe; a government that cannot act, that cannot respond satisfactorily to its citizens' demands, loses its legitimacy.

Supporters of the filibuster argue that it promotes deliberation; by slowing the legislative process, it provides an opportunity for second thoughts and perhaps for cooler heads to prevail. Furthermore, many argue, it gives extra weight to intensity in the process, allowing an intense minority to protect itself from a tyrannical majority.

In reply one can argue that, quite apart from extended debate in the Senate, the legislative process advantages intensity. For example, the committee assignment process (in which members' preferences are given substantial weight) and members' considerable freedom in both chambers to choose the issues to which they will devote their time result in greater influence being exercised by those with the more intense preferences on an issue (Shepsle 1978; Hall 1987). Deliberation is promoted by ensuring that a minority has time to attempt to raise public opposition to a proposal it believes unwise, but guaranteeing the minority an opportunity to publicize its views does not require such a difficult cloture procedure. If Rule 22 were altered so that the longer a measure is debated on the floor, the smaller the supermajority needed for cloture, the minority would have the floor time to make its case but would not be able to block action on majority-supported legislation forever.

Individuals and small groups of senators have frequently used the Senate's permissive amending rules in combination with extended debate to highlight neglected issues and policy proposals. Their aim has been to get their issue on the public agenda, to push it to the center of debate, and perhaps to pressure the Senate into legislative action. Now the minority party regularly uses this strategy to force onto the agenda issues the majority party would rather not consider. The minority party's aim is to raise the issue's visibility, to compel a wide-ranging debate, and to pass legislation if possible. Yet within the current climate, the result more often than not is neither debate nor legislative action on either the minority's or the majority's agenda. The majority uses procedural devices to prevent debate and action on the minority's agenda, and the minority reciprocates by blocking the majority's agenda. This state of affairs requires remedy if the Senate is to function at all adequately. A deal in which the minority party receives a right to full floor consideration of its issues in return for the majority party's eventually getting a simple majority vote on passing its bills would seem to be to the advantage of both.

Assessing Unorthodox Lawmaking

Overall, then, how do we rate unorthodox lawmaking? A broader assessment of unorthodox lawmaking requires some discussion of the appropriate criteria for judging Congress. Unless we are clear about what it is we want Congress to do, how are we to evaluate the impact of unorthodox lawmaking?

Certainly, we expect Congress to represent us; we expect members to bring into the legislative process the views, needs, and desires of their constituents, and we expect Congress as an institution to provide a forum where the interests and demands of all segments of society are expressed. But, while we want Congress to be a forum for debate where the full range of views is expressed, we also want Congress to make decisions—to pass laws.

This second criterion has sometimes been labeled lawmaking, but obviously not just any laws will do. In characterizing what sort of laws Congress is expected to pass, two criteria are frequently mentioned and often conflated. First, Congress should pass laws that reflect the will of the people; that is, Congress should be responsive to popular majorities. Second, Congress should pass laws that deal promptly and effectively with pressing national problems. These two criteria, which can be labeled responsiveness and responsibility, are distinct. Only in a perfect world would what the majority wants always accord with what policy experts deem most likely to be effective. Both responsiveness and responsibility are values we would like Congress to further in its lawmaking, yet at times they may come into conflict.

In popular and journalistic discourse, members of Congress are admonished to "do what's right, not what's popular." But do we really want Congress to regularly thwart popular majorities? Furthermore, and critically, uncertainty about the link between a specific policy choice and the societal outcome means that, in most major policy areas, legitimate differences of opinion as to what constitutes good public policy exist. Members of Congress are also told to pay attention to the people, not to the special interests or the out-of-touch experts; yet how should Congress respond when what the people want is based on faulty logic or incorrect information, a not infrequent occurrence given citizens' inattention to public policy problems? And what if the majority in question is a slim or relatively indifferent one and the minority passionately dissents?

Some tension among the values of representation, responsiveness, and responsibility is unavoidable. The institutional structures and processes most conducive to each are not necessarily the same. A decentralized, open, permeable body in which individual members have considerable resources and autonomy of action has great potential for representation—for articulating the broad variety of opinions and interests in our society. A more centralized, hierarchical body is more capable of expeditious decision making. Decision-making processes highly exposed to public scrutiny further responsiveness; those that are less visible may promote responsibility. Representation takes time, especially when there are a great variety of viewpoints; by definition, lawmaking requires closure, an end to debate, and, implicitly or explicitly, a choice among competing alternatives. Thus, it is logically impossible to maximize all three values simultaneously. It would require an institution and a legislative process that make decisions quickly and slowly at the same time, ones that both expose members to the full force of public opinion and also provide some insulation.

If we expect a Congress that gives all interests a full and fair hearing on each issue and then, in every case, expeditiously passes legislation that both satisfies a majority, preferably a large one, and effectively addresses the problem in question, we are doomed to disappointment. Congress has never been able to come up to that standard, and the environment in which the contemporary Congress functions makes that even less feasible than in the past. The problems facing the country are highly complex. On many, there is little consensus among the experts about the appropriate governmental response; on others, the experts' prescriptions are unpalatable. Citizens are divided, unclear, and often ambivalent in their views as to what they want government to do. Political elites, including the representatives citizens elect, are sharply divided with regard to what they believe constitutes good public policy.

If, as I have argued, it is logically impossible for Congress to be perfectly representative, responsive, and responsible at the same time, and if the climate in which it currently functions is a difficult one, how should we evaluate unorthodox lawmaking? I would argue that so long as unorthodox lawmaking facilitates Congress's ability to make decisions without sacrificing deliberation or restricting significantly the range of interests with access to the process, it performs an extremely important function.

Unorthodox lawmaking has made it possible for Congress to carry out its essential function of lawmaking during an exceedingly tough time. And that in a very important sense is the bottom line; "representation" by a body powerless to make decisions is just meaningless talk. Institutions, like other complex organisms, are faced with the challenge of adapting to their changing environment or succumbing. In the case of the Congress, the threat is not that the institution will cease to exist but that it will become irrelevant. If it does not and cannot carry out its legislative functions satisfactorily, those tasks are likely to be taken over, in fact if not in form, by other entities—the executive branch most likely.

The development of what I have called unorthodox lawmaking is the latest chapter in an ongoing story of congressional adaptation and change. Confronted by a political and institutional environment that made lawmaking difficult, congressional leaders modified and sometimes transformed existing procedures and practices as they attempted to do their job of facilitating lawmaking. The result, unorthodox lawmaking, is often not neat and not pretty, especially on those highly salient and contentious issues that are most likely to lead the news. It is, however, highly flexible and so can be tailored to the problems—political, substantive, and procedural—that a particular major measure raises. To be sure, one component of unorthodox lawmaking—the frequent use of extended debate in the Senate—has contributed to gridlock. The difficulty of changing Senate rules threatens the adaptability of the chamber.

Even so, unorthodox lawmaking on balance represents successful adaptation to a tough environment. During much of the past two decades, all of the ingredients for gridlock have been present: divided control of the presidency and Congress, large and deeply felt differences in policy preferences between the parties, big deficits that make the policy choices facing politicians unpalatable ones, and a public divided and ambivalent about what it wants. Yet throughout this difficult time, Congress has with few exceptions produced essential legislation and kept the government functioning; the failure to do so in 1995–1996 resulted in such negative public opinion that Congress is unlikely to shut down the federal government again. The Congress has also managed to pass some significant measures that were not simply must-pass bills (Mayhew 1991). Unorthodox lawmaking has given Congress the capacity to produce such legislation within an environment more conducive to gridlock. To be sure, the political system has failed to solve a number of the big problems facing the country—how to shore up or reform Social Security and Medicare, the big entitlement programs, and what, if anything, to do about the growing inequality of wealth, for example. However, with the federal budget deficit having been transformed into a surplus, the problem that seemed most intractable has been resolved, though there is little agreement as to whose policies should get the credit.

Furthermore, unorthodox lawmaking has made it possible for Congress to make decisions without, most of the time, sacrificing deliberation or restricting significantly the range of interests with access to the process. The development of expertise is still rewarded and deliberation is still fostered by the committee system. Overall, Congress as an institution and its legislative process are much more open to the full range of societal views and interests than in the prereform era, and although the procedures and practices of unorthodox lawmaking can narrow participation, they more frequently broaden it.

Unorthodox lawmaking has not made it possible for Congress consistently to make laws that both reflect the will of the people and deal promptly and effectively with pressing national problems. No process can ensure that. It has made it possible for our most representative branch to continue to perform its essential function of lawmaking in a time of popular division and ambiguity; it has thereby given us all the opportunity to work toward a political system in which the branch closest to the people better performs the tough tasks we assign to it.

References

Bach, Stanley. 1994. "Legislating: Floor and Conference Procedures in Congress." In *Encyclopedia of the American Legislative System,* vol. 2, ed. Joel Silbey. New York: Scribner's.

Bach, Stanley, and Steven S. Smith. 1988. *Managing Uncertainty in the House of Representatives.* Washington, D.C.: The Brookings Institution.

Beth, Richard. 1994. "Control of the House Floor Agenda: Implications from the Use of the Discharge Rule, 1931–1994." Paper presented at the annual meeting of the American Political Science Association, New York, September 1–4.

_____. 1995. "What We Don't Know about Filibusters." Paper presented at the meeting of the Western Political Science Association, Portland, Oregon, March 15–18.

Binder, Sarah. 1996. "The Partisan Basis of Procedural Choice: Parliamentary Rights in the House, 1798–1990." *American Political Science Review,* March 8–20.

_____. 1997. *Minority Rights, Majority Rule: Partisanship and the Development of Congress.* New York: Cambridge University Press.

Binder, Sarah and Steven S. Smith. 1997. *Politics or Principle? Filibustering in the United States Senate.* Washington, D.C.: The Brookings Institution.

Burger, Timothy J. 1995. "After Defeat House Leaders Must Regroup." *Roll Call,* July 17, 1, 22.

Canon, David. 1992. "Unconventional Lawmaking in the United States Congress." Paper presented at the annual meeting of the American Political Science Association, September 3–6, Chicago.

Carey, Mary Agnes. 1999a. "Managed Care Overhaul Shows New Signs of Life." *CQ Weekly,* January 16, 129–134.

———. 1999b. "Momentum, for the Moment." *CQ Weekly,* October 9, 2357–2361.

Carney, Dan. 1999. "Beyond Guns and Violence: A Battle for House Control." *CQ Weekly,* June 19, 1426–1432.

Cheney, Richard B. 1989. "An Unruly House." *Public Opinion* 11:41–44.

Cloud, David S., and George Hager. 1993. "With New Budget Deal in Hand, Clinton Faces Longest Yard." *Congressional Quarterly Weekly Report,* July 31, 2023–2028.

Cloud, David S., George Hager, and Alissa Rubin. 1993. "Deal on Deficit Sets Stage for Senate Floor Fight." *Congressional Quarterly Weekly Report,* June 19, 1542–1545.

Cohen, Richard E. 1992. *Washington at Work: Back Rooms and Clean Air.* New York: Macmillan.

———. 1996. "Appropriators Losing Clout." *National Journal,* January 20, 130–131.

Congress and the Nation. 1993. Washington, D.C.: Congressional Quarterly.

Congressional Quarterly Almanac. Various years. Washington, D.C.: Congressional Quarterly.

Connelly, William, and John Pitney. 1994. *Congress' Permanent Minority? Republicans in the U.S. House.* Lanham, Md.: Rowman & Littlefield.

Cooper, Joseph. 1981. "Organization and Innovation in the House of Representatives." In *The House at Work,* ed. Joseph Cooper and G. Calvin Mackenzie. Austin: University of Texas Press.

Cooper, Joseph, and Cheryl D. Young. 1989. "Bill Introduction in the Nineteenth Century: A Study of Institutional Change." *Legislative Studies Quarterly* (February): 67–106.

Cox, Gary, and Mathew McCubbins. 1992. *Legislative Leviathan: Party Government in the House.* Berkeley: University of California Press.

Cranford, John. 1987. "Highlights of HR 3, the House-Passed Trade Bill." *Congressional Quarterly Weekly Report,* May 2, 813.

Davidson, Roger H. 1981. "Two Avenues of Change: House and Senate Committee Reorganization." In *Congress Reconsidered,* ed. Lawrence C. Dodd and Bruce I. Oppenheimer, 2d ed. Washington, D.C.: CQ Press.

———. 1989. "Multiple Referral of Legislation in the U.S. Senate." *Legislative Studies Quarterly* 14:375–392.

Davidson, Roger H., and Walter Oleszek. 1977. *Congress Against Itself.* Bloomington: Indiana University Press.

———. 1992. "From Monopoly to Management: Changing Patterns of Committee Deliberation." In *The Postreform Congress,* ed. Roger H. Davidson. New York: St. Martin's.

Dodd, Lawrence C., and Bruce I. Oppenheimer. 1977. *Congress Reconsidered.* New York: Praeger.

DSG (Democratic Study Group). 1994. "A Look at the Senate Filibuster." *DSG Special Report,* June 13, 103–128, Appendix B (compiled by Congressional Research Service).

Eilperin, Juliet. 1996. "House Bills Bypass Committee Process." *Roll Call,* March 18, 1, 27.

Ellwood, John W., and James A. Thurber. 1981. "The Politics of the Congressional Budget Process Re-examined." In *Congress Reconsidered,* ed. Lawrence C. Dodd and Bruce I. Oppenheimer, 2d ed. Washington, D.C.: CQ Press.

Evans, C. Lawrence. 1999. "How Senators Decide: An Exploration." Paper presented at the Conference on Senate Exceptionalism, sponsored by Vanderbilt University, Nashville, Tenn., October 21–23.

Evans, C. Lawrence, and Walter J. Oleszek. 1995. "Congressional Tsunami? Institutional Change in the 104th Congress." Paper presented at the annual meeting of the American Political Science Association, Chicago, August 31–September 3.

———. 1999. "The Procedural Context of Senate Deliberation." Paper presented at the Conference on Civility and Deliberation in the United States Senate, sponsored by the Robert J. Dole Institute, University of Kansas, Washington, D.C, July 16.

Fenno, Richard. 1973. *Congressmen in Committees.* Boston: Little, Brown.

Fessler, Pamela. 1993. "If People Get Behind President, Congress Is Likely to Follow." *Congressional Quarterly Weekly Report,* February 20, 380–381.

Fiore, Faye. 1995. "Unyielding GOP Freshmen Lead Balanced-Budget Siege." *Los Angeles Times,* December 21, A1.

Foerstel, Karen. 1999a. "Debate on Managed Care Legislation Diverges along Familiar Lines." *CQ Weekly,* March 20, 710–702.

———. 1999b. "GOP, Industry Trying to Shift Attention from "Patient Rights" to Aid for the Uninsured." *CQ Weekly,* May 8, 1079–1080.

———. 1999c. "Managed Care Struggle Shifts to Unpredictable House." *CQ Weekly,* July 17, 1775–1721.

———. 1999d. "Managed Care Fight Finds GOP Torn Between Doctors, Insurers." *CQ Weekly,* July 31, 1861–1863.

Gamm, Gerald, and Kenneth Shepsle. 1989. "Emergence of Legislative Institutions: Standing Committees in the House and Senate, 1810–1825." *Legislative Studies Quarterly* (February): 39–66.

Gilmour, John B. 1990. *Reconcilable Differences?* Berkeley: University of California Press.

Gold, Martin, Michael Hugo, Hyde Murray, Peter Robinson, and A.L. "Pete" Singleton. 1992. *The Book on Congress: Process, Procedure and Structure*. Washington, D.C.: Big Eagle Publishing Co. Supplements published biannually.

Granat, Diane. 1984. "The Big Conference: Getting to Be Old Hat." *Congressional Quarterly Weekly Report*, June 2, 1298.

Hager, George. 1993. "President Throws Down Gauntlet." *Congressional Quarterly Weekly Report*, February 20, 355–359.

_____. 1995a. "House GOP Pushes Budget Cuts as Political Stakes Mount." *Congressional Quarterly Weekly Report*, March 18, 794–798.

_____. 1995b. "Senate Drafting Session Delayed to Build Support for Cuts." *Congressional Quarterly Weekly Report*, April 29, 1166.

_____. 1995c. "Caustic Four-Day Scrap Portends a Long Haul in the Senate." *Congressional Quarterly Weekly Report*, May 13, 1302.

_____. 1995d. "Tax Cuts Dominate Agenda as Conference Begins." *Congressional Quarterly Weekly Report*, June 10, 1619.

_____. 1995e. "Pivotal Floor Votes Are Up Next as GOP Budget Lurches Ahead." *Congressional Quarterly Weekly Report*, October 14, 3119.

_____. 1995f. "In the House, GOP Leadership Scores Comfortable Win." *Congressional Quarterly Weekly Report*, October 28, 3287.

_____. 1995g. "Budget Battles Set to Continue after Christmas Cease-Fire." *Congressional Quarterly Weekly Report*, December 23, 3874–3878.

_____. 1996. "Congress, Clinton Yield Enough to Close the Book on Fiscal '96." *Congressional Quarterly Weekly Report*, April 27, 1155–1157.

Hager, George, and Alissa J. Rubin. 1995a. "With Cuts Ahead, GOP Works to Build a Sense of Urgency." *Congressional Quarterly Weekly Report*, May 6, 1227–1230.

_____. 1995b. "Congress Gives Resounding Yes to Balanced-Budget Plan." *Congressional Quarterly Weekly Report*, July 1, 1899–1905.

_____. 1995c. "As Budget Talks Break Down, Finger-Pointing Escalates." *Congressional Quarterly Weekly Report*, December 16, 3789–3792.

_____. 1996. "Chances of a Budget Deal Now Anyone's Guess." *Congressional Quarterly Weekly Report*, January 13, 89–91.

Hager, George, and David S. Cloud. 1993a. "Leaders Scramble to Win Votes for Deficit-Reduction Bill." *Congressional Quarterly Weekly Report*, May 22, 1277–1279.

_____. 1993b. "Democrats Pull Off Squeaker in Approving Clinton Plan." *Congressional Quarterly Weekly Report*, May 29, 1340–1345.

_____. 1993c. "Democrats Tie Their Fate to Clinton's Budget Bill." *Congressional Quarterly Weekly Report*, August 7, 2122–2129.

Hall, Richard L. 1987. "Participation and Purpose in Committee Decision Making." *American Political Science Review* 81 (March): 105–127.

Hibbing, John, and Elizabeth Theiss-Morse. 1995. *Congress as Public Enemy.* New York: Cambridge University Press.

Hook, Janet. 1993. "In Fight for Votes, White House . . . Here, There and Everywhere." *Congressional Quarterly Weekly Report,* July 31, 2023–2028.

———. 1995a. "Congress Passes Landmark GOP Plan to Balance Budget." *Los Angeles Times,* June 30, A28.

———. 1995b. "Budget Battle Forces Gingrich into the Trenches." *Los Angeles Times,* October 21, A20.

———. 1996. "White House, Congress Reach Deal on Budget." *Los Angeles Times,* April 25, A1, A15.

Hook, Janet, and Paul Richter. 1996. "House GOP Leaders, in Shift, Act on Shutdown." *Los Angeles Times,* January 5, A1, A16.

Hosansky, David. 1995. "Chipping Away at Opposition, Senate Passes Mandates Bill." *Congressional Quarterly Weekly Report,* January 28, 276–279, 307–309.

Katz, Jeffrey L. 1995. "Provisions of House Welfare Bill." *Congressional Quarterly Weekly Report,* March 18, 815–818.

King, David. 1994. "The Nature of Congressional Committee Jurisdictions." *American Political Science Review* (March): 48–62.

Koszczuk, Jackie. 1995a. "Gingrich Puts More Power into Speaker's Hands." *Congressional Quarterly Weekly Report,* October 7, 3049–3053.

———. 1995b. "Gingrich's Abortion Strategies." *Congressional Quarterly Weekly Report,* November 4, 3376.

———. 1999. "GOP's Fragile Unity Fractures in Managed Care Decision." *CQ Weekly,* October 9, 2354–2356.

Koszczuk, Jackie, and David S. Cloud. 1995. "GOP Leaders Tell the Troops, It's Time to Lock Hands." *Congressional Quarterly Weekly Report,* September 16, 2769–2770.

Krehbiel, Keith. 1988. "Spatial Models of Legislative Choice." *Legislative Studies Quarterly* (August): 259–319.

Kuntz, Phil. 1992. "Drawn-Out Denouement Mirrors Character of 102nd Congress." *Congressional Quarterly Weekly Report,* October 10, 3127–3128.

———. 1994. "Hard-Fought Crime Bill Battle Spoils Field for Health Care." *Congressional Quarterly Weekly Report,* August 27, 2485.

Lawrence, Christine C. 1988a. "Senate Breaks Deadlock, Passes Anti-Drug Bill." *Congressional Quarterly Weekly Report,* October 15, 2978.

———. 1988b. "Drug Bill Delays Conclusion of 100th Congress." *Congressional Quarterly Weekly Report,* October 22, 3032–3036.

———. 1988c. "In Its Last Act, Congress Clears Anti-Drug Bill." *Congressional Quarterly Weekly Report,* October 29, 3145, 3170.

Lipinski, Daniel. 1999. "Communicating the Party Record: How Congressional Leaders Transmit Their Messages to the Public." Paper presented at the annual meeting of the American Political Science Association, Atlanta, September 2–5.

Longley, Lawrence, and Walter Oleszek. 1989. *Bicameral Politics*. New Haven: Yale University Press.

Matthews, Donald E. 1960. U.S. Senators and Their World. New York: Vintage Books.

Mayhew, David R. 1991. *Divided We Govern: Party Control, Lawmaking, and Investigating, 1946–1990*. New Haven: Yale University Press.

Oleszek, Walter J. 1996. *Congressional Procedures and the Policy Process*. 4th ed. Washington, D.C.: CQ Press.

Oppenheimer, Bruce. 1994. "The Rules Committee: The House Traffic Cop." In *Encyclopedia of the American Legislative System*, vol. 2, ed. Joel Silbey. New York: Scribner's.

Ornstein, Norman J., Thomas E. Mann, and Michael J. Malbin. 1990. *Vital Statistics on Congress 1989–1990*. Washington, D.C.: American Enterprise Institute.

_____. 1998. *Vital Statistics on Congress 1997–1998*. Washington, D.C.: Congressional Quarterly.

Owens, John E. 1996. "The Return of Party Government in the U.S. House of Representatives: Central Leadership-Committee Relations in the 104th Congress." Paper presented at the annual meeting of the Political Studies Association of the United Kingdom, University of Bristol, January 4–6.

Peterson, Jonathan, and Paul Richter. 1995. "Budget Talks Accepted after Pointed Accusations." *Los Angeles Times*, December 21, A24.

Risjord, Norman K. 1994. "Congress in the Federalist-Republican Era." In *Encyclopedia of the American Legislative System*, vol. 1, ed. Joel Silbey. New York: Scribner's.

Rohde, David. 1991. *Parties and Leaders in the Postreform House*. Chicago: University of Chicago Press.

Rubin, Alissa J. 1995a. "Finishing the 'Contract' in Style, House Passes Tax-Cut Bill." *Congressional Quarterly Weekly Report*, April 8, 1010–1014.

_____. 1995b. "Spadework on Medicare Pays Off for GOP." *Congressional Quarterly Weekly Report*, September 23, 2895.

_____. 1995c. "Finance Committee Republicans Divided over Tax Cut." *Congressional Quarterly Weekly Report*, October 7, 3058.

_____. 1995d. "Unified GOP on Senate Finance Approves $245 Billion Tax Cut." *Congressional Quarterly Weekly Report*, October 21, 3189–3192.

_____. 1995e. "Senate GOP Appeases Moderates, Gets Majority Behind Bill." *Congressional Quarterly Weekly Report*, October 28, 3290.

_____. 1995f. "A Flurry of Amendments." *Congressional Quarterly Weekly Report*, November 4, 3359.

____. 1995g. "Reality of Tough Job Ahead Dampens Joy over Deal." *Congressional Quarterly Weekly Report,* November 25, 3397–3399.

Rubin, Alissa J., and George Hager. 1996. "Chances of a Budget Deal Now Anyone's Guess." *Congressional Quarterly Weekly Report,* January 13, 89–91.

Salant, Jonathan D. 1995. "Term Limits: Procedure OK'd on Floor Vote." *Congressional Quarterly Weekly Report,* March 18, 787.

Schick, Allen. 1980. *Congress and Money.* Washington, D.C.: The Urban Institute.

Shepsle, Kenneth. 1978. *The Giant Jigsaw Puzzle: Democratic Committee Assignments in the Modern House.* Chicago: University of Chicago Press.

Sinclair, Barbara. 1983. *Majority Leadership in the U.S. House.* Baltimore: Johns Hopkins University Press.

____. 1989. *The Transformation of the U.S. Senate.* Baltimore: Johns Hopkins University Press.

____. 1991. "Governing Unheroically (and Sometimes Unappetizingly): Bush and the 101st Congress." In *The Bush Presidency: First Appraisals,* ed. Colin Campbell and Bert Rockman. Chatham, N.J.: Chatham House.

____. 1995. *Legislators, Leaders and Lawmaking.* Baltimore: Johns Hopkins University Press.

____. 1996. "Trying to Govern Positively in a Negative Era: Clinton and the 103rd Congress." In *The Clinton Presidency: First Appraisals,* ed. Colin Campbell and Bert Rockman. Chatham, N.J.: Chatham House.

Smith, Steven S. 1989. *Call to Order: Floor Politics in the House and Senate.* Washington, D.C.: The Brookings Institution.

____. 1995. *The American Congress.* Boston: Houghton Mifflin.

Smith, Steven S., and Marcus Flathman. 1989. "Managing the Senate Floor: Complex Unanimous Consent Agreements since the 1950s." *Legislative Studies Quarterly* (August): 349–374.

Stockman, David Alan. 1986. *The Triumph of Politics.* London: Bodley Head.

Strom, Gerald, and Barry Rundquist. 1977. "A Revised Theory of Winning in House-Senate Conferences." *American Political Science Review* 71 (June): 448–453.

Taylor, Andrew. 1995. "Line-Item Veto Compromise Easily Passes Senate." *Congressional Quarterly Weekly Report,* March 25, 854–856.

____. 1999a. "House Republicans Grope for Strategy to Avert Collision over Spending Bills." *CQ Weekly,* May 29, 1261–1263.

____. 1999b. "GOP's Tweaked Budget Plan Still Short on Workability." *CQ Weekly,* June 12, 1366–1369.

____. 1999c. "No Time To Compromise: GOP Tax Cutters Charge Ahead." *CQ Weekly,* July 24, 1783–1785.

Thurber, James, and Samantha Durst. 1993. "The 1990 Budget Enforcement Act: The Decline of Congressional Accountability." In *Congress Reconsidered,* 5th ed., ed. Lawrence C. Dodd and Bruce I. Oppenheimer. Washington, D.C.: CQ Press.

Tiefer, Charles. 1989. *Congressional Practice and Procedure.* Westport, Conn.: Greenwood Press.

Waldman, Steven. 1995. *The Bill.* New York: Viking.

Young, Gary, and Joseph Cooper. 1993. "Multiple Referral and the Transformation of House Decision Making." In *Congress Reconsidered,* 5th ed., ed. Lawrence C. Dodd and Bruce I. Oppenheimer. Washington, D.C.: CQ Press.

Zuckman, Jill. 1993. "Echoes of Slavery." *Congressional Quarterly Weekly Report,* July 24, 1960.

Index